THE OWL DELIVERED
THE GOOD NEWS ALL NIGHT LONG

Also by Lopamudra Maitra Bajpai

Stories of Colonial Architecture: (Kolkata–Colombo)
India, Sri Lanka and the SAARC Region:
History, Popular Culture and Heritage

THE *OWL* DELIVERED THE GOOD NEWS ALL NIGHT LONG

Folk Tales, Legends, and Modern Lore of India

Edited by
Lopamudra Maitra Bajpai

ALEPH

ALEPH

ALEPH BOOK COMPANY
An independent publishing firm
promoted by *Rupa Publications India*

First published in India in 2021
by Aleph Book Company
7/16 Ansari Road, Daryaganj
New Delhi 110 002

ISBN: 978-93-90652-74-7

3 5 7 9 10 8 6 4

Printed in India

For Baba and Mini
...from one chapter to the next—as the storytelling
continues....

Contents

Editor's Note

This book is the first publication of its kind and a comprehensive effort has been made to explore folk tales and modern legends across India, spanning genres from oral tradition to digital media. With a focus on languages and dialects, expressions and their representations, I have included all twenty-eight states and eight union territories (UT) of India (at the time of publication of this book), including the recently formed union territories of Ladakh, Jammu and Kashmir, Dadra and Nagar Haveli and Daman and Diu. I have covered as many as fifty-seven languages and dialects. While many of the dialects are from prominent language families, there are many which are often missing from discussions at present; as are many languages that do not have a script, and many languages which are, at present, spoken by very few people.

The stories in this book have been arranged alphabetically according to the states and union territories from where they possibly could have originated from, as quite like languages, narratives cannot be compartmentalized into water-tight geographical locations. Three stories have been selected from each state and union territory and across these stories run an essence of folk tale, myth, oral tales, and modern lore from postcolonial decades to the digital age. Each of the represented stories belong to three categories. First, a folk tale belonging to the official state/UT language (with few exceptions, for better language representation) or a language spoken by the majority of the people. The second story is also a folk tale and belongs to a language, other than the language spoken by the majority in a region or the official state language. In few instances, this section has been represented by certain less spoken dialects or languages of a region—for better language illustration. The third is a modern story, mostly from the period after Independence and speaks of inspirational people and their diligent work. These are narratives which I feel hold promise of resonating across generations and contributing to the vast oral literature of intangible cultural heritage in times to come.

The 108 tales in the book revolve around various themes such as friendship, lost love, wit, humour, righteousness, courage, and nature. Melioristic legends of modern times ranging from social reformers, conservationists, and environmentalists, to feminists and emancipationists also feature in this book in an attempt to look at folklore, fables, mythologies, and legends from an 'updated' and contemporary frame-of-reference. This is of imperative necessity in present times, keeping in mind the layers of changes within texts and discourses within narratives, which are also representations of socio-economic, cultural, political, and religious perspectives across a wide spectrum. The expansive collection has been made possible through the personal tellings, narrations, and contributions of sixty authors and translators from across South Asia. Many stories represented here are part of a family or local lore and thus, do not carry textual references. I have personally collected these stories through many interactions with the narrators, authors, and translators. The outcome has been as fascinating for me as it has been for each and every contributor, I hope. Many a times, such a telling has helped to bring to the fore, a forgotten narrative within a family or a village and helped to reconnect with an incident from the past.

I hope this rich volume inspires readers around the world as much as a scholar of Indian or South Asian history, culture studies, communication or intangible cultural heritage and that, they will discover several new perspectives, approaches, and contexts through the stories presented here.

Introduction

I vividly remember a series of Bengali folk tales that my father often narrated to me as a child. These were stories of a foolish tiger and a sly fox, in which, invariably, the tiger would be fooled by the fox. I must have been around four or five years old and had just begun my pre-primary school in Kolkata. Among all the stories my father told me, a particular story immediately appealed to my young mind because it seamlessly integrated a traditional folk tale from the erstwhile Bengal region, with events from the present time. It created a wondrous as well as a determining experience for a young listener. In order to maintain the essence of the tale, I would like to narrate it as closely as possible to the original:

> In the jungles, there lived a crocodile. He was a very nice man and had seven wonderful kids. The crocodile children were a joyous lot and loved to play around the whole day, however, the father crocodile was very sad as he was facing real challenges to have his kids admitted to a school. He travelled across Kolkata looking for a school including your [my] school, but no school was willing to accept crocodile babies in their school. You see, it is very difficult to have crocodile and human kids in the same classroom. So, the father crocodile was really sad and worried, lest his children remained uneducated all their lives.
>
> Now, one day, he got to know that that there was a school in the jungle, run by a fox. It was quite famous and all the children of all the animals attended that school. Thus assured, the father crocodile started off for the school run by the fox, with his seven smiling crocodile children in tow.

On meeting the fox, the father crocodile was very happy as he thought that the fox was a clever teacher. The cunning fox however, thought differently. On seeing the baby crocodiles, he felt greedy and thought, 'This is wonderful. I can eat one kid every day and the foolish crocodile will not even get to know. When he comes to meet his children, I will show him one of the kids more than once. That's all.' And the sly fox laughed to himself. Now, since it was a residential school, the crocodile kids were supposed to live in the school premises. So, the crocodile father bought school uniforms, bags, lunch boxes, and water bottles for his childen and off they packed their bags and went to live in the new school hostel. Soon they reached the school and after settling the kids in their new 'home', the father crocodile left with a heavy heart promising them to visit every day.

The next day, when the father crocodile came to meet his children, the cunning fox had already eaten one crocodile kid. So, when the father crocodile wanted to see his kids, standing at the entrance of the classroom, the scheming fox showed them one by one at the door and he showed the last kid twice. The next day, when the father crocodile visited again, the sly fox had eaten a second kid. This time, the fox showed the father crocodile the last kid thrice. Thus, each day, as the wicked fox ate a kid, he repeated the last one as many times so that, to the foolish crocodile, the number of children would still seem to be seven.

The father crocodile never suspected anything. Thus, after seven days, when he visited the school and called out for the fox, he was extremely surprised to get no answer. He called out again and again and still got no answer. Then he called out the names of his kids, still no answer. Now, he started to suspect something was not right and entered the classroom. To his utter horror, he saw the floor of the classroom littered with the bones of young crocodiles and the fox teacher nowhere to be seen. The school was empty.

Struck with grave dismay, anger, and shock, the father crocodile went out in a frenzy, searching for the fox and suddenly spotted the fox, swimming across the river, along with his wife and kids. No one can beat a crocodile in swimming. He jumped into the river and quickly reached the fox and tightly caught hold of one of his hind legs. The fox felt that he was going to die for sure but immediately thought of a cunning idea. He shouted out to the crocodile, 'Dear brother crocodile, you are so foolish. You have mistakenly caught hold of my walking stick, instead of my hind leg.' The crocodile thought, 'Oh my God, it is indeed so embarrassing to commit such a blunder.' He immediately let go of the leg and caught hold of a cane that the fox was holding. The sly fox lost no time in jumping out of the river, along with his wife and kids and shouted, 'Foolish crocodile, see how I tricked you. You will remain foolish forever.' And saying thus, the sly fox ran away and never returned, while the crocodile slowly trudged home, wiping his tears.

The original folk tale is part of an oral collection from erstwhile Bengal (including present-day Bangladesh) and also appears in the book, *Tuntunir Boi,* compiled, edited, and published by Upendrakishore Ray Chowdhury around 1908.[1] For more than a century now, the story has been reproduced

---

[1] Published by Sukumar Ray from Sukia Street and printed by Haricharan Manna at the Kantik Press on Cornwallis Street. The book was priced at 8 annas. The illustrations were line drawing sketches by the author himself. It is a collection of twenty-seven folk tales for children. According to the introduction, the folk tales seem to have been greatly influenced by the author's original hometown, Mymensingh, which is now located in Bangladesh.

in many children's books, each one enriched with a different illustration or supplemented by intonations, pauses, and music in audiobooks for children—to enliven storytelling sessions. My story hour was unique too. The repeated narration of this improvised version of the story by my father had its special moments. The storyline used to be infused with incidents from my childhood, including the name of my school and several other areas in our vicinity. The fact that the crocodile father scurried along the busy streets of Kolkata, seven children in tow seemed to me like any passers-by on a regular road. The description of the kids playing would often include the games that I played with my little sister as a child, and they would often fight amongst themselves—in a similar manner my sibling and I did. The school uniforms, bags, lunch boxes, and water bottles of the crocodile kids were very similar to mine and equally colourful. To a child's mind, these descriptions would make the story immediately come alive with a personal association—to which was added the original version which I knew so well from *Tuntunir Boi*. I remember, actually imagining the crocodile father from the book, walking down the streets of Kolkata with his seven children, and enquiring at various schools. Somehow, the context and place never really bothered me. Thus, no question ever arose as to how a crocodile can get transferred from a jungle to the busy city of Kolkata within minutes, considering the fact that there is no jungle in sight near Kolkata any more—at least not a green jungle. No question also arose about the location of the school of the sly fox, but I always remember feeling terribly sorry for all the poor seven kids and the father at the end. The sorrow of the father somehow resonated with my young mind. The most rewarding thing, however, followed after the story was over. Almost every telling ended with a series of discussions, including, what might have happened thereafter, whether the fox was punished or not, amongst others. This discussion with my father would also entail highlighting the 'good' and the 'bad' things about life and the people in it. To an innocent mind, this was explored in piecemeal courses and as I struggled to figure out the meaning of these, I would delve further into more questions. Thus, the discussions would continue, till, more often than not, I would find my father dozing off and I would be left imagining by myself—keeping further questions and answers for the next time—when we would start all over again.

My storytelling sessions with my father remain a beloved part of my childhood memories which has come alive many years later when I retold the same story to my daughter when she was around six or seven years old. The story from the east in erstwhile Bengal travelled across the streets of Kolkata to the west in Pune, Maharashtra, where I now live with my family. The story had reinvented itself once again through a retelling, weaving in experiences from recent times and merging it with the original storyline.

A narration builds up its own repertoire, movement and through its general spontaneity, weaves a significant sense of association with the listener or the spectator. In terms of folklore, it is well understood that 'actions' and 'characters' are units of semantic analysis, where the 'actions' highlight any process or variation which is relevant to the gradual development of the story and the 'characters' undergo changes by the qualifications attributed to it, while remaining relatively permanent in time. Both 'characters' and 'actions' in a storyline reflect themselves through a surface narrative as well as a deep narrative structure. While the former is reduced to a small number of categories, the latter sees the abstract oppositions that establish classifications of the world and codes of behaviour.

Folklore, in its own flow of spontaneity, has its natural resonance amidst listeners. A lot also depends on the narrators and, of course, the connectivity through the local or regional language or dialect. The personal association with each and every listener is different as each and every listener interacts with the story differently and responds to it separately as well. It is, thus, important to understand the basic structure of the emission and dissemination of folk tales. The meaning of a narration often changes, and it occurs primarily at three stages. At the very beginning, a narrator/teller changes the story. In recent times, one must also consider a varied array of narrators and narrations, including electronic media and the internet, along with traditional oral narration, print publications, theatrical performances or plays, puppet shows, dance and musical performances, festivals, rites and rituals, vrat-kathas (religious oral narrations of mythological stories concerned with a specific deity), amongst others. The second change occurs during the time of transmission. Here, the mode of communication is to be considered once again as well as any small changes within the surface structure of the narration. At this level, one can also further witness variations like suppressions, additions, or dominant tones. These are significant to keep in mind, especially with the changing times and in the present global context. Finally, there is the third change when audience reception takes place. Here, too, one has to keep in mind the mode of communication and also the specific sociocultural context, space, and time of the audience.

As I have mentioned in the Editor's Note, the stories presented in this book have been made possible by the diligent transcribing efforts of sixty narrators and translators. In order to help readers, I would like to share the various methods I have followed in preparing the stories for this book. Many stories have been 'written' by various authors who have recollected (from memory and from various retellings, often across childhood and at home) and written the stories in the English language. No translation took place while transcribing these stories. On the other hand, there are many stories, which have both been 'narrated' and 'translated'. These are stories, which have been narrated in a regional language to the translator, who in turn has translated it into English. To this category belong many of the stories I have collected over my research and fieldwork from various parts of India, and these have been 'written by' or 'transcribed by' myself into English. I have also helped in the translation of several stories from the Hindi, Bangla, Marathi, and Assamese.

Thus, it is important to understand the process of transmission of stories across various stages—right from being a part of oral traditions to the modern reflections in digital formats. A narration goes through several layers of filters, for instance, the editor, collector, or storyteller. Storytellers collect or assimilate stories from their vicinity, primarily, sociocultural proximities; however, they narrate, from time to time, only those stories, which are popular. The collector, on the other hand, collects stories from the storytellers and not necessarily, all stories. Finally, the editors tend to collect stories from both storytellers and collectors but not necessarily all stories. These changes in narration and transmission are particularly significant in present times, as the retelling of traditional folk tales, myths, fables, and legends have been greatly influenced through the development of technology and modern publishing. The narration greatly differs, coursing from its traditional approach of being part of an oral discourse to the modern digital age. For example, a story, narrated orally, will be greatly different from its versions in print or electronic and audiovisual media. Also, the reach of a folk tale is greatly influenced by the incorporation of digital technology.

In a similar manner, the reception of a story, its understanding, and interpretation by the audience, can vary vastly, depending on a number of factors. Some folk tales touch upon a sensitive chord with a group of people and also perhaps bring tears to their eyes, while many others will make people burst out laughing or leave them with food for thought, however, it is not the same with all folk tales. The reaction of the listeners, to a great extent, depends on the time and space of the narration/performance or retelling. This brings to mind a recent narration by my friend Arindam Sarkar from Kolkata about a modern urban legend. The narration was part of a storytelling session, one evening, at a friendly gathering at a homestead farm near Mirik. This is a place close to Darjeeling in northern West Bengal, named Khushi's Farm, owned by my friends from Darjeeling, Swapna and Bhaskar Rai. After dinner, as the guests gathered around the light of a lantern, the only audible sound in the distance was the murmur of a rushing Himalayan stream nearby, occasional croakings of toads, and staccato sounds of crickets. Arindam proceeded to begin his narration by mentioning that he had told this story earlier too, to different people, on different occasions. As the story slowly proceeded towards the climax, we waited for the finale in anticipation. I am reproducing the same story here in first person in order to keep to the original narration as close as possible.

This is a story based on a true incident which happened to my father a few decades ago. My father had his own clothes printing factory at the time. In those days, they used to print batik design on saris, especially silk saris and they were quite popular. This printing press was located in an area which had many similar small workshops, factories, and other printing presses as well. The incident took place at the printing factory when the busy season of Durga puja was round the corner. The press was very busy to finish a large order of saris and the workers used to work well past midnight and until the wee hours of the morning. Then they would rest for a while and again assemble for work at around eight in the morning. My father used to be also present at all times for a proper supervision.

One night, as the workers were busy with their printing

work, they heard a very faint tinkling sound. At first nobody cared, then the sound started to gradually become louder and clearer. It was the sound of a lady's anklet and it was tinkling quite loudly. At first, one of the workers heard it. Then another one, followed by a third, and so on. Finally, even my father heard the sound. As the sound kept getting louder and louder, it almost seemed as if it was approaching the printing press. Suddenly, the sound reached the doorstep of the press and stopped. In the meantime, as the sound was getting louder and louder, the workers had stopped working and were looking up— especially at a window. The sound felt like coming from just outside the window. It seemed, someone was actually standing there. In fear and anxiety, the workers had stopped all their work and everyone, including my father, were looking at the window, silently, not knowing what to anticipate. All of a sudden, a woman's face appeared at the window. She was laughing out loudly and shrieking at the same time. In the dim lights of the street, her face was faintly visible. Her hair was dishevelled. Her eyes were big and round and full of terror and everytime she shrieked, her head jerked back, and her hands moved violently.

This vision was enough to scare all the workers immediately. All of them backed off from the window— as far away as possible. However, my father, though frightened at the beginning, composed himself and stepped out of the printing press to inspect the window. As he reached, the shrieking lady outside immediately took off at full speed and vanished into the night.

After much investigation, it was found out that, in the same locality, a group of thugs operated thus. They knew that it was a busy season for the small factories, workshops, and printings presses in the vicinity to meet the bulk orders for the upcoming season. They also knew that in order to meet deadlines, most factories would be working till the wee hours of the morning. Thus, they deduced a ploy to frighten the workers, so that they would run away in fear, leaving the factory doors open. This was the time when they used to enter and rob the small factories and workshops. This was their modus operandi and they never repeated it more than once at a place, lest they get caught. This was a big revelation for all the workers at the printing press. They, in turn, became more careful, but they also learned not to get scared as all such supernatural experiences were the creations of miscreants. But one thing was certain—all of them remembered the incident from the night for years to come.

In the dark of the night, under the lamplight, with the rushing water of the Himalayan stream next to our hut and the clear night sky above lit with a million stars, the urban legend almost seemed too real to be dismissed as untrue. Arindam's intonation, pauses between words, slow hand gestures and movements, and eye contact with each and every member of the audience, added to the desired impact which a storytelling session should have. Indeed, as the story ended, all of us were happy to hear a positive ending and according to the narrator himself, the story never had such an appeal, outside of that night—created at a specific time and space. Within the context of the session and the ambience, the story left a significant impression on all the listeners. Arindam, who was not professional storyteller, had made his mark as an excellent storyteller.

This brings us to an important aspect of a story—the beginning and ending. Just like the stories about the crocodile and the sly fox or the urban legend above—every story emphatically introduces itself in a very unique way. The crocodile stories mostly used to begin with 'Once, there was a very sad crocodile as he was facing real challenges to have his kids admitted to school...' and ended with '...thus the sly fox ran away and never returned, while the crocodile slowly trudged home, wiping his tears'. Both descriptions helped my young mind to visualize the crocodile, slowly walking back into the forest as the sly fox trotted along—probably for another adventure. The urban legend story above began with an introduction, 'This is a story based on a true incident which happened to my father....' and the narrator proceeded and reached the end as he signed off saying, '...all of them remembered the incident from the night for years to come'. The emphatic introductory and end notes helped to transfer the listeners from the silent night at the farm, into a distant space, into one of the by-lanes of the busy city of Kolkata where the story took place. Such beginnings and endings act as important parts of communication for folk tales, myths, and legends. While a definite beginning draws the immediate attention of the listener or spectator, an equally important ending, conveys the culmination and an attempt to disassociate with the 'world of stories'. The American folklorist and anthropologist William Bascom, in the mid-1960s, had spoken about these attempts to act like a 'frame to enclose folk tales' and which sets them apart from not only myths and legends, but also 'from normal conversations, and from other forms of serious discourse'. Giving examples of folk tales from Ashanti, Yoruba, and Kimbundu of Africa and the Marshallese of the Pacific and also how these are very similar to the ones from various parts of Europe, which often begins and ends respectively with 'Once upon a time....' and '...They lived happily ever after', respectively. Bascom had further pointed the differences between factual prose narratives and fictional ones in some cultures—which are often understood by the time of the tellings by the narrator, for instance, amongst the Marshall and Trobriand Islanders and also Fulani and Yoruba, a folk tale is only told after dark and also through the conventional opening formula. A. K. Ramanujan, in his *Folktales from India*[2] also explains this within an Indian context to provide a frame and a sense of time and space and that these helped to 'editorialise' a telling and incorporate proper feelings, resembling adjectives, which the 'story tells itself'. Interestingly enough, Ramanujan speaks of these beginning and ending frames as resembling keys which help listeners to 'turn the key for our entry into a tale-world and a tale-time, and let us cross a threshold into another kind of space' and the 'closure break away any identification with the characters, separate our world from those of the stories, emphasise their fictive nature, their artifice and fantasy'. Ramanujan cites examples of a traditional closure from regional folklore from India, for example, in Assamese, a tale often would end with the words: 'We had to send our clothes to the washerman, so we came home', in Telugu, often a folk tale found an ending through the phrase: 'The story went to Kanchi and we came home', and in Kannada, often the ending phrase of a folk tale would be: 'They are there, we are here.'[3] The examples cited in this introduction, also further explain the emphatic need for a 'beginning' and an 'end' and their significance in framing a narration—to initiate an imaginary journey and to leave a lingering thought at the end.

It is important to mention here that these 'beginnings' and 'endings', just like the frameworks of stories, have evolved and changed over a period of time and at present, are very different from the traditional ones which many of us have grown up listening to. While researching for this book, barring some examples from Arunachal Pradesh (which is also part of the Galo stories from Arunachal Pradesh in this book), I rarely came across an occasion, where a story had a traditional beginning or ending in any specific language, including Assamese, Telugu,

---

[2]A. K. Ramanujan, *Folktales from India*, New Delhi: Penguin India, 1992.
[3]Ibid., p. xxxv.

or Kannada. I remember, growing up, listening to innumerable Bengali folk tales, where most narrations would end with a traditional Bengali 'chhara' (a specific form of poetry). The 'chhara' had no direct connection with the essence of the story but speaks of a small story by itself, through the form of a dialogue from everyday life. Some popular 'chharas' are given below:

'My story is over and the amaranth green plant crept on the ground.'
'Why do you creep so plant?'
'Why does the cow eat me up?'
'Cow, why do you eat the amaranth green creeper?'
'Why doesn't the cowherd take me for grazing?'
'Cowherd, why don't you graze your cattle?'
'Why doesn't my wife serve me my supper?'
'Wife, why don't you serve supper?'
'Why doesn't the banana plant give me leaves so that I can serve food on it?'
'Banana plant, why don't you serve this lady some leaves?'
'Why isn't there enough rainfall for my leaves?'
'Rain, why don't you fall?'
'Why doesn't the toad croak?'
'Toad, why don't you croak?'
'Why does the snake eat me up?'
'Hey snake, why do you eat up the toad?'
'Why not? Shouldn't I eat what I am supposed to and slither away?'[4]

I visualize this as a gradual transformation from the world

---

[4]Original 'chhara' in Bengali oral traditions. It also appears in *Chhele Bholano Chhara* (Chhara for children) by Nityanandabinod Goswami, 1948, p. 63, and also in *Thakurmar Jhuli* (Grandmother's Bag of Tales) by Dakshinaranjan Mitra Majumder, 1907, p. 228.

of imaginary kings, queens, talking crocodiles, sly foxes, and foolish tigers to the real world, with real problems that operate in tandem and in a cyclical manner—and the ending imparts a practical solution in a rather matter-of-fact way. A song (of closure of traditional folk tales) with an exact storyline was also often seen in Assamese folklore. This Assamese song is about a lady, who loved gardening. On a certain day, with utmost care, she planted a particular flowering plant. This plant refused to flower even after months of careful tending to and thus, one day, she decided to speak to the plant and thus follows the same 'chhara' as mentioned in the Bengali translation above. Within both Bengali and Assamese contexts, these traditional closure songs or 'chhara' creates a typical environment or mood for the listeners and also renders voice to the characters.

Another typical ending of most traditional Bengali folk tales[5] goes as:

There was once a king
Who loved to eat the sweetmeat—khaja
His queen, loved to have the sweetmeat—pheni,
Their servant, he went on a trip,
The king's drawbridge closed up,
All words end here.

It is assumed thus, with the drawbridge, the world of imagination also closed up like a chapter of a book—till it is ready to be brought down for further communication, the next time.

However, it is important to mention that most stories, at present, rarely use such traditional frameworks. Rather, each story adheres to a specific time and context for its telling. These demarcate them as folk tales, vrat-kathas, myths, and

---

[5]The original 'chhara' in Bengali is from the book *Thakurmar Jhuli*, p. 227.

so on and depending on this, they are specifically associated with occasions and events. This is also evident in this book, for example, the funeral poetry from Meghalaya, the vrat-katha narrations from Madhya Pradesh, the Evrat Jeevrat vrat-katha from Dadra and Nagar Haveli and Daman and Diu, the stories of goddesses Sammaka from Telangana or of Kannagi from Tamil Nadu, Kerala and also Sri Lanka, amongst others. Each narration is bound to specific occasions, events, and time as well as contexts. The narration also has to take place within certain settings, for example, a place of worship or a temple, or a worship being performed in the house by the womenfolk or a prayer in a house of mourning, and so on.

Folk tales have travelled a lot in terms of expressions from the days of colonial reconstruction of the past. They have moved from a simple narration of what was considered as 'simple village or rural life'. It is also important to mention here that it is time to reconsider different perceptions in understanding folk tales as not simply being the representations of so-called 'backward' groups—a mistake and oft repeated reflection which I have seen to be a part of far too many studies. In an attempt to understand the transmission, continuation, progress, changes, etc., in folklore, it is significant to also understand that narratives should not be taken to represent divisions between societies. This is rather an approach that brings in a racial intonation and imparts a veil in moving forward from the colonial reconstructs. It is also time to move further in our approach towards an understanding of oral traditions as being the basis to comprehend sociocultural layers and ethos between 'greater' and 'lesser' traditions—an approach prevalent even some decades ago. New approaches are needed to understand their significance, survival, and continuity in present times and perceive them to be engaging in newer conversations, often questioning several established or commonly accepted societal norms and processes. Though, over the last few years, folklore as a discipline has grown much to include various approaches, it needs to further include several perspectives, including narratives of marginalized voices of caste, gender, and sexuality or of matters relating to understanding ecology and biodiversity or of popular culture and history of a nation or a region.

STORIES INCLUDED IN THIS VOLUME

An important aspect of oral traditions is the fluidity with which it travels across a considerable geographical area. I have also tried to highlight some of examples in the notes, at the end of the book, which provide information about the similarities between stories and regions. The stories (three stories each from each state or union territory) presented in this book belong to a wide genre of folklore, including folk tales, myths, fables, and modern legends. They are representative of fifty-seven languages and dialects, namely, Telugu, Hindi, English, Galo, Assamese or Axomiya, Chakma, Magahi (earlier Magadhi), Maithili, Urdu, Chhattisgarhi, Sindhi, Konkani, Marathi, Gujarati, Rathwi, Haryanvi, Punjabi, Mandyali, Kangri, Kashmiri, Santhali, Ho, Kannada, Tamil, Malayalam, Bundeli/Bundelkhandi, Marathi (including an older dialect, which was spoken during the time of the Peshwas and across the Konkan region), Meiteilon or Manipuri, Thadou, Ladakhi/Bhoti, Garo, Khasi, Mizo, Lai, Lotha, Odia, Kui, Marwari, Dhundhari, Malwi, Nepali, Lepcha, Lambada, Kokborok, Bengali, Awadhi, Nicobarese/Nicobaric, Andamanese, Bagri, Garhwali, Kumaoni, Dhodia, Kukna, Varlie, Hindustani (an amalgamation of Hindi and Urdu and is closer to the Ganga–Jamuna tehzeeb from present times and rarely referred to at present), Jasari, and Sadri. Details of the official state languages are available in the Government of

India 2011 Census data.[6] This data consists of 'an alphabetical abstract of languages and the mother tongues with speakers' strength of 10,000 and above at the all-India level, grouped under each language. There are a total of 121 languages and 270 mother tongues. The twenty-two languages specified in the Eighth Schedule of the Constitution of India are given in Part A and languages other than those specified in the Eighth Schedule (numbering ninety-nine) are given in Part B. The same number of Scheduled Languages was twenty-two even at the time of presentation of the 2001 Census.[7] These twenty-two languages are Assamese, Bengali, Bodo, Dogri, Gujarati, Hindi, Kannada, Kashmiri, Konkani, Maithili, Malayalam, Manipuri (excludes figures of Paomata, Mao–Maram, and Purul subdivisions of Senapati district for the 2001 Census. Manipuri includes Meitei), Marathi, Nepali (Nepali includes Gorkhali), Odia, Punjabi, Sanskrit, Santhali, Sindhi, Tamil, Telugu, and Urdu.[8] The manner of collection and presentation of the language data is based on the same principles as those adopted for the earlier 1971, 1981, 1991, and 2001 censuses, including ascertaining the speaker strength as 10,000 or more speakers. The table includes a division of Part A–which includes the Scheduled Languages (as mentioned above which is twenty-two) and Part B–which includes the Non-Scheduled languages and is mentioned to be ninety-nine in 2011, against 100 in 2001[9](with the inclusion

---

[6]Paper 1 of 2018, Language-India, States and Union Territories (Table C-16), Office of the Registrar General, India, New Delhi, available at <http://censusindia.gov.in/2011Census/C-16_25062018_NEW.pdf- CENSUS OF INDIA 2011>.

[7]Ibid., p. 4.

[8]Abstract of 'Speakers' Strength of Languages and Mother Tongues', Government of India Census Data 2011, available at <http://censusindia.gov.in/2011Census/Language-2011/Statement-1.pdf>.

[9]The decrease is due to the exclusion of Simte and Persian (which were not returned in sufficient number in 2011).

of Mao[10]). Of the total population of India, 96.71 per cent have one of the Scheduled Languages as their mother tongue. The remaining 3.29 per cent comprise other languages. The data also provides a total of 270 identifiable mother tongues, which have a number of 10,000 or more speakers each at the all-India level. This total number includes 123 mother tongues, which are grouped under the Scheduled Languages (Part A) and remaining 147 mother tongues, which are grouped under the Non-Scheduled Languages (Part B). There are innumerable other mother tongues as well and in the census data, these Languages, which have less than 10,000 speakers each, have been classified under a particular language and are included in 'Others' under that specific language.

With the plethora of stories collected for this volume, there was a need to understand them across linguistic groups and also accord a geographical identity. There are languages and dialects which are similar across many regions and while compiling the stories, I found an increasing need to observe, analyse, and thereby further reinterpret folk tales, myths, and legends from a new perspective in present times. This cannot be observed in isolation alone and has to be viewed through comparative understandings of specific sociocultural, religious, and political contexts within specific regions. This is an imperative necessity, as time and again several narrators helped to highlight specific critical situations, emotions, and expressions through their retellings. With the diversity explored in these stories, a need arose to analyse folklore from a very different perspective, especially as most of the narrations are based on personal tellings and often related to childhood memories, friends, or family units. Here, it is also important to mention that the gender reflections within stories are not necessarily influenced by the gender of the teller, as might

---

[10]This had more than 10,000 speakers at the all-India level at the 2011 Census.

be commonly believed. This is particularly observed regarding women-centred stories in this collection, which reflect specific expressions, symbolisms, and emotions and thereby weave a significant genre of communication by itself. It is also important to mention about therianthropy across several stories from Northeast India. Therianthropy is the reflection of shapeshifting of humans and has been mentioned across several cave-art forms, folklore, and mythological stories from around the world and throughout history. These stories generally speak of a transformation of a tiger or a tree into a woman and can possibly suggest a man–nature relationship through a close-knit bond of the regenerative powers of Nature which is reflected in the dominant picture of a tiger as well as a woman. There are also some interesting stories associated with the idea of the supernatural. As timeless classics, a representation of the fear of the unknown and the mystical or paranormal has always prompted a rational explanation from mankind. These stories reverberate across regions and also often help to highlight specific undertones of migration, exclusion, isolation or social seclusion, including gender discrimination, physical, sexual and emotional exploitation. Last but not the least, this book attempts to look at love stories from a very different perspective through the concept of 'lost-love' and from a close study of a large number of similar stories which have been narrated from across the world. I decided to include this section especially after being awed by the number of sad love stories that I had come across in the course of my research. Almost all the people who narrated a love story, spoke about stories, forlorn with grief, anguish and heartache. In fact, there were so many in number, that at a point, I started to believe that the 'traditional' love stories are hard to find any more. It was only after several discussions with many storytellers that I realized that it was not loss of trust but the rising anxiety in homes and houses, and an oft repeated discord within marital relationships that are reflected in these stories of 'lost love'. Love seems to find its own ways of expression in the modern global world—leading to an oft-lingering emotional scar.

All the 108 stories in this book have further been sub-divided into wider groups of nine, for a better understanding. These sub-divisions are primarily based on a perception of the narrative structure of the 'characters' and 'actions' as well as their representation, discourse, and context in present times. This will further aid to critically observe each story, the deeper meanings, functionality and also relevant historical and cultural issues. These nine divisions are— Friendship, Lost Love, Wit, Women-centred, Humour and Stories from Rumour, Righteousness and Courage, Creation Stories, Ghosts and other Revenants and Urban Legends, Nature and Melioristic Legends from modern times (includes social reformers, conservationists, environmentalists, feminists, emancipationists, and reformists).

FRIENDSHIP

This is a special genre, exploring various aspects of relationships, through layers of diverse sociocultural norms and traditions which finally translate into trust, mutual respect, and above all, friendship. During the course of my fieldwork, many such stories were highlighted by the narrators and translators and I felt that it was important to keep them under a special theme in present times. These are also stories of assurance, certitude, and reliability, inspite of various adverse situations and circumstances—reasons which themselves need a spotlight at present, to strengthen the simplicities, against the complexities of life. These stories are 'The Copper-tiled House' and 'Friend' (both from Maharashtra), '1956: A Love Story' (Goa), 'Galngam: The Thadou Kuki Idol' (Manipur), 'A Tale of Two Brothers' (Nagaland), and 'Of Love and Mutual Respect' (West Bengal).

LOST LOVE

Prose, poetry, and art from around the world often highlight how the world moves with love and kneels before it in awe. A popular genre for artistic expressions, love stories occupy a special place amidst genres of stories too, including folk tales. In this collection, several of the stories could actually belong to popular genres such as 'suitors' or 'lovers'. However, the title of 'lost love' is assigned to comprehensively represent all the storylines, which portray a continuing pattern—love that gets lost and the maiden or suitor is left bereaved, or deceased at the end. This also might lead to a common assumption that is often carried with such storylines, that the basic idea which is propagated through the story is a 'just' punishment, accorded due to a confrontation of the 'established' societal norms and thus, the unhappy ending and the suffering of the protagonists. I would perceive it as a clichéd notion and would rather move away from the perspective and analyse this discourse through a significant new platform. The sheer amount of such stories which I have encountered during my research is a reflection of the fact that there seems to be a growing recognition of the important role of women in determining the outcome of a courtship and this has found a new meaning in the present age and is a fast-growing part of the present societal scenario. Within this subgroup, the stories are 'Tatora and Vimaro', 'The Fairy Princess of Havelock' (both from Andaman and Nicobar Islands), 'Jaayww Bonv' (Arunachal Pradesh), 'The Tale of the Cat's Daughters' (Assam), 'Mirza and Sahibaan' (Chandigarh), 'Heemal and Nagrai', 'The Only Son' (both from Jammu and Kashmir), 'Grapmangtata—Funeral Song', 'Two Orphans' (both from Meghalaya), 'Chiasung and Manghan', 'Kaptluangi and Rema' (both from Mizoram), 'Songmo and her Tree-lover' (Nagaland), 'Moomal and Mahendra' (Rajasthan).

WOMEN-CENTRED STORIES

Let me begin by mentioning why there is a 'women-centred' and not a 'men-centred' subgroup in this book. The decision was fairly simple—looking at the sheer number of stories collected, which highlighted various achievements of women. This was also an added incentive to chart a new graph for understanding folk tales in the modern global age. In earlier times, a colonial reconstruction or telling of the past visualized gender and caste as static and historically unchanging. Though such a concept still persists within ideologies of religious nationalism, it is often questioned by social scientists, seeking an answer about specific 'unanswered' data and questions. The folk tales in this subgroup especially highlight some of these questions. They speak of the status, contribution, and most importantly, the pivotal role of women within a particular context, including a family, but not only limited to it alone. Though several of these stories have a traditional mould, there are many others, which carry an essence to break away from the stereotypical representation of women and combine cleverness, selflessness, moral, and often physical courage and barring few, many are interestingly reflective of a freedom from religious dogma and didacticism and also emphasize that gender is primarily a product of nurture and not nature. Interestingly enough, it should also be mentioned that the gender of the teller of the stories centred on women was not limited to women alone. The stories within this subgroup are 'Mother' (Bihar), 'Amrita Pritam' (Chandigarh), 'The Magical Garuda Pillar', 'Ranjana' (both from Chhattisgarh), 'The Divaso Festival and the Evrat Jeevrat Vrat Story' (Dadra and Nagar Haveli and Daman and Diu), 'Begum Jamila Khwaja' (Delhi), 'The Wicked Mother-in-law' (Goa), 'Kalpana Chawla' (Haryana), 'Kodai and Poovatha: A Strange Relationship' (Karnataka), 'The Tale of the Brave Lady' (Kerala), 'The Single-handed Legal Battles of Akkatai

Teli' (Maharashtra), 'Chungkham Rani, the Creator of Rani Phi' (Manipur), 'Women Empowerment and the Colours of Phulkari' (Punjab), 'Tinchari Mai: An Ascetic with a Difference' (Uttarakhand), 'Gymnast Dipa Karmakar: Inspiring the Youth' (Tripura).

WIT, HUMOUR, AND STORIES FROM RUMOUR

Humour has a many layered perspective, amongst which, it is also important to understand, as the American folklorist Alan Dundes pointed out, 'Humour is a veil barely concealing an expression of most of the major problems facing contemporary society'[11]. This can be further explained to include the term 'society' in a general manner and almost every other social circle around us. Common sense and intelligence are considered essential ingredients for survival in both animal and human worlds. Innumerable stories thus speak of wit with the help of which, a so-called ordinary person can defeat more powerful forces (which can be in any sociocultural context). The stories in this subgroup also include an important section which has evolved through local rumours. This is an important aspect as it also helps to highlight a significant part of erstwhile history, which gave rise to the rumour in the first place. It is also to be borne in mind that in order to understand the validity of a rumour or any tale from wit and humour, there is an imperative necessity of historical assessment, which has been attempted in this collection. The stories in this subgroup include 'The Story of Tenali Raman' (Andhra Pradesh), 'Bimbin Tabo' (Arunachal Pradesh), 'Harhi Pond' (Bihar), 'The Mahua Tree' (Chhattisgarh), 'Scandal Point' (Himachal Pradesh), 'Liquor Saves Pondicherry' (Pondicherry), 'Through

---

[11]Alan Dundes, 'Introduction: The Analytics of Alan Dundes', Simon J. Bronner (ed.) *Meaning of Folklore: The Analytical Essays of Alan Dundes*, Louisville: University Press of Colorado, Utah State University Press, 2007, p. 4.

the Eyes of Buaji' (Rajasthan), 'Lalu Sardar: The Short Man'
(Telangana), 'Chamadbhai in the Forest', and 'Dug-a-dug, Dug-
a-dug, Digging' (Gujarat), 'Tsi-zo Lha-wang and Shing-zo Lha-
wang' (Ladakh), 'The Moon and His Light' (Uttarakhand),
'The Foolish Son-in-law' (Assam).

RIGHTEOUSNESS AND COURAGE

Several stories in this book were included to specifically
highlight an important genre of traditional folk tales. These
are the stories which spoke of bravery, courage and mostly
ended with a decision to choose the 'right' from 'wrong'. As
clichéd as it may sound, I found it interesting to note that
several narrations from recent times also tend to highlight the
same messages as the ones from the past, though they are not
traditionally part of folklore. These stories included expressions
of present complexities within the sociocultural milieu, which
often resonate across various layers of the society and more
often than not, attempt to raise vital questions against existing
societal norms. Thus, a need was felt to highlight such a genre
or subgroup and the stories include 'Danveer Karna' and 'An
Old War Folk Song' (both from Haryana), 'The Himalayan
Mystery: Shikari Devi' and 'Pahadi Gandhi: Baba Kanshi Ram'
(both from Himachal Pradesh), 'The Forgotten Hero: Maqbool
Sherwani' (Jammu and Kashmir), 'The Clever Fox' and 'The
Story of the Tana Bhagats' (both from Jharkhand), 'The Tale
of the Lady With the Ruby Anklet' (Kerala), 'The Story of
Shaligram and the Butcher' (Madhya Pradesh), 'The Skull of U
Syiem Syad Lukhmi' (Meghalaya), 'Stories of Osakothi Rituals
in Ganjam' (Odisha), 'Baba Farid and Beera Bai' (Punjab),
'Ageing: A Child's Tough Question' (Sikkim), 'The Righteous
King', 'The Story of Thirunaallaipovar: He Who Will Go
Tomorrow' and 'Insatiable Fire' (all three from Tamil Nadu),
'Fists Against Spears' (Telangana), 'Guns That Were Kind'

(Uttar Pradesh), 'The Story of Madanmohan of Bishnupur' (West Bengal), 'Thinnan: The Story of a Loyal Devotee' (Andhra Pradesh), 'Baba Farid' (Chandigarh), 'Delhi Is Still Far Away' (Delhi), 'Father's Gift' (Gujarat), 'The Wish-fulfilling Well' (Ladakh), 'The Survivors' (Punjab), 'The Legend of Pampum Palli of Amini Island' and 'The Legend of Farangiya Aruta Kunnu of Andorth Island' (both from Lakshadweep).

CREATION STORIES

This genre is perhaps a universal one which also runs across various cultures across the world. I have remodelled the concept to include all stories of formation and creation, including the many microstructures within a larger sociocultural platform. Thus, along with the basic understanding of the creation of the earth, this genre also includes stories of the formation of elements and structures within, for example, society and states or cities, crops, insects, flowers and rivers, amongst others. The stories in this subgroup include 'Submergence' (Dadra and Nagar Haveli and Daman and Diu), 'The Loose Nail' (Delhi), 'Thangchhawli' (Mizoram), 'Origin of the Dongria Kondhs' (Odisha), 'The Creation' (Pondicherry), 'Lepcha Folk Belief on the Origin of Insects' (Sikkim), 'Pyonli' (Uttarakhand), 'The Lepcha Legend of the Teesta and Rangeet Rivers' (West Bengal), 'The Owl Delivered the Good News all Night Long But the Woodpecker Got the Reward of the Golden Crown' (Tripura).

GHOSTS AND OTHER REVENANTS AND URBAN LEGENDS

This is a popular subgroup and includes not only reflection of apparitions, but all magical flora and fauna. More often than not, there is a lingering element of negative reflections across all the stories, causing harm, loss, or death of the protagonists. It is important to mention that this group also contains several stories which come under the subgroup of urban legends. These are significant expressions as they highlight transformations within present urban sociocultural and religious milieu and also struggles of survival, hope, questions about social identity, voices of the marginalized and threatening dangers. These often encircle responses and questions of laymen of present urban areas which arise out of the growing complexities of a rapidly changing landscape. This group consists of a wide range of supernatural stories and the stories vary widely from one to the other. These stories are 'The Ghost in the Hostel Room' (Bihar), 'The Potter's Girl and the Divine Cow' (Goa), 'The Shepherd and the Tiger' (Jharkhand), 'The Story of the Magical Mango' (Karnataka), 'The Chudail Who Stayed Back' (Madhya Pradesh), 'Henjunaha and Lairoulembi' (Manipur).

NATURE

It was indeed interesting to notice the survival and portrayal of several folk tales which highlight concepts of preservation and conservation of flora and fauna. These stories are still retold within families as well as public spaces and are pleasantly repeated to highlight even traditional knowledge about environment protection. Preservation and conservation of nature finds a new voice through the likes of 'The Story of Preservation of Hoka Trees' (Dadra and Nagar Haveli and Daman and Diu), 'Khichan's Demoiselle Cranes and a True Reflection of Atithi Devo Bhava' (Rajasthan), 'Panduk Chidiya', and 'The Hurricane and the Foolish Leopard' (both from Uttar Pradesh), 'How A Brother and Sister Transformed into Elephants' (Tripura).

MELIORISTIC LEGENDS FROM MODERN TIMES

Finally, this book features stories about the benevolent and philanthropic work done by many people in the last eight

decades after India's Independence. During my research
something interesting caught my attention. During a discussion
on modern lore or stories that one can remember from the
immediate past or within families or villages, I came across
storylines that had a very similar reverberation through all.
These were stories that reflected hopes of reconstructing a
positive future through the work and contributions of benevolent
people. The strong storylines, along with the equally robust
and vivid emotions thus necessiated the narratives to be part
of a very different genre and thus was born the sub-theme of
'Melioristic Legends from Modern Times'. The areas of work
of these significant people are as varied as the types of stories
and include various selfless and magnanimous work and social
service, as well as work related to environment protection and
conservation, education, agriculture, archaeology, and history,
football training, food-blogging, amongst others. The stories
in this subgroup include 'The Story of a Teacher' (Madhya
Pradesh), 'The Legendary Work of A. P. Mohammad' (Andaman
and Nicobar Islands), 'The Legacy of Mastanamma, the Oldest
Food Blogger' (Andhra Pradesh), 'Gohen Bam' (Arunachal
Pradesh), 'Messages Through Wall Art' (Assam), 'Saalumarada
Thimmakka' (Karnataka), 'The Revival Story of Navara Rice'
(Kerala), 'The Spear Cry Out: Narrative of a Naga Archaeologist'
(Nagaland), 'From Khasi Cup to World Cup: A Journey of
Odisha's Hockey Culture' (Odisha), 'Know God, Know Peace'
(Pondicherry), 'Tikalal Niroula: An Eminent Personality from
Sikkim' (Sikkim), 'Water, Forest, Land' (Telangana), 'The Ice
Man of India' (Ladakh), 'Ali Manikfan: A Traditional Scientist
and a Genius' (Lakshadweep).

　　Folk tales and oral traditions are not a static phenomenon
and are being constantly reworked upon and thus are the
products of a specific individual bearer as part of a social group.
It also helps to represent what a teller feels to be a true reflection
of real relationships between various sociocultural interactions,

including groups in a class, ethnicity, and gender, amongst others. Legends take the ethos a little further as they delve into the arena of oral expressions which tells of extraordinary events in the life of so-called ordinary people, and these are narrated as significant historical accounts. These are also passed on orally from generation to generation and more often than not carry details of local specifics to further validate the telling. Many a times, during my fieldwork, several legends were also locally compared to newspaper stories and most details within these stories were considered to be credible information within specific regions. This also further helps to build up the story and the information related to it.

Finally, the tales in this book were contributed by a wide range of authors and narrators and are as steeped in tradition as they also move away from it, with a determined approach to chart out new expressions and identities. These stories are as much for children as for any story aficionado or a researcher or an academic of intangible cultural heritage of India or South Asia. Thus, several of the stories might even seem familiar to narratives known to many, including the creation stories—'Submergence' (Dadra and Nagar Haveli and Daman and Diu) and 'Origins of the Dongria Kondhs' (Odisha) or well-known fables, like the story of 'The Clever Fox' (Jharkhand) or similarities with the stories from *The Jataka*, like the story of 'Ageing: A Child's Tough Question' (Sikkim), amongst other—one has almost come across any or many of these stories at any point in life. They are sometimes fondly remembered or serve as conduits to explore a happier connection with childhood or delved deeper at present, to find reflections of socio-cultural representations and acculturations. The understandings from story remains personal, as I mentioned earlier and that's one of the biggest significant takeaway from each narrative.

Times have changed and the format and need of storytelling and narration have itself found several new platforms of expressions. Children probably no longer need folk tales to stay awake or go to sleep as they are more or less attached to the technological versions of stories. Adults, on the other hand, find new expressions amidst storytelling sessions across corporate offices, as the art of narration is often utilized as an effective tool for imparting several aspects of learning and behaviourial trainings through workshops and seminars in the workplace. Storytelling is also often utilised as an effective method in various modern therapy or counselling sessions. Finally, the pandemic caused by the coronavirus has thrown open and reinvented some more and varied genres, techniques, platforms, methods, ideologies, and expressions of narratives. The present has shown how storytelling can be a part of non-virtual as well as the virtual world to render different approaches of understandings, to reach people of all ages and across all countries and across hundreds of occupations. The global world has become one big platform to express narratives creating a niche and path for themselves and to be remembered in the future showing us truly how times have vastly changed and stories and narration often reinvent themselves through new approaches.

This comprehensive volume aims to add to this nouveau approach and is a first of its kind to cover all the states and union territories of India, including a large number of languages and dialects in the process. I hope this book opens dialogue across time, conversations of socialization, acquisition of knowledge and rediscovers itself amidst the modern, global, digital age, and at the same time, it continues to exist for its primary purpose—to entertain, amuse, and enrich us or soothe a tired mind or simply add to the fun of reading a story.

ANDAMAN AND NICOBAR ISLANDS

....

1

Tatora and Vimaro

Once upon a time, several thousand years ago, the Car Nicobar Island had several inhabitants who belonged to the Mongoloid race. On that island were two villages, namely, Pasa and Lapati. In Pasa village, there lived a handsome boy called Tatora. He had a reputation amongst the Nicobarese of being a helpful person. Thus, he was always invited to various festivals and ceremonies. He wore his traditional dress and carried a wooden sword tied around his waist at all times. It was believed that the wooden sword had magical powers and Tatora never allowed anyone to use it or even touch it.

One day, as he was strolling on the beach, he heard a beautiful song. He was so enamoured by the lovely tune that he followed the tune and discovered a beautiful maiden singing. However, the young girl was taken by surprise and stopped singing immediately. Tatora asked her, 'Why have you stopped singing midway? It was such a beautiful tune.' The woman replied, 'Who are you and why are you questioning me? I am not bound to answer you as I do not know you.' However, Tatora was awestruck by the beauty of the girl and forgot to answer her; instead, he once again asked his question, 'Why did you stop singing? You have such a lovely voice.' The girl replied in amazement, 'This is not the reply to my question. I have never seen you around my village—Lapati.' Once again, the awestruck Tatora repeated the same question.

This time, the maiden replied in anger, 'Why are you not answering my question? Don't you know that your behaviour is disgraceful and that such behaviour is not tolerated in my village?' Saying this, she started to walk away. Suddenly, Tatora woke up from his trance and said, 'Please forgive me. This is the first time in my life that I have been overwhelmed in this manner. I will not stop you from leaving, but please tell me your name.' The girl felt sorry for him and introduced herself as Vimaro. Tatora said, 'That is a beautiful name. Will you come here again tomorrow?' Vimaro smiled and started to walk away. Tatora shouted behind her, 'Do come tomorrow again. I am Tatora.'

That night, both Tatora and Vimaro could not stop thinking about each other. The next evening, Tatora went back to the beach and was overjoyed to see that Vimaro was waiting for him. They hugged each other and realized that they were deeply in love. They kept meeting each other and desired to get married; however, they knew that it was impossible. Pasa and Lapati villages were sworn enemies and a marriage alliance between the two villages was practically impossible. Nevertheless, the lovers refused to give up and tried their best to convince the village elders.

After a few days, it was time for the pig festival. Tatora was not interested in the ceremonies, instead, he kept searching for Vimaro. Suddenly, he saw her sobbing behind a coconut tree. At that moment, Vimaro's mother came searching for her and saw the two of them together. She was livid and started to scold Vimaro and abuse Tatora. Hearing her abuses, Tatora grew very angry, took out his wooden sword and plunged it deep into the sand with all his might. He then started to walk away, dragging the sword behind him and making a deep depression in the sand. This deep cut started to grow wider and gradually divided the land into two parts. On one side of the divide, Tatora kept shouting Vimaro's name and on the other, poor Vimaro kept screaming Tatora's name. Tatora lost his senses soon after. When he regained consciousness, he saw that the two landmasses had completely separated. He lay helplessly, thinking about Vimaro while she kept running wild calling Tatora's name. It is said that Vimaro's screams has haunted the island for centuries.

....

2

The Fairy Princess of Havelock

Once upon a time, Havelock Island was a land frequented by fairies. There used to be a beautiful lake on this island and every night, beautiful fairies used to descend on the lake for a swim, along with their princess. This princess had special magical powers and wherever she would pass, a trail of light would follow her. Thus, her parents kept her locked away inside her home all day, but at night, she would fly out of the house with her friends. The whole lake would glisten with the fairy lights. Just before the crack of dawn, all the fairies would leave the lake and return to fairyland.

One night, there was a violent storm. That night, the princess's friends decided not to visit the lake and also warned her from doing so. However, the princess was overwhelmed with a desire to visit the lake. All around, the sea was making terrible noises with the ferocious crashing of the waves. The princess was a little terrified, but she gathered enough courage and descended upon the lake. Every time, before she entered the water, she would take off her wings and keep them aside on the lakeside. That night too, she carefully took off her wings and kept them aside. As she walked towards the lake, she saw a handsome man lying unconscious. She was both intrigued and curious as she had never seen a good-looking man as this one. While she realized that she should leave, she was also eager to speak with the handsome man. Finally, she decided to save the man. Thus, she went to the lake and filled her palm with water and sprinkled it on the man's face. Soon, he gained consciousness and was amazed to see a beautiful lady on the deserted island. As the man tried to sit up, the princess asked, 'Who are you and what are you doing here? This island belongs to me and I'm the princess of this island.' The man replied, 'I am the prince of the eastern kingdom. I was sailing on the sea and my ship got wrecked in the furious storm. I somehow managed to jump into the water, but lost consciousness immediately after. I do not remember anything after that or how I managed to reach this island.'

The princess listened in silence and felt sorry for the prince. Both sat silently, looking at each other and in deep thought, as if connecting and communicating in silence. Finally, the princess said, 'O prince! It is almost morning and it is time for me to return home. You may stay here till the storm subsides. I will take you to a safe resting place. I will come every day to meet you. After midnight, when the first star of dawn is visible, I will come to the lake. You may come and meet me there.' Though the prince requested her to stay back, the princess left for her home, but both of them kept thinking about each other and their love brought them together every night. They would meet near the lake and the princess would leave by dawn.

Several days passed by in this manner. One night, as the princess came to meet the prince, she saw that he was looking sad and sitting silently. On being asked, the prince replied that he was feeling homesick and wanted to meet his parents. He was the only son of his parents and he thought that his parents would be worried at his long absence. However, the princess got anxious as the storm was yet to subside. She feared that the prince would drown. Suddenly, the prince said, 'I can think of a way to escape the storm, if you agree to help me.' The princess was eager to help the prince as she was in love with him. Thus, the prince suggested, 'I can go home with the help of your wings, if only you would take them off and give them to me. I will go home, tell my parents about you, and return to marry you.' The princess readily agreed and took off her wings and gave them to the prince. While handing over the wings, she said, 'These wings are my identity. I will not be able to fly without them. I will wait for you on this island until you return.' Then she put her wings on the prince, taught him how to fly, and the prince flew away into the night sky. Days passed but the prince did not return, and the princess remained stranded on the island—waiting and crying her heart out.

It is believed that the lake still exists in Havelock Island and in the early hours of the morning, one can notice wet footprints on the shore and sometimes even hear sobbing in the late hours of the night.

3

The Legendary Work of A. P. Mohammad

Shri A. P. Mohammad did not receive any formal education but created a benchmark in the region of South Andaman to the extent that people remember his work fondly and consider him a legend of the modern times.

A. P. Mohammad's forebears were from the Malabar region of the state of Kerala. In 1921, many people were deported from the Malabar region to South Andaman as a form of punishment by the British government. Through sheer hard work, they managed to make the place habitable. Mohammad's grandfather, Late Moinuddin, was a freedom fighter and fought against the British in 1921. He was arrested and deported to the Andamans at this time. Mohammad's father, Late Ayutti, was a farmer and struggled to make the place suitable for agriculture. A. P. Mohammad was born on 7 March 1942 in Stuartganj. After the death of his father, Mohammad took on the responsibility of looking after his family.

In his early days, Mohammad started his career in a small vegetable shop in Port Blair's Ghanta Ghar area. It was during this time that his interest in politics grew. Within a short time, he became an active and leading member of the Congress party of South Andaman. People would come to him, seeking help. He would render all possible help including financial assistance. Thus, his popularity grew. His helpful nature would also often drive him to argue with various officials for social causes. As he continued his social work, it occurred to him that he should contribute to the sphere of education. In those days, there was no English-medium school in the region. One day, he came across an article in a magazine which spoke about selfless services for the upliftment of poor Muslims in the area and he started to feel that education will provide the necessary enlightenment to improve the living conditions of the people in the region. Thus, in 1977, he started a school—MES (Muslim Education Society School)—with four children in his own home. This school was started with the help and support of all his family members. Soon it became popular. As the number of students grew, the school required more space to accommodate the students. The local authorities donated a piece of land to build a madrasa. In the course of his work, A. P. Mohammad received official recognition for educating the children and youth.

It was an emotional moment for Mohammad and the principal of the madrasa when the Islamic Development Bank of the Kerala branch sanctioned a loan of rupees eighteen lakhs for the construction of the madrasa building. Thus, the school started in earnest and became popular within a short span of time. It also began to receive regular donations from the government. At present, the school has several branches across South Andaman where education is imparted at various levels, including a school till the twelfth standard in the Azad Nagar region, one till the tenth standard at Ograbanj and Wimberleyganj, and in Shore Point area till the fifth standard. Today, the schools boast of several reputed alumni, including ten in medical and engineering professions.

A. P. Mohammad has also contributed considerably to the discipline of regional journalism. Though he was a non-Hindi speaker (Malayalam being his mother tongue), he managed to start a daily, *Sahil ki Aur* (Towards the Shores) in 1996, with an ideology that the news from South Andaman should reach the various corners of the Andaman and Nicobar Islands. Later on, this daily was transformed into a weekly. For his contributions towards journalism and social services, he was awarded by the lieutenant governor of the island with a commemorative certificate.

A. P. Mohammad also helped resettle 129 people in the Little Andaman region. He also worked for the people who suffered in the 2004 tsunami and arranged for a grant of rupees nine lakhs from the central government for resettling various families.

A. P. Mohammad also helped recognize and duly award all the freedom fighters who were deported to the South Andaman from the Malabar region.

ANDHRA PRADESH

Thinnan: The Story of a Loyal Devotee

There was once a hunter named Thinnan. His parents lived in Uduppur, a village near Srikalahasti in Andhra Pradesh and his father was the head of the tribe. The village was surrounded by green forest all around and all the villagers were hunters and experts in archery. They used to wear the claws and teeth of wild animals that they had hunted as ornaments. There was a story about the birth of Thinnan—his parents remained childless for a long time and after worshipping Lord Muruga, his mother conceived. The entire village celebrated the birth of the baby boy. His father made animal sacrifices to please Lord Muruga and named his son Thinnan (strong), as he found that the baby was heavy and strong, even at birth.

Thinnan began to grow up playing with wild pigs, snakes, and jackals. He could fearlessly put his hand into the mouth of a tiger. When he was a little bigger, his father decided to give him lessons in archery. On the day his training began, it was a grand initiation ceremony and Thinnan's father arranged a grand feast for all the hunters that day. Thinnan mastered archery in a short span of time and when he was sixteen, his father made him the head of the tribe. Thinnan continued to lead his tribe on hunting expeditions. One day, Thinnan and his fellow villagers went on a hunt. They caught many wild animals, but a wild boar escaped and ran off into the woods. Thinnan chased it and finally noticed it standing near the base of a hill. He killed it and flung it across his shoulder.

As Thinnan was returning to the village, he noticed a Shiva linga and felt that he should offer puja to the deity. He went to a nearby river, filled his mouth with water, plucked flowers, placed them on his hair, and carried some flesh of the animal in his hands. He returned to the Shiva linga, offered the flowers and flesh and spit out the water, in order to bathe the idol. He also decided to stay for a while longer and requested his friend, Kadan, who was accompanying him, to inform his parents about his decision.

Now, there lived a sage named Shiva Kochariyar, who also worshipped the same Shiva linga. When he arrived for his daily rituals, he noticed the raw flesh in front of the linga. He cleaned up the place and decorated the area with fresh flowers. The very next day Thinnan came again, spit water on the deity and made his offerings—the same way as he had done the day before. Soon after this, the sage also visited. Just like the previous day, he was infuriated. He cleaned the place and offered fresh flowers once again. In this manner, both devotees continued to make their offerings to Shiva. However, the sage was getting very irritated with the offerings of flesh and wished that Lord Shiva would tell him who was behind this. One day, the Lord appeared in his dream and mentioned that it was being offered by a very strong devotee and if the sage wanted to meet him, he should come in the early hours of morning and hide behind a bush.

Thus, the sage hid behind a bush the next day. After some time, he saw Thinnan arrive and offer flowers and flesh. As usual, he spit out water from his mouth to bathe the idol. Suddenly, the sage noticed that the left eye of the deity was bleeding. Though Thinnan tried to stop it by wiping it with a corner of his cloth and by applying crushed medicinal leaves, the bleeding continued. Finally, Thinnan gorged out his left eye with an arrow and offered it to the idol. Thinnan placed it in the left eye of the deity and the blood stopped flowing. Though he was injured, Thinnan was happy and danced all around the deity. Within a few seconds, the right eye of the deity also started to bleed. The one-eyed Thinnan lifted up his right leg, placed it in the area of the right eye of the deity and thus balancing himself, took out an arrow and started to gorge out his right eye as well. Suddenly, Lord Shiva appeared before Thinnan and stopped him. He fell at the Lord's feet. Thinnan and the sage, both were blessed with the presence of Lord Shiva. The sage finally understood the extreme love and devotion of Thinnan for Lord Shiva. Since Thinnan offered his eye to Lord Shiva, he became known as Kannappa (the one who had offered his 'kannu' or eye). Later, he became one of the sixty-three Shaivaite saints (Nayanars) and was popularly known as Kannappa Nayanar.

5

The Story of Tenali Raman

Tenali Ramakrishna, popularly known as Tenali Raman, was born to Garlapati Ramayya and Lakshmamma in the village of Tumuluru in Andhra Pradesh. His father was a temple priest and unfortunately passed away suddenly, when Raman was still a small child. Immediately after his father's death, Raman's mother took him and left for the city of Tenali, her native place. There Tenali Raman lived in his maternal uncle's home with his mother. Raman's mother wished to make her son a great scholar, but she failed to find a good teacher for him. There were many scholars in and around the city, but they were Vaishnavites and worshipped Lord Vishnu. They refused to accept a student like Raman as he was a Shaivite and worshipped Lord Shiva. Raman was, however, happy with his playmates in Tenali. They roamed around the village, played and ate fruits which they stole from the gardens in the neighbourhood. His mother used to work as a housemaid and earned just enough to tend to her son's needs but she was anxious about her son's future.

When Raman was a young adolescent boy, he suddenly grew conscious of his lack of education. He did not know how to read or write. Following his mother's instructions, he started to wander in search of a good teacher. He approached a few Shaivite scholars who lived in Tenali but they refused him as they were themselves poor and could not afford a student. Raman's search continued and finally he found a Vaishnavite Brahmin teacher who taught his students in the courtyard of his house. Raman decided to hide behind a big tree and listen to him every day. In this way Raman's education started from behind the tree. One day, however, one of the students caught Raman hiding and brought him to the teacher. Raman told the truth and expressed his desire for learning. The teacher was reluctant to accept a student who was a Shaivite. He told Raman that if he accepted Raman as his student, he would be made an outcast by his community members. But he blessed Raman and wished him a fruitful future.

A heartbroken Raman walked aimlessly across a forest and reached the doorsteps of an old mansion. He sat down and started to cry loudly. Suddenly, to his surprise, a sage came and asked him about his sorrow. Raman narrated his sad story. The sage consoled him and advised him to pray to Goddess Kali who would suggest a solution for his sorrows. The sage also whispered some chants into his ears. Raman continued to chant for eleven days, without eating or drinking. Finally, Goddess Kali appeared before him and asked him to open his eyes. Raman slowly opened his eyes and saw the terrifying Kali seated on a lion, with thousand flaming tongues and thousand pairs of red eyes. When Raman looked at the ferocious thousand faces, he forgot himself and started to laugh instead. The goddess wondered and asked the reason for the mirth. Young Raman replied that he was imagining what if the goddess caught a cold and had a running nose, how would she manage to wipe the thousand noses with her mere two hands. Hearing his witty reply, the goddess too started to laugh out loud. She blessed him and asked him to go and meet Krishnadeva Raya, the king of Vijayanagara.

Tenali Raman went to Vijayanagara with his mother. As he enquired, he understood that King Krishnadeva Raya liked intelligent people in his court. Though Raman tried his best he could not get an appointment with the king. He did not give up hope and finally one day, as a drama troupe came visiting the palace, Raman got his opportunity.

This troupe had come to perform the Krishna Leela. Raman noticed that several characters were dressed as cowherds for the play. Raman took a churning stick and got dressed as a cowherd to get an easy entry into the palace. However, a guard stopped him at the gates. Raman convinced the guard that he would share half of the gifts that he would get from the king with the guard. This pleased the guard and he allowed Raman to enter through the main gates. As Raman reached the Durbar hall, he was once again stopped by a guard and this time, he promised to give the guard the other half of his gifts that he got from the king. Thus convinced, the second guard also allowed him to enter the palace.

Inside the palace, Raman started to act as part of the troupe. The audience was bored and sleepy with the same dialogues that were repeated in every show. However, Raman's tricks soon changed the dynamics of the play and the stage became a laughing riot. Raman accidentally hit the actor who was playing Krishna with his churning stick and the actor fell down. Raman made up some dialogues and pronounced loudly that Lord Krishna who could kill King Kamsa, Krishna's demon-uncle and a treacherous ruler, who could lift up a heavy mountain to save people and kill the poisonous snake, Kaliya, could not bear the blow of a mere churning stick. For strength and courage, Krishna should now pray to Goddess Kali. The actor, who played Krishna, actually got up and started to pray to Goddess Kali on the stage. This unconventional sequence had the audience rolling with laughter. The king was also entertained and was amused. He wanted to meet the witty cowherd boy; however, the troupe stated that Raman did not belong to their troupe. On being asked by the king, Raman narrated everything. The king was not happy on hearing this as he considered Raman to be trespassing. He ordered a hundred whiplashes for Raman. Raman brought the two guards along with him—one from the main gate and the other from Durbar hall as he had promised to share the king's gifts with them equally. Raman then requested the king to divide the whiplashes between the two guards and narrated to the king the whole story about entering the palace. The king appreciated his cleverness and appointed Tenali Raman as his court jester.

....

6

The Legacy of Mastanamma,
the Oldest Food Blogger

In 2017, the 106[1]-year-old Karre Mastanamma was seen in an audiovisual blog (that went viral) explaining her favourite dishes—vegetables, lentils, fish, prawn, and egg curry, and the secret to happiness. Her secret was 'Cook a lot of curries and eat well'. She is considered to have been the oldest food blogger spreading her message through audiovisual social media platform in modern times. She had over 300,000 subscribers and 52 million views on YouTube at the time of her death. Mastanamma the YouTube sensation has left behind a legacy— the power of love, reflected in the many dishes she shared with millions of viewers across the world. The ever-smiling Mastanamma's recipes had a wide variety and some of them were especially liked by viewers, including her baingan bharta, catla fish curry, and most of all, the watermelon and chicken curry, with over 75 lakh views of the video. Mastanamma was known as the grandmother with a toothless smile and was best known for making cooking enjoyable, with a homely touch.

Karre Mastanamma was born in Kopalle, near the village of Gudiwada, in Guntur district of Andhra Pradeṣh on 10 April 1911. She got married at the age of eleven and settled down in the village of Gudiwada, 10 kilometres from Tenali Mandal in the same district. She described her in-laws as being affectionate

---

[1]In a BBC interview (for BBC Monitoring) in 2017, Mastanamma claimed to be 106 years old. Though there was no birth certificate to prove it, Mastanamma's age was famous across her village.

towards her. She had five children. Today, all of Mastanamma's children have passed away. Her eldest son, David, passed away in 2018. Mastanamma often described her early life to be of great hardship, but it was always her feisty spirit that kept her going. She also worked briefly as a chef at one of her son's restaurant and always liked to cook and serve people. It is this very love that changed her life over a summer day in 2016. As the story goes, one of Mastanamma's grandson's, K. Laxman, paid her a visit, along with a friend, Shrinath Reddy. Reddy and Laxman were publishing audiovisual materials online and what they witnessed over their brief stay at Mastanamma's house, made the tech-savvy duo visualize a concept, which resulted in a ground-breaking journey that reached almost all corners of the world. This started with both Reddy and Laxman watch Mastanamma cook a delectable brinjal curry for them. Inspite of her age, she would finish the cooking within minutes, without any help from others. This brinjal curry was an epiphany for Reddy and Laxman who thought it would be a great idea to record Mastanamma's cooking and circulate it online. They both felt that her excellent recipes should be known to the world.

Thus began Mastanamma's audiovisual blog *Country Foods* in 2016. Reddy and Laxman planned and regularly uploaded a video. Mastanamma never shied away from the camera and reflected a carefree yet cordial persona through her reel-life presentations. Her previous experience of working as a chef was also helpful. People immediately started to like her videos, and this continued across 200 online recipes. Initially, Mastanamma didn't understand the concept of an audiovisual blog. Gradually when her fame spread and people started to visit her from neighbouring states, she came to realize the basic concept of how her recipes had gained popularity outside her village through the help of technology.

Though Mastanamma only spoke Telugu and cooked mostly

authentic Andhra cuisine, yet, there were variations in her cooking. At times, she could be seen to display different versions of a plate of French-fry style chips—with a very different variety of seasoning than what is served in a fast-food joint. In a similar manner, she also prepared chicken burger with slices of melting cheese, emu egg fry, bread omelette, or a simple snake gourd and milk curry—all with her special touch and ingredients. Whether it was an authentic Andhra cuisine or not, they were all liked by people all over the world and each video was well-received. Adding more to her style of cooking was her presentation, which brought a homely touch through the videos. Mastanamma never used a formal cooking range, instead, cooked with large traditional metal pots and pans, wood, in an open fire, in a field close to her house. She cut her vegetables on the traditional Indian knife known as the Kathipeeta in Telugu (which is famous in various parts of India and is known by different names across many regional languages—boti in Bengali, arivalmanai or aruvamanai in Tamil, addili in Konkani, vili or morli in Marathi, panikhi in Odiya, and so on). Finally, she would serve the dish on a plaintain leaf to her near and dear ones, who would also be seen relishing her cooking with a smile on their faces. Towards the end of 2018, Mastanamma's health started to fail, but somehow, she managed to find time for a new recipe and a last recording.

Mastanamma passed away on 3 December 2018. At the time of her death, her cooking blog had over 12 lakh subscribers. She left behind a legacy with her unique style of cooking and lived her life to the fullest through the love that she received from around the world.

ARUNACHAL PRADESH

7

Jaayww Bonv

Jaayww Bonv, Jaayww Ja
Korum yu ogo yu, Jaayww Ja
Jimi yu ogo yu, Jaayww Ja
Korlo yu ogo yu, Jaayww Ja

This story of Jaayww Bonv begins in ancient times when silence prevailed everywhere.

Jaayww Bonv was the name of a charming girl. She was the daughter of Hicww—Earth. She was the most beautiful girl in the land and the ornaments she wore further enhanced her beauty. Her beauty surpassed everything. The story of her beauty spread far and wide. Suitors from different lands came to woo her but nobody could succeed in winning her heart. Among these suitors were two young, attractive men, Diiduu-Kuubo, a man from the forest and Bwr-Tapuu, a man from the realm of water.

Diiduu-Kuubo owned the forest and Bwr-Tapuu possessed the world of waters and neither of them knew about their common interest in Jaayww Bonv. Both were powerful and skilful in their own ways and tried to woo Jaayww Bonv on different occasions by offering her gifts. Diiduu-Kuubo professed his love for her in his own way, 'Jaayww Bonv, I have hunted the whole forest for the best meat, and I offer you fresh meat of the animals that live in my forest.' Jaayww Bonv happily and cheerfully accepted the gift. Soon, Bwr-Tapuu came to meet Jaayww Bonv and said, 'O Gorgeous Lady!

I bring unto you fresh fish from the waters as a token of my love.' This gift too was joyfully accepted by Jaayww Bonv.

Jaayww Bonv was happy with all the attention she was getting from the two charming young men. Though she accepted the gifts, yet she was confused, 'I am passionate about both of them. Both of them shower me with the best of gifts that they can offer. Diiduu-Kuubo brings me the best meat from the forest and Bwr-Tapuu presents me with the best fish from the water. How can I choose between the best?' Since she could not decide for herself, she decided to seek her mother's help. She went to her mother and said, 'Mother, who do you think deserves to be my suitor? Diiduu-Kuubo or Bwr-Tapuu?'

Her mother thought for a while, took a deep breath and said, 'Jaayww Bonv, my daughter. Diiduu-Kuubo and Bwr-Tapuu, both are good and bring you the best of gifts. The meat offered by Diiduu-Kuubo is no doubt fresh from the forest but is hard, whereas the fish offered by Bwr-Tapuu is fresh as well as soft to eat. Therefore, I would suggest you consider Bwr-Tapuu.' Following her mother's advice, Jaayww Bonv chose Bwr-Tapuu and left with him for the water world, to be with him for the rest of her life. She made the waters her home and was happy living there.

When Diiduu-Kuubo came to know that Jaayww Bonv was living with Bwr-Tapuu, he was furious and vowed to take revenge on both of them. He felt deeply insulted and cheated. Though he devised several nefarious plans, he failed miserably and waited for the right time to seek revenge.

One fine day while sauntering through the woods, Diiduu-Kuubo came across a weak and sickly civet. He was shocked to see such an unhealthy animal in the forest. Out of curiosity he asked the civet, 'What happened to you? Why do you look so sick?' The civet replied with great agony, 'By mistake I ate the poisonous berries of the muutv tree. This made me ill.' Diiduu-Kuubo was truly grieved and showed the civet a particular plant that could cure him, but he became curious. He asked the civet, 'Could you show me the tree that caused you the sickness?' In his mind, he started to think of an idea to do away with both Bwr-Tapuu and Jaayww Bonv. Thus, just as soon as Diiduu-Kuubo was shown the poisonous tree, he started to collect as many berries as possible. After he felt that he had collected enough, he brought all the poisonous berries to the spot where Bwr-Tapuu and Jaayww Bonv lived. He pounded these and mixed them with water. As he sat crushing the berries, he went on cursing fiercely:

Jaayww Bonv ne, Bonv hikw tummo ruuko
Bonv dorso go pagmo ruuko
Lwwlv yudwr v dwrru dag bv
Lwwtak yubar v barji dagbv
Bwtv lwwru vm, itv lwwru vm
Kacww eekuka....

The poison should cause immeasurable suffering to Jaayww Bonv. Let the extract of the poison reach each and every corner of the waterbody and crumble the boulders into pieces.

Jaayww Bonv and Bwr-Tapuu! This is what you both deserve for what you have done to me. You both are going to suffer for your deeds.

The extract from the berries soon mixed with the water and the poison gradually spread across the entire waterbody. The poison killed all types of life forms that lived in the water. The contaminated water also entered the house of Bwr-Tapuu and Jaayww Bonv, causing them great pain and finally their death. Thus, Bwr-Tapuu and Jaayww Bonv met with their unfortunate end because of Diiduu-Kuubo.

Thus, according to the people of the region, the use of poisonous berries to poison the waters by Diiduu-Kuubo was the first instance of herbal fishing and beginning of the tradition. Ever since, this method has been passed on through generations and herbal fishing has become a popular method of community fishing and an important part of the traditional Galo knowledge system.

....

8

Bimbin Tabo

Jinv Bimbin Tabo v goiyv,
Korum ogo yu goiyv,
Jimi ogo yu goiyv,
Korlo ogo yu goiyv

This story of Bimbin Tabo begins in ancient times when silence prevailed everywhere.

Long time ago, there was a man named Bimbin Tabo. He had two wives who were devoted and took good care of him but he was a greedy and uncaring husband.

One fine morning, Bimbin Tabo told his wives, 'Today, I will go to the forest in search of small game.' Saying this he set out for the forest. On reaching the woods, he started to set up traps at various locations. After setting up the traps he waited quietly for the animals to fall into the traps.

The whole day he waited eagerly but without much luck. It was getting dark in the forest. Just then he saw a civet caught in his trap. His happiness knew no bounds. The sight of a trapped civet after spending the whole day starving in the forest brought much relief to his growling stomach.

Bimbin Tabo looked at the trapped civet and thought, 'If I take this home, I will have to share the meat with my two wives.' Therefore, he decided to have it all by himself. He made a small fire in the forest with dry leaves and twigs lying around, roasted the catch, and ate the meat. Not to leave any traces, he put the bones in a small leaf, wrapped it tightly and threw it far away in the forest. Afterwards, he collected mushrooms for his two wives.

At home, handing over the leaf packet containing mushrooms, he told his wives, 'I spent the whole day in the forest looking for game with no success. Mushroom is all I have got. Here it is.'

A few days passed and Bimbin Tabo decided to go to the forest again for hunting. After reaching the forest, he looked for an appropriate location to set up the traps. He set the traps and waited anxiously. This time he was lucky. Within no time, three birds were caught in his trap. He couldn't thank his luck enough. Happily, he picked up the birds, put them in his bamboo basket and headed home. Cheerfully, he returned home with his catch of the day. Sitting around the fireplace in the evening, he took out the birds from his basket and showed them proudly to his wives. Soon he was faced with a predicament.

He took a deep breath, and said, 'Taaku pwum v, xii aaum v, achen aren ma.' Here are three birds and three people, how are we going to divide it amongst us?

The first wife immediately responded, 'Let us take one each. Isn't that fair?'

Hearing this Bimbin Tabo flared up in anger, picked up the bamboo tongs lying nearby and hit the first wife. Instantly, she ran out of the house.

Bimbin Tabo settled down in his place still looking perplexed. He asked the same question to his second wife. This time the second wife, who had witnessed the whole incident, suggested cautiously, 'Why don't you have two birds and sister (the first wife) and I share one bird.'

Hearing this Bimbin Tabo felt relieved and satisfied. He happily announced, 'Vgem ruma bv tatte donmv.' This is exactly what I wanted to hear.

After the deal was settled, the first wife was called back

inside the house and accordingly, the food was shared among the three. However, both wives weren't happy with the way their husband had treated them. On earlier occasions too, Bimbin Tabo had shown no consideration to the needs of his two wives.

After a few months had passed, it was the season for cultivation. Day and night Bimbin Tabo worked in the field. He burned the undergrowth and meticulously cleared the debris. When the land was ready for sowing, he went to his two wives and said, 'The field is ready for sowing now. Please go to the field and sow the seeds.'

Both wives knew that at the time of sowing, Bimbin Tabo would need their help. And they wanted to teach him a lesson for being unkind to them. Therefore, they went to the field but instead of sowing paddy they put dust and instead of maize they put pebbles in the holes made by the dibbling stick.

They both knew that Bimbin Tabo wasn't a good husband to them. He neither shared food equally nor treated them well. Therefore, they both decided to leave him and run away.

Bimbin Tabo mwv goiyv, si kubbe yu goiyv
Riji kubbe yu goiyv, ximar kubbe yu goiyv
Kabji kubbe yu goiyv, jinv bimbin e goiyv

When Bimbin Tabo came to the field, he couldn't find his wives. He looked everywhere but in vain. He then realized his folly; the way he had mistreated his two wives. He cried and cried but it was too late.

....

9

Gohen Bam

A dream doesn't become reality through magic; it takes sweat, determination, and hard work.

In the 1950s, the NEFA (North East Frontier Agency), presently known as Arunachal Pradesh, was highly inaccessible to the outside world due to its difficult mountainous terrain. There was no proper means of communication and even basic necessities were non-existent. Electricity was a distant dream in those days. It was during this time, in the midst of all practical difficulties, that the Late Gohen Bam began his journey to become an entrepreneur while he was still a teenager.

Born to Kargo Bam and Jumme Riba in one of the remotest villages, Bam, in the Lypaa Radaa district of Arunachal Pradesh, Gohen Bam was one among four siblings. Without any formal education, he started his career with no guidance, capital, or contacts. He began to work by peeling cane bark in the forest. To receive his first payment, he walked for several days through dense forest infested with wild animals. He covered a distance of around 180 kilometres, in undulating terrain, braving all odds from Daporijo to Ziro Valley. From the profit that he made, while returning, he bought a hundred cattle from Lakhimpur in the state of Assam, to start a cattle business.

A friendly person, he had no problems making new friends. In 1962, he met Mr Sood, a General Reserve Engineer Force (GREF) personnel and within no time they became good friends. Mr Sood later gifted him a generator and it was used in a function organized at Bam village to produce electricity. This was the first instance of an event with electricity in the region.

In the following years, he ventured into various small-scale business enterprises, including setting up the first rice mill in the village and supplying rice to the village school, followed by a wood business and the first furniture shop in the region, which popularly came to be known as Bam Furniture. He was also given the contract to build the government quarters in the Basar region and later, he donated land to the state government for the construction of government buildings in different locations. Seeing his hard work and his interest in village developmental activities, he was selected as Member of Anchal Samiti (rural local governments or panchayats at the intermediate level of the three-tier panchayati raj system) of Bam village in 1972, as well as the following two years. Apart from being a popular orator, he was also regarded as a repository of traditional knowledge. He had profound knowledge of folklores, myths, legends, fables, and folk tales. Therefore, he was regarded as a xikok—someone who is well-versed in folk literature. Often, during the performance of rituals, he would flawlessly recite and chant invocations along with the priest.

The late 1970s saw some more significant contributions by Bam. This was the time when Purana Bazaar was emerging as an important centre for business activities and witnessed different people from outside Arunachal Pradesh, coming in, settling down, and opening shops. Bam was one of the pioneers who were instrumental in the establishment of this township. He started the first Fair Price shop at Basar. Soon, Purana Bazaar developed into a full-fledged business centre catering to the basic needs of the people from Basar and nearby villages. He also opened a cinema hall at Purana Bazaar which became a famous recreation centre screening Hindi, English, Nepali, and Chinese movies.

Bam also helped to start bus services that connected Basar to Aalo, the headquarters of West Siang district. This proved to be a big step as commuting was very problematic due to

lack of vehicles and well-built roads. The bus service helped
the people of Basar to commute to Aalo easily, especially for
official work. Gohen Bam had a great business acumen. He was
popularly known as thikadar—contractor—among the people
because he was a famous contractor in the region.

Though he lacked formal education, yet he always remained
well-informed. His charismatic personality also helped him
befriend many government officials, who always helped him
willingly, whenever there was any need. Thus, he kept himself
informed of government-aided schemes meant for village level
development programmes and saw that the villagers duly
benefitted from them, including government schemes like the
Integrated Rural Development Programmes (IRDP), Biogas
and solar study lamp schemes. He also opened a fish pond
at Bam village with the help of the Fishery Department and
was involved in many developmental schemes related to wet
cultivation and horticulture.

On a personal level, he helped many young boys and girls
from the villages by providing them accommodation in his
own house and helping them continue their education. For his
significant contribution to society, he was awarded the state
Silver Medal on 26 January 2000 by the Honourable Governor
of Arunachal Pradesh.

ASSAM

10

The Tale of the Cat's Daughters

Once there was a cat that began craving fish so she asked her mistress to feed her some. The cat was pregnant at that time. The mistress told her that she did not have any fish and that the cat had to get her fish herself. So the cat went looking for some fish. She robbed some from her neighbours, and from wherever she could get her paws on, but she had a cruel mistress, who cooked and ate all the fish. The wicked lady only left the dry bones for the starving, pregnant cat. The cat asked her mistress, 'I got all this fish, I robbed them from so many places putting my life at risk, but you ate everything and did not leave anything for me. How is this done?' The owner snapped back and told her that it is either this or the cat could just forget about everything. Furious and seething with rage, the cat cursed the owner saying that whatever is there in the mistress's stomach should come to hers and vice versa.

It so happened that the wicked woman too was pregnant at that time and so, one day soon after, the cat gave birth to two human babies and the mistress, to a couple of kittens. Afraid of her owner's wrath, the cat took her daughters away to a safe place. She looked after her daughters with the utmost care, love, and devotion. Every day, the cat would go out looking for food and her kids, who were left behind, worried about their mother. One evening when she came back, her daughters implored, 'Mother, what if something bad happens and you don't come back one day? How will we know if you are fine, that a human being hasn't killed you?' The mother cat placed a bowl of milk under a tulsi plant and told them that if the tulsi plant dies and withers away, and if the milk turns black, they should know that she is not safe. The daughters were happy and satisfied with this explanation.

One day soon after, the plant died, and the milk turned black. Scared and worried, the daughters scurried out of the safe place to look for their mother. They walked for miles on end until they got thirsty and the younger sister asked her elder sibling to fetch some water. The elder sister found a river nearby and quenched her thirst, but when she was trying to take some water back, the river suddenly dried up and so did the water in her hands. Perplexed, she looked around and then she heard the voice of the River Prince. He commanded that she would have to remove her finger ring and throw it into the heart of the river and only then will she be able to take some water. The girl complied and took some water back. After quenching her thirst, the younger sister told the elder one that she should get her ring back from the river since she is not thirsty any more. The sister went back and searched for the ring but the prince dragged her into the river and she disappeared.

The younger sister was sitting and crying at the riverbank, calling out for her sister to no avail when a trader sailing by, saw her and offered help. The trader, who had two wives, took the younger sister home and married her. The other two wives soon became jealous of the younger wife because the trader fell deeply in love with her. Soon, the new wife got pregnant and gave birth to a bonny baby boy. However, without the knowledge of the young wife, the two jealous wives threw the newborn baby into the river right after he was born. They told the cat's daughter that she had given birth to a piece of wood which is why they did what they did. The daughter got pregnant and delivered another boy soon, but the wives threw the baby into the river this time too, having told her that it was a pumpkin this time. When the trader got to know this, he thought that his new wife was a cursed woman, so he made a small hut at the trash site outside the house and moved her there. Meanwhile, the River Prince had married the elder sister who was earlier thought to have been missing. He also found two newborn baby boys in the river and took them into his fold.

One day, while the trader was sailing by, the River Prince caught hold of his boat and it just wouldn't budge. For a long time, the trader made efforts to release it. The prince then told the trader from the depth of the river, 'I'll only let you go if you make me two promises. One, you'll have to organize a big public feast and invite all the villagers. Two, you'll have to throw your xasoti[2] and your walking stick into the water.' With no other option but to agree, the trader made the promises and left. Meanwhile, the elder daughter called her sons and told them everything about her own journey and how they were found, right from the beginning when she was born to her cat mother.

Informed, on the day of the big feast, the two sons took the xasoti and the stick and went out looking for their mother and, by sheer luck, met their real mother—the younger cat daughter. The boys instantly knew that she was their mother. They were hungry and tired and said, 'Mother, can we take shelter here for some time and do you have some food and water for us?' The young mother did not recognize them at first and got angry thinking that they were mocking her. The sons told her that they were her boys and unravelled the whole mystery by showing her the trader's xasoti and the stick.

The news that the prince's sons had stopped by at this cursed woman's house in the village soon reached the place of the feast and the story was unfolded. To prove the truth behind it, the boys showed the xasoti and the stick to everyone as

---

[2]A packet of betel nut and leaves wrapped in a gamusa, the traditional Assamese cloth.

well. In the end, the two elder wives confessed and repented for what they had done. The trader accepted his mistake and took his young wife back to his house. Everyone returned home and they all lived happily ever after.

....

11

The Foolish Son-in-law

It was Magh Bihu and the father-in-law felt that it would be nice to invite his jowai, son-in-law, to dinner. So the entire family lost no time in inviting the son-in-law and excitedly went about making preparations for dinner.

On the day of the dinner, the son-in-law started a little late in the afternoon. As he started walking, he noticed that his own shadow was also walking along with him, but he did not realize it to be his shadow, instead, he thought that it was someone who was accompanying him. He felt that his father-in-law would be upset if he arrived at his house with a stranger. He immediately said to the shadow, 'Hey, what do you want? Why have you come? Go away!' But the shadow neither replied nor left. So, he asked once again, 'Hey! Why don't you speak up? Do you need my cheleng?' Saying so, he wanted to dismiss the shadow and he motioned with his hand in a manner, as if he wanted the shadow to leave. The shadow, instead, made a similar hand gesture. The son-in-law thought that the shadow may only be interested in his cheleng, so he left it on the ground and continued to walk. But to his surprise, he noticed that the shadow continued to walk along with him. Quite perplexed, he gradually gave away his dhoti and gamchha too. At this point, as he stood thinking about ways to get rid of the shadow, the sun started to set in the horizon and it soon became dark.

Unfortunately, the son-in-law suffered from partial night-blindness and he could not see clearly in the dark. Thus, as dusk set in, he could barely move and kept standing, thinking about a way out. Suddenly, he could see something on the horizon, and it looked like one of the white cows that belonged to his father-in-law. It was indeed a white cow. He thought it was the best way to reach his in-laws' house as he could not walk any further in the dark. In his condition of semi-visibility, he somehow fumbled and caught hold of the cow's tail and went along. Thus, after some time, he reached the house of his in-laws. However, he felt ashamed to enter the house as he was not wearing a dhoti and so he thought of hiding behind a banana tree. However, as he could not see properly in the dark, he did not realize that the banana tree where he was hiding was actually the place where his in-laws throw the kitchen waste.

In the meantime, the xahur, father-in-law, who was waiting for his jowai, thought that the latter would not turn up as it was already dark. So, he finished his dinner and went to bed and the xahu, mother-in-law, cleared the kitchen, collected the kitchen waste and threw them out of the window, as she always did. The garbage fell on the jowai's head and made him wet and dirty. In shock, the jowai uttered the word 'Ah!' loudly and his xahu heard this. She immediately recognized the voice and realized that the jowai was standing outside the kitchen window. She felt sorry and ashamed and called him in and also gave him some spare, clean clothes. Then, she served the jowai rice with liquid jaggery. The jowai did not know what the liquid was and said that he did not want it. To this, the xahu replied, 'Do have it. It is very sweet and tasty. I prepared it especially for you.' Now, on being requested by his xahu, as the jowai tasted the liquid jaggery, he liked it very much and asked to see where all the jaggery was kept. The xahu pointed to a clay pot suspended from the ceiling and mentioned, 'Can you see that pot? I keep all my jaggery in that.'

After the jowai had finished his dinner, the xahu prepared his bed and bid him goodnight. As both the xahur and xahu slept, the jowai kept thinking about the tasty jaggery and could not sleep. He got up, went to the place where the clay pot was hanging and made a hole at the bottom of the pot. The sweet, liquid jaggery kept trickling down through the hole and the jowai kept licking to his heart's content. After some time, when the jowai realized that the pot was empty, he suddenly felt that his upper body was covered with sticky jaggery. As he was wondering how to get rid of it he dimly saw some cotton nearby, which was to be used in preparing a mattress. The jowai rubbed his body against the cotton to wipe off the sticky substance; instead, his entire upper body was covered with white, fluffy cotton. He felt he looked like a white goat and suddenly he could faintly see the goatshed where the goats lay peacefully. He entered the goatshed and thought that he could lie there for the night. Alas, that was not to be as two thieves entered the goatshed soon after. They wanted to steal the best goat and decided to choose the one with the softest fur. They saw the jowai and thought that he was the softest goat and thus decided to carry him with them.

The thieves tied the jowai to a bamboo pole and carried him off to a nearby riverbank. At a particular spot on the bank, the thieves could see that the water was shallow and they began to cross the river. As they were wading across the water, they did not notice that the bottom of the animal which they were carrying was touching the surface of the water. The jowai was extremely uncomfortable at this and said loudly, 'Lift me up, lift me up, you foolish thieves!' The thieves, on the other hand, got very frightened and thought that it was a supernatural occurring. They threw the goat in the water and ran away in fear.

Since the water was shallow at that point, the jowai did not drown and the water washed away all the sticky jaggery and cotton. He cleaned himself well and came out of the river and sat down on the bank. The sun was already appearing on the horizon and it was soon dawn. In the meantime, the xahur, who could not find the jowai inside the house came out looking for him. He reached the riverbank and saw the jowai sitting there and took him home. The xahu was waiting at home with a scrumptious breakfast and they fed the jowai well. After a hearty meal, the jowai bid his in-laws farewell and started off for home.

12

Messages Through Wall Art

Earth, beautiful Earth, and out of this is my motherland Assam, eternally blissful Assam, full of wide-ranging species of plants and animals is my Assam. If we humans are the most superior beings, we must save this ailing Mother Earth and Assam.

Thus goes the narration as part of an early morning session in a primary school in Assam by Kiran Gogoi who originally hails from Chabua town in Upper Assam. Gogoi's classes are well attended by students as well as teachers. The children stand in queue and their teachers stand close to them. All listen in rapt attention to Gogoi. The children even touch the ground with their fingers followed by their forehead in an act of paying obeisance to Mother Nature. Kiran Gogoi's special classes teach one to respect nature and be thankful for what it unconditionally bestows upon us. Gogoi was formally employed as a teacher at a private school and was always enamoured of the natural beauty of Assam. Unfortunately, his school shut down due to lack of financial assistance. It was at this time that Gogoi decided to devote a considerable amount of time to his true love—nature. Being also inspired by the songs of the famous Assamese singer Bhupen Hazarika, Gogoi always felt a deep sense of closeness and association with the natural beauty of Assam and the mighty Brahmaputra River. Inspired through the magical touches of verdant Assam, Gogoi's passion took shape in 1994, through the initiation of his NGO Baichitra

Dharitri. It began with the vision of highlighting aspects of nature amongst school children and spreading awareness about safeguarding the environment. Initially, his special classes in various schools aimed at teaching children through impromptu poetry on environment; however, over the last several years, Gogoi's attempts to spread positive messages have taken an important form of dissemination of messages—through wall art and writings.

Gogoi writes in Assamese on walls, using limestone powder, boiled into a paste in water. He started this even when he was a schoolteacher though it was limited in nature. Gradually, over the years, it has become an important method of mass communication. He is often seen to carry a small earthen pot with a mixture of limestone paste and a small brush. He dips the brush and creates messages and art pertaining to nature on several walls. This is Gogoi's attempt to reach out beyond the school premises. So far, his work has incorporated over a thousand writings on walls across various regions of Assam, including both big and small towns and cities and also various districts, such as Guwahati, Kokrajhar, Dhubri, Silchar, Dibrugarh, Nagoan, Morigaon, Tezpur, Kaziranga, Jorhat, Sibsagar, Golaghat, Tinsukia, amongst others. One can even find him writing his messages on walls on hot, humid or scorching days of the summer months. Sometimes, when Gogoi works continuously at a stretch for four to five days and without any protection or gloves, the limestone causes bruises and burns on his hands and he ends up with bleeding palms and fingers. However, Gogoi's love for nature has always inspired him and kept him going.

Gogoi's diligent efforts have paid off. There are various organizations that have offered to help him in his tree-plantation drives by providing free saplings. He has successfully managed to reach out to places beyond Upper Assam and communicate with a cross-section of people from across the state of Assam.

He is also often invited to various environmental programmes, and workshops. So far, Gogoi has conducted more than 9,000 meetings in schools to create awareness amongst the students on how to conserve and preserve nature. A silent worker, Gogoi's wall art leaves behind important messages such as:

> With knowledge, nature will survive.
> This is nature loving Assam.
> You are the wonderful earth, and we are your sons.
> Rhino killing is a world sorrow.
> Different species of plants and animals are a treasure.
> Will alcohol stop consuming humans?
> The sons of earth may live long.

BIHAR

13

The Ghost in the Hostel Room

A jay gained consciousness gradually at the sound of the villagers around him. He was still near the pond and was feeling drowsy. He could not remember for how long he was lying unconscious, till the folks of Grin Surya village discovered and rescued him. When he opened his eyes, he was lying half upright, leaning against the big tree next to the pond. At least seven to eight people were gathered around him, anxiously peering into his face, which was dripping with water sprinkled on him from the pond nearby. He was bombarded with questions, especially because the villagers knew him well and was overjoyed to see him return to the village for the first time since he had left for his higher studies in medicine in Patna, a year ago. However, Ajay did not reply to any of the questions and all he could think of was what happened just before he passed out. That was also the last time he had seen Pradip. He had passed out even before Pradip left.

After this incident, days passed into weeks, but Ajay never recovered his health. He was always ailing. He lost his appetite for food and he hardly touched water. As he lay starving and forlorn, he went back to the very beginning of his medical college days several times in his mind...exactly a year ago.

Ajay had got admission in MBBS in a reputed medical college in the big city of Patna. Hailing from a village, which was several hours away, Ajay took residence at the boys' hostel. He entered his room to find Pradip as his roommate—a student of third year MBBS. Pradip smiled and greeted him. To Ajay, Pradip looked a bit serious and a recluse. Ajay didn't really mind and almost never disturbed Pradip, but Ajay never saw him attending any classes. Pradip was always in his room whenever Ajay entered—be it any time of the day. However, it was within a couple of months that he had to confide in Pradip and mention that he has to change the room. Pradip, however, replied calmly, 'But why do you want to change rooms and roommates now? Are you having any trouble? I am very comfortable with you.' Ajay thought for a while for a suitable answer and before he could reply, Pradip added, 'You did see me one of these days, right? Isn't it so?' Pradip sounded stern and was looking at Ajay with piercing eyes. Ajay was frightened and fumbled, 'Yes, I...I...noticed that you do not get...o-out of the bed t-t-to switch off the light. The-the other day, when I asked for a g-glass of water, you got it next to my bedside, even without getting down from your bed.... I-I saw you extending your hand, a-all the way over to the o-other corner of the room to do chores....' Ajay was stammering and his voice trailed off. Not only was he frightened now, he was pale and shivering and was feeling sick. Pradip was still looking sternly at Ajay and replied in a threatening tone, 'Very well. So, you know everything. I have been living in this room for twenty years. I was a medical student once like you and used to reside in this room and I will never leave this room, neither can anyone make me leave. I have never allowed anybody to occupy my bed. When the hostel wardens worry too much about this fact, they suffer in agony. So, don't be foolish. I will not harm you, however, do not speak about me to anyone, or else....' Pradip walked away, still looking at Ajay.

After that day, Ajay could hardly wait for the semester to get over. He was anxious to reach his village. Soon, it was time for summer vacation and Ajay started off for home. As he reached his village, he heaved a sigh of relief to have escaped the nightmare of the hostel and his room. He was generally thinking and walking briskly towards his home, when he noticed his childhood friend, Vijay Pal, sitting next to a large pond, which was situated just on the outskirts of the village. Vijay waved at Ajay and he waved back. Vijay walked towards Ajay with a wide smile, 'Come, come, doctor sahib. Tell me, how have college and hostel life been...?' and almost instantly added, '...but you look terrible. What happened? Are you sick?' Ajay could take it no more. It was as if an answer to his weeks and months of anxiety and emotional trauma. He blurted out his experience to Vijay who listened carefully. Finally, Vijay replied, 'Oh that's terrible, but how did the hand extend? Was it like this?' and suddenly Vijay transformed into Pradip and his right hand started to extend towards the tall tree next to the pond. As the hand grew, Ajay heard Pradip saying loudly, 'Didn't I tell you not to tell this to anyone. Now that you have broken your silence, you will suffer....' Ajay remembered no more and probably passed out at this moment. It was only after the villagers rescued him that he could reach his home....

A few weeks later, it was the end of the summer vacation. All the students returned to their classes. The medical college campus was buzzing with greetings, smiles, and laughter but Ajay was missing. Ajay had died in his village home from starvation two weeks after he had reached home.

14

Harhi Pond

In ancient times, there was a fisherwoman by the name of Harhi. She used to go from door to door, selling fish in different areas of Darbhanga. Harhi used to carry a large bowl on her head filled with fish. One day, as she was on her way, a vulture swooped down and snatched away a big and heavy rohu fish. The vulture flew away with the rohu before Harhi could stop it. The fish was still alive when the vulture snatched it and it started to suffocate in the clutches of the vulture. The vulture was on the lookout for a resting place to enjoy its food and took it atop a tall tree. In the meantime, Harhi was following the vulture upto a certain distance. However, she finally realized that she couldn't retrieve her fish and stopped chasing the vulture. After some time though, Harhi noticed that the fish had fallen from the tall tree, after it had freed itself from the clutches of the vulture. She quickly started to move towards the tree and laughed heartily, looking towards the vulture, as it could not control a small fish.

Passers-by thought that Harhi was laughing because she got her fish back and a traveller asked, 'Hey Harhi! You sell fish every day, but why don't you cover the fish in the bowl so that the vultures may not snatch them? Today the fish was dropped; otherwise it would have been your loss. However, I don't understand why you are so thrilled. What exactly is the matter?' Harhi replied, still smiling, 'Baba, if a small piece of fish is eaten by a vulture or a crow, what does it matter? But this heavy fish of more than a ser not being able to be controlled by this huge vulture, is indeed a matter to laugh about. Oh God! Human beings are gradually becoming weaker and smaller by the day and as I can see, so are birds and animals! Wise people remark that once upon a time, the hands of human beings were as heavy as one maund and on top of that, they would wear ornaments of the gods, as heavy as ten sers. Such heavyweights could be, however, carried by vultures for hundreds of miles but in modern days, vultures cannot carry a fish of a ser or so! This is indeed funny.'

Listening to these words of Harhi, the traveller replied, 'Harhi! How do you know that the hands of people were as heavy as one maund and they used to wear ornaments of ten sers which could be carried by vultures for hundreds of miles?' Harhi replied with a smile, 'Hey Baba! I was a vulture in my previous birth. When the battle of Mahabharata was waged, we used to go to the battlefield, greedy for human flesh. Once I saw the hand of a brave warrior lying on the ground. It must not have been less than two maunds and his wrists, fingers, and arms had ornaments of not less than five paseris. I caught hold of that hand, clutched it with my claws and flew in one breath to the branches of a nearby peepul tree and ate the flesh to my heart's content. Even now if the place is dug, one can find the bones of that hand and the ornaments!'

The traveller, of course, didn't believe Harhi's story, but gradually this story began to spread, and it reached the court of the king. The Darbhanga maharaj ordered Harhi to be present in his court and tell him the full story. He obtained the location of the peepul tree and commissioned hundreds of labourers to dig the area. At last, a big bone of a hand was found, which was still adorned with paseris of gold, silver, and other costly jewels. The king awarded Harhi handsomely and the place became famous as Harhi Pond.

15

Mother

'Vishnu Pad is not even half a kos away from Nadra Gunj, and we have lived here always, in peace with the Hindus. I am not scared of any rioters, I am not leaving my home to go to Pakistan, and there will be no more discussion.' Amma was steadfast in the face of persuasion.

'But, bhabi,' Chhote abba persisted, 'the reports from Tilhara will make you shudder. It is no longer safe for us to remain here. India is no longer safe for Muslims.'

'Really!' Amma looked at her younger brother-in-law in the eye. 'I was born here. My husband is buried here. So is my father...and my mother. I will not leave their graves; I will not leave my home.'

The same evening as cries of 'Jai Bajrang Bali' resounded outside, and the horror of the communal riots that rent the country asunder seemed closer home, the women and children of Zaman Manzil huddled together. Shafi, all of seven years and Amma's youngest son, crept closer to his mother.

'Amma, are you not scared?' Shafi asked her.

'No, beta', she said. 'We are in our home, and we are safe. Remember, I am Shah Chand's daughter, and the prayers of my Baba will protect us all.' That night, the entire household, including neighbours, lay huddled, bleary-eyed and praying.

The next morning brought a fresh onslaught of counsel. Chhote abba, Shafaqat mamu, Yusuf Khalu, and Ahmadullah nana...all the men in the family gathered in Amma's aangan, the hallowed courtyard.

'I work in the Eastern Railways, bhabi, the government will

provide us with a beautiful home, you needn't worry,' Chhote abba said. And there will be a wagon for us to take all our belongings to East Pakistan. And more importantly, do you feel safe after what happened yesterday?' he added.

Amma relented. 'Okay, start loading your railway wagons.' Everyone sighed in relief. The wagons were loaded with furniture, clothes, and all our belongings. Provisions came next: rice, wheat, oil, dal, spices and even goitha, cowdung cake for fuel. A week before the departure, the wagon, loaded with all our worldly possessions was flagged off from Gaya for Dhaka.

And then came the final day. And Amma stood like a rock. 'I will not leave, bhaiyya, your elder brother is buried here in Gaya. If his spirit comes looking for his wife and sons, what will he find here in Zaman Manzil? Silence and abandonment? I will not leave. Take your wife and children and go, because I cannot stop you from a better life. And no one can touch me in your brother's home. I know.'

The whole household has been packed up and sent. 'Bhabi....' Chhote abba was not above pleading. 'No, bhaiyya, I will not leave my home.' Amma was unwavering.

Chhote abba's voice trembled as he spoke. 'Bhabi, haven't you heard of the stories from Tilhara? Women and children had to jump into wells to escape from the rioter's ill intentions, to save their honour. Do you know the wells have all been filled up to the brim with dead bodies, no one was spared in the riots, and Tilhara isn't far from Gaya. The arson and looting will reach here very soon.'

Amma looked him in the eye once more. And the steel in her tone softened. 'There is a well in my aangan, bhaiyya, and I will also know what to do if the rioters come to my doorstep. You take everyone and go. Shafi and I will stay here,' she pulled her son closer, as he clung to her aanchal, the loose end of the sari.

'I can't take my wife and children, bhabi, and leave my

brother's wife and children in peril,' said Chhote abba. 'They will stay back with you, but I have to join my job day after. Do you promise to come to East Pakistan should you feel the least bit threatened, bhabi?'

'Yes,' Amma said, 'should I feel unsafe in my home, I will let you know.' No one left the home. Not Amma, not her family, not Chhote abba's. Not one family from Mohalla Nadra Gunj migrated to Pakistan during the Partition of India. If Ameeruddin's young widow with four small boys was not scared of rioters and arsonists, who would be?

And years later, in azad Hindustan, Amma, the proud grandmother to so many grandchildren, passed away peacefully in her sleep, surrounded by her sons, sisters-in-law, daughters-in-law, and neighbours—in the same home she had first stepped into as a young fourteen-year-old bride.

Yet, several years later, Shafi still remembers how the women of the family bathed her dead body gently with the water from the same well, which was to protect her honour, should the rioters reach her doorstep, and Shafi could see the smile on Amma's face. A smile that said: 'I came to Zaman Manzil on the shoulders of four kahaars, palanquin bearers, who carried my palki, and I will leave on the shoulders of my four grown-up sons. With as much honour, joy, and peace.'

CHANDIGARH

16

Mirza and Sahibaan

L ong ago, in a small hamlet called Khewa (near present-day Jhang in Pakistan), between the Ravi and Chenab rivers, a woman named Nooran, gave birth to a son. However, she succumbed to the painful childbirth and the baby boy was nursed by a wet nurse, who had a suckling daughter of her own. As per the tradition during those days, the baby boy and the baby girl, being nurtured by the same woman, became cousins. The boy grew up to be the chief of his village and came to be known as Khewa Khan, while the girl grew up to be Fateh Bibi and was married to a man from the Khurral tribe in Dananabad. Geographically, Khewa and Dananabad were a day's ride away on horseback. If one started in the wee hours of the morning, one could reach by dusk.

Sahibaan, who was Khewa Khan's daughter, was brought up in the lap of luxury and Mirza grew up basking in the warmth of the love showered by his family, especially his mother, Fateh Bibi. When Mirza was around eight years old, he was sent to Khewa Khan's house as he was his maternal uncle. Little had he known that this would be the harbinger of a great love and a greater loss in his life. Mirza and Sahibaan were enrolled in the local mosque, where they were guided through lessons by a strict maulvi. The close proximity started to stir feelings that were incomprehensible to the young Mirza and Sahibaan. As adolescence moved into adulthood, the attraction became evident and they fell deeply in love with each other. The strikingly handsome Mirza was the perfect match for the unparalleled beauty of Sahibaan. Piloo, the Punjabi poet, extolls the beauty of Sahibaan, by saying that grocers made errors while weighing goods, the moment they saw her luminous beauty and farmers stopped ploughing when she passed through the fields, like a whiff of fresh air. Mirza, on the other hand, was an epitome of courage and bravery. He was so handsome that even the sun's rays were blinded by his sight. Not only was he brave, he was also an expert marksman, with none to match his skills in archery. He was known to have never missed a target. As their love grew, so did the rage of Sahibaan's kins. This unabashed display of affection and love became a stigma on the fair name of Khewa Khan's family. Mirza was immediately sent back and Sahibaan's marriage was finalized to someone named Tahir Khan. Sahibaan, in desperation, sent a woeful message to Mirza to save her. He defied all the logic delineated by his family members and stuck to his decision of rescuing his lover. He set out on his journey and reached just in time before Sahibaan's marriage could be solemnized. He climbed into Sahibaan's room and they both left the house. They galloped into the dark and uncertain night, with the certainty that their love would eventually overcome all obstacles and would prevail.

Mirza decided to take a break after a non-stop and arduous flight into the night but Sahibaan begged him not to do so, as she had this foreboding that her brothers would catch up with them. Mirza was too confident about his prowess and laughed her fears off. He dozed off under a shady tree. Meanwhile, Sahibaan was plagued by a gamut of emotions and the more she thought, the more her loyalties started getting divided between her family and her lover. Deep down in her naïve heart she believed that her brothers would not harm Mirza. So, she quietly placed Mirza's quiver of arrows on a high branch so that he would not be able to reach it and bloodshed could be averted. However, her wish for peace was not destined to be. Her brother, Shamair, took Mirza by surprise and pierced his throat with an arrow. Completely taken aback by the attack, Mirza looked for his quiver, but could not find it anywhere and was struck relentlessly with a shower of arrows. As he looked questioningly at Sahibaan's eyes, she fell on him to protect him from the sudden and senseless assault, but to no avail.

Mirza and Sahibaan, in their last moments, immortalized a love which was pure and genuine. Since that day, the heart-breaking story of Mirza and Sahibaan has become an important story of love in the Land of Five Rivers (present-day Punjab region in India and Pakistan). When a minstrel or a poet looks for a verse, the tale of Mirza and Sahibaan rises to life and looks for their unfulfilled love in a desolate countryside.

17

Baba Farid

Long ago, in the heart of undivided Punjab, lived a naughty boy named Sheikh Farid. He loved to question his mother about all things that intrigued him. His mother, who was a very pious lady, wanted him to be good, kind, compassionate, and a God-fearing man when he grew up, so one day, she asked him to pray to Allah five times a day. Little Farid, however, was not an ordinary child. He always wanted a reason for doing anything. Farid's mother had told him that Allah would give him sweet, succulent dates, if he prayed with sincerity. Farid was delighted because nothing pleased him more than juicy dates. He asked his mother how he ought to pray. She placed a mat and demonstrated how it was to be done. He immediately took the cue and started to pray with his eyes closed and fervently asked Allah to give him dates. His mother quietly placed a few dates on the mat. When Farid opened his eyes, he was overjoyed to see the dates. This continued for some time and Farid started praying religiously. One day, his mother forgot to place dates on his prayer mat. However, she was extremely puzzled to see that Farid was eating dates after concluding his prayer. She asked him where he had got the dates from and he replied that Allah always provided him with dates. That was the time when his mother realized that Farid had a divine streak.

When Farid grew up, he defied traditional forms of worship, much like Guru Nanak. There are several stories that show that he did not follow meaningless rituals. When he was much older, he decided to suspend himself upside down in a well every day in order to meditate. He did it daily for twelve years in the hope that one day he would find God. He grew so weak over the years that crows started pecking on his shrivelled flesh. He begged the crows to peck anywhere but to leave his eyes alone as he wanted to witness Allah's face one day. He was so overwhelmed with weakness and emotion that he started wailing. The supreme God, Kabir, appeared and asked him why he was subjecting himself to that kind of torture. Farid told him that he wanted to see Allah. Kabir asked him what he thought Allah was like, to which Farid promptly replied that Allah was omnipresent, invisible, and formless. Kabir chided him saying that it was preposterous of him to think that he would be able to see Allah since He was indeed formless! Farid realized that there was truth in those words and that he had been blindly following his guru. The divine realization that God cannot be attained with meditation and other forms of physical discomfort dawned on him. He also became enlightened with the knowledge that Allah resides in the heart and that there is no need to seek him anywhere outside.

There is also another anecdote where someone brought Farid a pair of scissors he put it aside and asked for a needle. When asked why he had done that, he said that his purpose in life was not to cut but to bring together and join!

Baba Farid, as he came to be known in the undivided Punjab region, was one of the greatest Sufi saints. He tried to make people introspect and understand their lives with the help of poetry and analogies. His healing touch gave comfort and relief to all those who were suffering from the vagaries of life.

18

Amrita Pritam

'Jahaan bhi azaad rooh ki jhalak pade, samajh lena wahi
mera ghar hai.' (Wherever you see a glimpse of a free
spirit, understand that it is my home.)

Amrita Pritam

On 31 August 1919, a beautiful baby girl was born to Kartar
Singh Hitkari and Raj Bibi. They named her Amrit Kaur.
Little did they know that one day the delicate baby that they
held in their arms would become the famous writer, Amrita
Pritam. They were certainly not aware that she would personify
the free spirit inherent in every young woman in Punjab and
that she would shake the very foundations of a society that
had made constricting rules for women.

Amrita lost her mother at a very young age, which made
her lose her faith in God. She was an impressionable young
woman, a keen observer, and a silent spectator of life. The
loss of her mother sparked a revolt inside her and she took
to writing poetry defiantly and aggressively, something that
the Punjabi society had not witnessed before in a woman. As
a valuable member of the Progressive Writers' Movement in
pre-Partition British India, she challenged the authority of the
British. Her unhappy marriage with Pritam Singh came out of
the closet as her poems grew bolder and had a marked feminist
voice. She confessed that her marriage lacked compatibility
and companionship. Even though Pritam Singh came from an

affluent family, she was not willing to live a life based on shallow values and sought a divorce.

She decided to fly rather than live like a bird in a gilded cage. She became the voice for many women suffering silently behind closed doors. Amrita Pritam grew to be a prolific writer who held the torch for many women through her inspiring and iconic poetry. She taught women that they had every right to live, love, and follow their hearts, no matter what the price. This was unheard of in a society that has been dominated by men. Her personal hell turned her poetry into a blazing fire, and she wrote like no woman had dared to write. Her spirit sought to empower and enlighten not only herself but also many women who were crushed and felt that they had no reason to live. Her poetry brought solace and comfort to many. Her rise to the pinnacle of literary excellence despite her trauma is indeed commendable.

Amrita found pure and eternal love in the artist, Imroz. The brilliantly talented painter painted the canvas of her heart with colours that would last forever. Their love was so strong that they did not feel the need to get married to give it a legal status. Their love demonstrated to society that commitment is in the heart and not on a piece of paper. Her immortal love story reinstated love in the hearts and minds of people.

Amrita passed away in 2005, but she left behind a legacy in the hearts of the people of Punjab. Even today, no poetry society or poetry gathering in Chandigarh is complete without mentioning Amrita Pritam. In every lane and street, if a poet writes a verse, he or she invariably seeks the blessings of Amrita Pritam. Such is her stature and luminescence. She personified the phrase 'Life is short, but love is long'.

CHHATTISGARH

19

The Magical Garuda Pillar

Slowly and steadily, the dark night passed on the baton to an intensely dim dawn light. One that was the engine of an early morning, shrouded completely in the chillness of a late December winter and laced with mist in millions of its atoms and molecules. Calm yet echoing with the tunes of morning tea vendors who were calling out 'chai chai'. It was not long before the wheels of the carriage slowed down considerably; they kept chugging along before the final application of brakes made them still. The slight backward reaction induced a small jerk, just good enough to open the eyelids! A glance outside depicted a station board: 'Welcome to Jagdalpur'. A couple of steps ahead and it was 'Alight here to visit Chitrakut Waterfalls–45 kilometres; Tirathgarh Waterfalls–35 kilometres'. Clearly an alluring sign to commune with nature in the tribal heartland!

Excited, he pulled up his backpack and they started to move outside the platform towards the taxi stand.

'Madam, aap ko kahan jaana hai?' enquired the cab driver.

'Dantewada', replied Sone Ki Chidiya (SKC), the golden bird, with aplomb

'Accha. Minimum do ghante lagenge.'

'Koi nahi. Aap apne hisab se le chaliye.'

They put the backpack into the dicky and climbed into the back seat of the taxi.

The steering wheel kept doing its job effortlessly.

It is now almost an hour into the ride. Replete with glimpses of forests, green fields, tribal settlements, and road bends (at times)!

74 *Lopamudra Maitra Bajpai*

'Why are we going to this place?' asked Awara Banjara (AB), the traveller.

'Well, every district, city, town, and village of my country has a tale to narrate. This place is no different. In fact, there's an interesting legend associated with it in addition to a historical anecdote,' said SKC beaming with excitement!

'Of what?'

'Royalty, deity, festival, beliefs, etc. Do you want to live this story?'

'Wow! I cannot wait to hear the story.'

It was the cycle of Satya Yuga. Prajapati Daksha humiliated Lord Shiva. Deeply frustrated at this and not being able to withstand this insult, his consort, Goddess Sati, then immolated herself in the fire pit of the yajna. This, in turn, angered Shiva to the core. The very fact that he was eternally in love with Sati only took him into a state of trance carrying her dead body on his shoulders. This Tandav Nritya, mad trance, had the potential to destroy the entire cosmos. Foreseeing this annihilation and also to free Shiva from the grief of his loss, Lord Vishnu, using his Sudarshan Chakra, cut her dead body into fifty-two pieces. These body parts then fell on the earth and was scattered across the entire Indian subcontinent (present-day India, Pakistan, Bangladesh, Nepal, Sri Lanka, and even Tibet). The locations sprung up with temples which also came to be referred to as Shakti Peeths (fifty-two in total), meaning, the goddesses here are worshipped as incarnations of Shakti—the female force. It is believed that Sati's teeth fell in Dantewada and the temple that came up over it came to be called as Danteswari Temple.

'Loved every bit of this. And what about the historical anecdote out here?' the eager listener asked.

Time, as usual didn't wait for anyone. Yuga cycles changed. In fact, there were four. Satya Yuga gave way to the fourth cycle—Kali Yuga. Thousands of years passed. We finally come to the fourteenth century. The armies of the Delhi Sultanate captured a large part of Telangana, including Warangal. The situation forced Annamadeva, brother of the last Kakatiya (subordinates of the Chalukya dynasty) ruler, Prataprudra II, to anoint his nephew to the throne and thence retreat into the dense Dandakaranya forest of Dantewada. Even then, as a royal tradition, he carried nothing but a statue of the family deity with him all along during these wanderings. Days went by. Then one night, he had a memorable tete-a-tete with her, in deep sleep, where she miraculously appeared in his dream stating that she shall be walking with him from there on. Further, blessing him with a boon that wherever he set his foot, he would acquire that part as his kingdom. Annamadeva was overjoyed. As he prepared to leave, she interrupted stating that there was a proviso to this boon. That if he turned back anytime during this walk, she would stop accompanying him and that point would become the boundary of his kingdom!

'Then?'

He kept walking for days in the jungles of Dantewada. One fine day, he reached the confluence of the rivers, Shankhini and Dankini. The riparian sight was a treat to the eyes. The calmness all around was conspicuous before something suddenly broke the silence. It was the tinkling sound of anklets. The sound and its echo so mesmerizing that it just stopped his walk altogether. Not just that, it forced him to turn back. The sight was even more divine. A live appearance of the goddess who had appeared in his dreams. For once, his joy knew no bounds. But the moment didn't last long enough. For he had broken the clause to not turn back. As he had been told, the Goddess stopped then and there.

Subsequently, Annamadeva started ruling over this place and built a temple here where he worshipped the goddess. The temple came to be called Danteshwari Temple and the goddess became the Kuldevi—the family deity—of the Bastar royal family!

'Fascinating! History is just so engrossing. Are there any religious beliefs attached to it?'

The temple has a garba griha, sanctum sanctorum; maha mandal, grand hall; mukhya mandap, main hall; and sabha mandap, assembly hall. There is a Garuda Pillar right at its entrance. It is said that one who is able to embrace it completely with both hands gets all his wishes fulfilled!

'Amazing. But how can a layman believe this wish-fulfilment story?'

Well, a culture is the evolution of beliefs, traditions, and customs over centuries. Over a period of time, some of them become so powerful that they get ingrained in the psyche of a community or clan. And their miraculous results overwhelmingly defy logic and science. Even otherwise, there are some things in life that are to be accepted without proof. Remember the concept of 'lemma' in mathematics? The more you explore my country, the more you will sway towards its secrets and mysteries!

20

The Mahua Tree

This is a very old folk tale. Once there was a village, where the sarpanch used to love hosting travellers and guests visiting the village and eagerly waited for visitors. He would spend his entire day thinking about innovative ways to entertain his guests and about the various kinds of food and drinks he would serve his guests. He wanted each of his guests to depart merrily and fully contented! This was his dream.

The guests, in turn, were happy too. They used to leave with joy in their hearts and a smile on their faces. They would always remark that they had not experienced such hospitality anywhere else. However, the sarpanch was still not satisfied. He continued to wonder, 'Why were the guests not dancing with joy even after being treated with wonderful hospitality?' His idea of revelry actually meant that the guests should sway and dance merrily and he was ready to do anything to witness this.

Each morning, the sarpanch would go looking for flowers and fruits in the forests, but alas, there was only one variety of fruit to be found. The sarpanch would gather as much as possible of whatever was available and later serve them to his guests visiting the village. The son of the sarpanch also shared his father's fervour. Both of them used to collect fruits and flowers in the jungle for their guests.

One day, one of the guests remarked, 'Are there any other varieties of fruits available here? I can only see one type of fruit before me. Where I come from, there is a wide variety of fruits available. Anyway, even this fruit, which you are serving, is also a good one and I am really enjoying it.'

To this, the sarpanch and his son looked at each other and then the sarpanch replied, 'We look for different types of fruits all day long in the forest, but this is the only variety available here.'

The guest replied, 'It really doesn't matter. I love your hospitality. Nowhere have I been served food with so much respect and festivity.'

That night the son told the father, 'I will go into the deep jungles to search for other varieties of fruits.'

The sarpanch's heart warmed up at the son's wish, 'Yes, son, you should go.'

The son searched the jungle for days but was unable to find any new variety of fruit. One day, after wandering for long, he was very tired and decided to rest under a tree. Suddenly, he saw a sparrow flying towards a tree. It was dancing and singing and gradually it flew away.

'Oh! This sparrow is dancing with joy!' thought the son. He looked everywhere and found many sparrows around him and all were having a merry time. The son became curious. He looked around to find the source of this merriment.

He saw a waterhole nearby. Many sparrows would fly, come to the waterhole, drink from it and fly away—gaily dancing and jumping with joy. After a while, he noticed one sparrow, which had not yet drank from the waterhole. It was neither jumping nor dancing. The son suspected that there must be something magical in the waterhole. It looked very tantalizing!

The sarpanch's son bent down and drank the water. 'Oh! This water is so weird. I feel like everything is dancing around me and I am dancing too. Surely there's some hidden magic in this water.' He looked around and saw that the tree above the waterhole was a mahua tree. The dried leaves from the tree were falling into the water. This also meant that there was something magical coming out of the leaves and getting mixed with the water.

The son was overjoyed. This was the fruit that he was looking for. He collected several fruits of the mahua tree and returned home.

In the meantime, the sarpanch was worried about his son as it was getting late. That day, three travellers had arrived. The wife of the sarpanch was lovingly serving food to the travellers but she was sad at heart. Both the sarpanch and his wife were looking towards the door every now and then waiting for their son to return.

Suddenly, there was a glow on the sarpanch's face. The wife understood that the son had arrived. Indeed, he arrived just in time when the travellers were about to leave and told his mother about the fruits in the water in the jungle and said that he wanted to offer it to the guests. However, his mother answered, 'But son, only after the fruits and leaves are kept in the water for a long time will it show its magic—this is what I have understood from your story. We cannot serve the water immediately to these guests.' Thus, the guests left and the family kept the fruits immersed in water for some days. They waited anxiously. After a few days, some more guests arrived. They were served with the magical water this time. When these guests left, the hosts were overjoyed to see that after a hearty meal when the guests departed, they were dancing and swaying with joy!

21

Ranjana

Ranjana was about a year old when her Sindhi family migrated to independent India. She has no memory of her family migrating across the border, but to this day, her heart is filled with numerous stories of how her family survived. It still seems bizarre to her how anyone can move from India to India. At the time of her birth, there was no India and Pakistan but now the name of her birthplace has changed from India to Pakistan and her entire family has also moved to India. Ranjana had eight siblings—five brothers and three sisters.

Ranjana had listened to numerous stories of their lives in Pakistan. She knew that they were diwans, landowners earlier. When India was divided into two, they were asked to move to India as they chose to continue being a Sindhi. A neighbour—a Pathan, helped them. For about a week they hid at the Pathan's home in the basement. Ranjana remembers her mother telling her how she used to put rolled-up pieces of cloth into her mouth to stop her from crying or making loud sounds to save the family from being heard by others who might be a threat to their lives.

Soon they migrated to India, in a fully loaded train with gold and jewels packed in pickle jars and roti containers. In the beginning, they had to stay as refugees in tents. They did not know anything about the new land, the language, or the food. The refugees were served makki di roti. This was new for them. Traditionally, they were wheat and barley eaters. Back home, the family knew Sindhi, Hatkani, Farsi, and other languages and their forefathers used a language that had no vowels. The new place felt alien. They would often ask the Almighty how they would be at home in a place which was not their homeland.

The family had to move many times, but gradually they found a place to settle down in Raipur. Schooling for the children was not difficult as Sindhi government schools were to be found in the region. After she turned ten, Ranjana's parents decided to send her to an English-medium school. She was a bright student and keen to study. She had to re-enroll as a first standard student as the medium of instruction had changed and the situation became difficult, not only because of the language barrier, but also because all the other girls seemed different. They smelled different, ate different kinds of food, and had different hobbies. While one of her hobbies was to save money in order to be able to buy a nice dress for Diwali, her friends would spend an equal amount every day, to buy fruits from the canteen. Her only dream until she turned fifteen was to be able to apply perfume. 'How and from where does this magical fragrance come from?' Her clothes smelled of a black soap, used to wash utensils by bhabi. Her mother was always bedridden and sick, probably because she gave birth to nine children and also suffered two miscarriages.

Ranjana got married at the age of sixteen. Though she tried her best to avoid being liked by the groom's family, yet, nothing worked. The day the groom's family came to see her to finalize the match, she tried to walk in a funny way and applied a lot of make-up. The groom's family thought the young Ranjana might be tired and sleepy. Finally, the marriage agreement was made between the two families. Within two days, Ranjana was married to a twenty-two year old man with curly hair and dirty feet. What a monster! His language was nothing but abusive and he loved drinking, smoking, and watching movies. He smelled funny and talked with lot of sarcasm and arrogance. A well-groomed, convent educated girl was packed and sent away to a completely new family. But Ranjana was also happy somewhere inside. As part of her marriage, she had received a gift that was the closest to her heart—a bottle of perfume. This was the only thing that would force her to wake up every day and get ready for the day and its activities. With time, Ranjana's life started to take shape in the new household. She wanted to work, which was initially considered a preposterous idea, but over a period of time, things started to change. Her husband became more understanding and they matured as a couple. Today, an aged Ranjana thanks the Almighty to have blessed her with an understanding husband and a loving family. She started working by sewing items at her sewing machine, making papads for the neighbours, and also teaching languages and giving tuitions for little kids in the neighbourhood.

In Chhattisgarh, Ranjana and her family had found the lovable home that the previous generation was missing after Partition. The new and secured life was a final sigh of relief for the entire family. They had difficulties in the first six to seven years but, soon, due to their diligence in business, they became successful in the region. The family ran a cloth business, which is still operational. They are one of the richest families in the community. Starting from a one-room house in the basement of a sugarcane factory, their residence has expanded, to a two-storeyed bungalow with six rooms. She is the proud grandmother of three grandchildren and all of them are on their way to becoming graduates.

DADRA AND NAGAR HAVELI AND DAMAN AND DIU

22

Submergence

S in was on the rise on earth. Brother quarreled with brother and father with son. No one cared about anyone. The path to truth was forgotten. It was as if the way of the world was nothing but to cheat one another. Greed and immorality reigned. The number of those who still maintained morality was getting smaller and smaller. To put an end to the situation, all the gods met Mahadev and complained in unison, 'O Mahadev, sinners dominate the earth and there seems to be no way to reform them; everyone is deviating from the path of truth and religion. Please find a way out of this.'

Even Mahadev himself was perplexed and finally it was decided that the best thing to do would be to destroy the earth and recreate again. After much deliberation, along with Naradev and the rest of the gods, it was decided that the earth would be inundated. Vayudev and Jaldev were asked by the gods to destroy the earth. Vayudev started first and the climate changed suddenly. The wind picked up. Dust rose all around. Trees were uprooted. Dark clouds also gathered in the sky. Frightened, the people on earth trembled. Lightning and thunder were so intense, their eyes and eardrums almost got torn out. Then it started to rain as if the sky was a mountain and a glacier was descending. Water filled up everywhere. The fear of death shook everybody to the bones. Everyone was trying to save themselves.

The current of the water dragged all forms of life with it. Those who were inside their homes were also dragged along with their homes. Within moments, the height of water rose as

high as seven palms and the whole earth was destroyed. The
gods watched this from atop Kem Mountain. The inundation
was complete, and the wicked world was destroyed. As night
fell, the satisfied gods slept on the mountain.

Meanwhile, Submergence thought, 'Oh, this mountain has
been spared from the inundation. Let me roll over it once.'
However, as much as Submergence tried to flood the mountain,
the mountain kept growing as the gods were residing on it.
Submergence said, 'O gods, I am only executing the order you
gave me and I will certainly flood this mountain.' The gods
had to let Submergence flood the mountain and they themselves
took shelter in Mahadev's court in the heavens.

Now Naradev and Brahmadev came forward to recreate
life and started wandering in search of soil to create a new
earth but since the earth was deep under water, finding soil
was almost impossible. Suddenly, Naradev noticed a gnat that
somehow had escaped Submergence and was looking for a
place to build her nest when Naradev exclaimed, 'Found it.
Found the soil.' And he told the gnat, 'Give us the soil you
carry in your mouth.'

The gnat said, 'I won't give it to you. I need it to build
my home.'

Naradev held her tightly by her waist causing the soil to
fall from her mouth. The gods immediately caught the soil in
their hands. But the gnat asked the gods, 'What was my crime
that you flattened my waist?'

The gods gave her a boon, 'You will find a place to build
your home inside the houses humans will build on earth. You
will give birth to a baby that will come out of the cocoon full
grown in forty-five days.'

This is why gnats are flat at the waist and build their nest
in the houses of humans.

The gods created a new earth from the soil they had
collected from the gnat but the question of steadying it came

up. They then built a pole. But who would be able to lift it? They called Bhimadev who employed his strength and made space between the earth and the sky and the netherworld. If the sky were to fall, it would fall on the earth and the pole would move, making the earth fall into the netherworld. To solve this problem, the earth was steadied with nine lakh nails (the stars).

Though a new earth was created, it was very rugged. So, the gods started to make the ground even. Toy-like animals were created from mud. Sunghyodev[3] then sniffed them to make them start breathing and Jivyodev[4] brought them to life. Bhimadev yoked a harrow to pigs but they kept poking their snout into the earth. Seeing them do this, the gods cursed them. Finally, when bullocks were yoked to the harrow, it was a success. The harrow worked on the soil and wherever mud was tossed, hills were formed. Then the harrow stopped as it snagged on a dry gourd. This is why there are only four continents whereas there are nine oceans on the earth. The mouth of the dry gourd was sealed with beeswax and it took some time to open it. When it was opened, a boy and a girl emerged from dry gourd. They were asked who they were, how had they escaped Submergence, and who hid them in the dry gourd. Here is their story:

A fishing excursion was undertaken. But fishes weren't found and everyone wanted some. So a priest was consulted and chalicomancy[5] was carried out. Then Jaldevi the life god appeared before them and said, 'Worship me. Then you'll all get enough fish.' They did accordingly and a large fish was caught. Everyone took some meat and had a ball. No one had told these two children about the

---

[3]Literally means 'sniff god'.
[4]Literally means 'life god'.
[5]Divination with chalk lines.

fishing excursion because they were orphans. When they
learnt about it afterwards, they reached with a basket
and an axe at the place but there was only the skeleton
of the fish left. However, when they tried to hack the
skeleton, the skeleton moved away. They wondered, 'When
everybody got some meat, why can't we even cut a bone?'

The fish said, 'Those who have eaten my meat are
going to be inside my belly soon. So, you should avoid
eating and pray to the gods. It will be good for you.'

The children heeded the advice and prayed to the
gods. As a result, Mahadev appeared before them and
gave them two seeds and said, 'Sow these seeds and water
them.' The seeds then grew into a vine and climbed onto
a tree and then gourds grew on it, but the children could
not reach the gourds. So, after praying to Mahadev, the
children meditated upon susalya dhurumaj[6] to reach and
drop the gourds. The gourds fell and in one of them,
Mahadev made arrangements for the children to live for
twelve years. He then sealed the mouth of the gourd for
twelve years.

Soon, the floods came, and everything went inside
the belly of the fish.

Now, to procreate the human race, there were the two
children but since they were brother and sister, another
problem arose. Mahadev again helped the gods out. He

---

[6]This phrase could not be understood. Either the words were misheard during
reproduction of the story or are ancient enough to have lost meaning for the
current generation. The dialect in which this story occurs is Kukna (an Adivasi
dialect from South Gujarat) and it couldn't be verified if these words exist.
A close meaning for the first word (susalya) is susala, which means 'mole'.
From the context it seems that this could either be an occupational title, if
at all, or the name of some person/animal who habitually climbs trees (with
vines on them). The second word (dhurumaj) doesn't seem to have even a
resembling word in the dialect.

made the children spin and move back and forth, and they then forgot that they were siblings.

Finally, new humans were born and thus the recreation of the earth was complete.

23

The Divaso Festival and the
Evrat Jeevrat Vrat Story

The story of the Evrat Jeevrat goddesses pertains to the
Divaso festival. According to this story, once, a childless
Brahmin priest, who was also a worshipper of Lord Shiva,
got a son after pleasing him on condition that the son, when
he grew up, should neither be not educated or not married.
As the boy turned five, the father decided that his son should
study. After some time, the child grew up to be a handsome
young man and the parents started to look for a bride for
him. Soon, a match was finalized, amidst several proposals.
When the wedding procession was returning from the bride's
house, they had to pass through a dense forest. While they
were in the middle of the forest, it started to rain heavily and
suddenly, a poisonous snake bit the son and he died instantly.
The accompanying people decided that the weather and the
place were unsuitable for a cremation ceremony, so they decided
to return to their village and come back the next morning for
the final rites. Thus, all the villagers left, but the wife stayed
back.

The poor woman, with much difficulty, dragged the body of
her dead husband into a nearby temple for shelter and bolted
the door from inside, to keep away wild animals. At the change
of prahar[7], Goddess Jaya Mata came to the temple and was
angry to see the dead body. The wife explained the terrible
conditions which brought her to the temple and promised to

---

[7]Sanskrit term for a unit of time, constituting almost three hours.

give her anything if she could bring her husband back to life. Jaya Mata stated that she would seek her wish later on and blessed the dead husband and left. The husband's right leg and thumb moved a bit. An hour later, Vijaya Mata arrived, asked the same question, and received the same reply. She too blessed the husband and left with a promise to seek her wish later on. The dead husband's right foot moved. In the next hour, Evrat Mata arrived, the same set of incidents took place and she too blessed the dead husband and the right side of the man's body moved. In the next hour, Jeevrat Mata arrived. When the entire incident was repeated and she blessed the man, he became alive and sat up. However, it was still dark outside, and the wife suggested that they should play paachika[8] till morning. In the morning, the villagers came to witness that the man was alive. His family members arrived hearing the news and took him and the daughter-in-law home amidst much gaiety.

By the end of the first year, the daughter-in-law was pregnant and finally gave birth to a son. On the very same night, Jaya Mata arrived and demanded that the baby be handed over to her. Since the daughter-in-law had promised the goddess to give her anything that she asked for, she could not refuse. So, she gave her newborn son to the goddess. The next year, when she gave birth to her second son, Vijaya Mata came and asked for the baby. In the following two years, the daughter-in-law gave birth to two more sons and Evrat Mata and Jeevrat Mata came and asked for the babies consecutively. The daughter-in-law had to keep her promise and gave away her babies. However, the family members and the villagers were suspicious and thought that the daughter-in-law was killing her own babies. Thus, on the fifth year, when the daughter-in-law gave birth to a baby girl, all the villagers kept a vigil. However, the baby survived. This time, the mother-in-law was convinced that the daughter-

---

[8]A game played with five stones.

in-law had herself killed all her baby boys. However, it was also the year when the daughter-in-law had to perform the Evrat Jeevrat Vrat puja. She called a few lady friends and went to the same temple for the celebration, where the four goddesses once had brought her husband back to life. She invited all four goddesses for lunch. Suddenly, four women, along with four young boys, arrived for lunch. The daughter-in-law did not know that these were the goddesses and that the four boys were her sons. She washed their feet and served them food. While the goddesses were departing, the daughter-in-law silently pinched her daughter and she started to cry. When Jaya Mata asked the reason for the child's crying, the daughter-in-law replied that the child didn't have a brother, so she was crying. On hearing this, Jaya Mata returned the first son. Soon again, the daughter started to cry again. When Vijaya Mata asked, she too received the same reply. Vijaya Mata returned the second son too on hearing the sad story. The same story was repeated with Evrat Mata and Jeevrat Mata as well and the daughter-in-law's third and fourth sons were returned to her. So, by the end of the day, the daughter-in-law returned home with her four sons and one daughter. Her family and the villagers praised her and were very happy. Thus, the Evrat Jeevrat Vrat came to be observed all over the region.

24

The Story of the Preservation of Hoka Trees

Hoka (*Hyphaene thebaica*) trees have a story of their own in Daman and Diu. Mostly limited to the areas of Moti Daman, hoka trees are a much-coveted attraction for tourists. These trees are also a specialty of the region and are not found anywhere else in India—making them a significant representation of the verdant flora of Daman and Diu. However, this rare section of greenery finds itself amidst a pall of gloom. Today, the tall palm trees stand as silent sentinels of the landscape facing an imminent threat of extinction. However, it is through the philanthropic work of local environmentalists like Ramesh Chandra D. Raval that the trees have found a new lease of life.

Hoka trees are also known as doum/doom palm or gingerbread tree. It is a dioecious palm and mostly grows up to 17 metres in height and it bears edible, oval-shaped fruits. It is considered that the Hoka trees are native to northern Africa and the Arabian Peninsula and according to popular belief, these trees travelled to the region during the Portuguese colonial times. Ramesh Chandra D. Raval's preservation work with hoka trees began in 2003, along with his conservation work of the lions in Gir Forest National Park.

The story of Ramesh Raval's work, however, did not begin with a formal training as an environmentalist but within the confines of a classroom. He settled in Diu as a Sanskrit language teacher at a government school in 1979 and taught the secondary classes. Inspired by a visit to the Gir Forest National Park in Gujarat, Ramesh decided to work for the conservation of lions. In 1993, his book entitled, *Singh Jeevan Darshan,* was published in Gujarati—which reflected his observations, experiences, and work with the lions during a period of twelve years. Even today, this book holds significance of being the only one of its kind with reference to a close study of the lions in the region. Ramesh speaks very fondly of his experiences that went into the making of the book, including keen observations about the behaviour of lions, their interactions within their packs, as well as with humans around them. Ramesh recalls how upon returning from the trip, he performed a puja, in a manner of paying respect to the Asiatic lion and to seek blessings to proceed with the documentation of his work. The book was an instant success and often also acted as an important document for environmentalists visiting the region. Ramesh has also been rewarded by local authorities for his conservation work.

Unlike his work with the Gir Forest lions, Ramesh Raval's work with the local hoka trees is not as well known. He first began to notice hoka trees on his various trips across the region. He realized that these Schedule I trees were on the verge of extinction. Since this is the only region in India which had hoka trees, Ramesh Raval decided to work for their preservation. Thus, in 2004, on his birthday on 4 December, he arranged for a tree plantation drive where 1,008 trees were planted with the help of several schoolboys.

A belief is associated with hoka trees that the saplings will grow into maturity when they are worshipped by a kumari, a pre-pubescent girl. Thus, a year later, on the same day, Ramesh Raval arranged for a puja of the saplings which were planted a year earlier by several kumaris. This programme was attended by various dignitaries of the region. In the course of one year, around 900 saplings had taken roots. Unfortunately, at present, several of these plants have been removed due to various developmental work in the region which required clearing of huge acres of verdant land cover. However, despite all odds and changing circumstances, Ramesh Raval's work of preserving hoka trees continues. His diligent efforts even saw an attempt to relocate several hundreds of saplings to Gujarat. He had gifted more than 200 saplings to the forest department as well. However, the saplings never took roots, inspite of utmost care. Ramesh Raval believes the climate and the environment of Diu to be conducive for the growth and development of the trees. His belief inspires his conservation work. Hopefully, his hard work will pay off and in the course of time, the story of hoka trees will continue to survive as symbols of inspiration.

DELHI

25

Delhi Is Still Far Away

One of the many visages of Dilli is of spiritualism, Sufism, culture, humanity, romanticism, and religion. It is also the city of shrines—of saints, holy people, and fakirs, where amidst the smouldering incenses and fragrant roses, the history is a narrative of a bygone era.

According to a legend, an old man once appeared in Hazrat Nizamuddin's mother's dream and declared that she would have to choose between her husband, Abdullah, and her son. Bibi Zulekha chose the apple of her eye, her son. It is said that Hazrat was merely five years old when he lost his father. It was under the guidance of his mother that he was brought up and educated.

It was the reign of Sultan Nasruddin when Bibi Zulekha brought Hazrat and his sister to Dilli. In those times, Dilli flourished in terms of politics, culture, and spiritualism. According to Amir Khusrau, poets, artists, Sufis, dervishes from all around the world had come and settled in Dilli.

The richness of the time was best reflected in 'Zilm ba amal Dilli Bukhara[9]'. Dilli was at a par with Bukhara when it came to science and education.

On their arrival in Dilli, these God-loving people took shelter at Miyaan Bazaar Sarai, also known as Namak Sarai.

---

[9]Bukhara was the centre of attraction for all civilizations from its early days in sixth century BCE. It was a centre of trade, scholarship, culture, and religion. By the time Hazrat Nizamuddin Auliya came to Dilli, it too was establishing itself on all those lines.

However, Hazrat moved out of Namak Sarai and went to live in different places.

Such was the state of poverty and hunger in those times that a bag was hung at the main door of the house and people used to put leftovers in it. Often when there was nothing in the bag, an empty dastarkhan[10] was spread and his mother would say, 'Today we are God's guests.'

Hazrat Nizamuddin Auliya was greatly influenced by his mother. Whatever he knew, he had learnt from his mother. At times, his mother would look at his feet and say, 'Nizam, your future is very bright. You will be like a tree which provides other people with its shade; it would be under your guidance that a lot of people will find peace.' Once, on the occasion of the new moon, Hazrat greeted his mother. His mother replied, 'Son, whom will you greet on the next new moon?' Hazrat understood what his mother was trying to warn him about and said, 'Under whose guardianship will you leave me?'

Bibi Zulekha said, 'I will let you know about it when the time is right.' After a few days, she fell ill and called for Nizam. On his arrival, she held one of his hands and looked up towards the sky and said, 'Nizam, I make the Almighty your guardian.' And then she closed her eyes forever.

Time passed, anxiety made a home in Nizamuddin Auliya's heart and in such an anxious state, he decided to leave the materialistic world and started a new life in the jungle. But the people were hungry for the aura of Khwaja Sahab's spirituality and followed him to the woods to seek wisdom and spirituality. People from different walks of life would come to him and there was a daily langar at the khanqah for everyone. Meanwhile, a new king was being crowned at the throne of Dilli, Sultan Ghiyassuddin Tughlaq, who established the Tughlaq dynasty. He

---

[10]A mat which is spread on the ground, floor, or table and is used as a sanitary surface for food, but it is also used more broadly to refer to the entire meal setting. It is part of traditional Central Asian cuisine.

continued with the traditions of his clan and started building a city of his own, which he named Tughlaqabad.

An order was passed that every labourer would work for the new city. On the other hand, a baoli had to be made for the khanqah of Hazrat. It so happened so that the workers used to work for the king during the day and for Hazrat Nizamuddin Auliya in the night. One day, the contractor caught the labourers yawning and after further investigation got to know that these workers were working double shift; one for the king and one for Khwaja Sahab. He forbade the workers to do so, but they did not pay heed to him and continued working like before. So when the king got to know about the whole situation, he was agitated and put a ban on the sale of oil at the khanqah of Khwaja Sahab. He knew well that without oil, people would not be able to light diyas and without diyas, there would not be any light, which would finally result in no work being done at the khanqah.

When Hazrat got to know about the work being halted at the baoli, he immediately called for his disciple Hazrat Nasruddin (who himself was a wali, a guardian or helper) and enquired about the situation. As soon as he got to know the reason behind it, Khwaja Sahab gave an order that the water from the well of the baoli should be put in the diyas instead of oil. Hazrat Nasruddin immediately implemented the orders and it was a sight to behold! The lamps were lit and they kept burning for nine consecutive nights till the work at the baoli was finished.

Since then Khwaja Nasruddin came to be known as Chirag-e-Dilli. Sultan Ghiyassuddin, on the other hand, was returning from a mission in Bengal and when he got to know about what was happening in Dilli, he was furious. He sent a message to Hazrat Nizamuddin Auliya that before the sultan sets his foot in Dilli, Hazrat should leave the city or else he would be hanged to death.

When Khwaja heard the sultan's command, all he said was, 'Dilli abhi dur hai.' (Delhi is still far away).

It was Khwaja's prophetic words that the sultan never saw Dilli again. While returning, at Afghanpur (near Meerut), the wooden pavilion which was set up for his reception collapsed, killing Sultan Ghiyassuddin and his second son. Wearied of the sultan's trickeries, Hazrat Nizamuddin Auliya cursed the place which was once the pride of the sultan. He said that from then on, that place would never flourish and never see a flourishing civilization.

Till this date, Tughlaqabad remains in ruins.

26

The Loose Nail

Many years ago, in the land of the Ganges, ruled the last of the Tomars. The year was around 1151 CE and the reign of the Tomars was succeeded by that of the Chauhans. The last Tomar king, Raja Bisaldev, had attacked Dilli and had conquered it, but the victory was turned into a peace agreement and it was agreed upon that the king of the Chauhans would marry the princess of the Tomars and their offspring would eventually inherit the throne of Dilli.

Thus, the marriage took place and the princess Karpuradevi married the king of the Chauhans, King Someshwara. Soon, the couple was blessed with a baby boy—who was to become the mighty Prithviraj Chauhan. He was the darling of both the Tomar and Chauhan clans. As Raja Bisaldev did not have a son of his own, he adopted Prithviraj. On his deathbed, Bisaldev declared Prithviraj Chauhan as his successor. This meant that the throne of both Dilli and Ajmer now belonged to Prithviraj Chauhan also known as Rai Pithora.

The fame of Rai Pithora spread far and wide—from the Himalayas to the Vindhyachal to the Narmada. People soon forgot about the wonderful reign of Anangpal Tomar and adapted themselves to the magnificence of the new king. Rai Pithora's rule became so famous that people from far-off places heard about his greatness. However, he was not known to be a calm and composed king. He was known for this hot temper and made several enemies, and this not only included mortal kings but the gods as well. He soured his relationship with the king of the earth, Vasuki Naag. Vasuki was the brother of Shesh

Naag and Manasa Devi. He would wrap himself around Lord
Shiva's neck and was known for his generosity and kindness
towards humans. According to Hindu mythology, King Vasuki
Naag is the king of this planet. He was impatient and thus,
kept moving continuously causing tremors and earthquakes.

It so happened, that once the high priest and the astrologers
of Dilli went to Rai Pithora and said, 'O King, as per our
astrological calculations, King Vasuki is resting beneath our
palace these days. If only we could do something to make him
stay here forever, then we need not fear the Chauhans. You and
your successors will rule forever.' Rai Pithora was excited to
hear this. He asked them for their advice to make this desire
come true. The high priest replied, 'We have a plan. Let us ask
the blacksmith to make a qeel—an iron nail—so long that we
can hammer it into the earth and pierce it through the fangs of
Lord Vasuki.' The logic behind this crazy idea was that once
the qeel was hammered into his fangs, King Vasuki would not
be able to move and would be forced to reside beneath Lal
Kot—Prithviraj Chauhan's palace. The king was really pleased
with the idea and immediately ordered the blacksmith to make
such a qeel. What a nail it was! It was no less than the length
of the serpent himself. The high priest and the astrologers
came together and calculated the exact position where King
Vasuki might be located and hammered in the qeel then and
there. However, Prithviraj Chauhan was not satisfied and was
anxious about the calculations and the qeel.

He ordered his servants to take out the qeel so that he
could investigate it himself. The moment the nail was uprooted,
everyone present in the court could see that the tip of the qeel
was smeared with blood. This time, the king ordered that the
qeel should be hammered in again at the same place. This sent
the high priest and astrologers into a frenzy. They exclaimed,
'Oh Lord! What have you done? What is the use of hammering
it in again now? King Vasuki must have travelled far by now.'

Thus, when the qeel was hammered in again, it only struck the flat earth because King Vasuki was far beyond their reach. Now that the qeel was struck in the barren land it remained loose and everyone in the court exclaimed, 'Qeeli dhilli' (the loose nail) and this wonderful city of Prithviraj Chauhan came to be known as Dilli.

27

Begum Jamila Khwaja

Begum Jamila Khwaja's father had bought the sprawling haveli behind Golcha, the famous Old Delhi cinema house, which belonged to Sir Syed's family. Begum Jamila Khwaja, known as Phuppho, grew up in privilege amongst the Old Delhi elite. She was intelligent and beautiful and decided to become a doctor. She joined Lady Hardinge Medical College but quit college for what she decidedly said was her calling. This was also the time of the Indian Independence movement followed by Partition. As an aftermath of Partition, the national capital struggled with an unparalleled refugee crisis amid spurts of communal rioting. Most of the ancient monuments witnessed the worst humanitarian crisis of the era and provided shelter to its victims. Purana Qila, Lal Qila, Humayun's Tomb, even the Taj Mahal, were converted into makeshift refugee camps.

A refugee demographic that is not talked of in the Indian narrative, or at least talked of seldomly and in hushed tones, found shelter within the ramparts of the Red Fort. These were the Muslims who stayed behind in India and became victims of communal violence in their own homeland. Of the ones who were displaced from their homes, some chose to go to Pakistan, and many did not have anywhere to go, because they were, and wanted to continue to be, Indians. Every morning, Phuppho would, with her bright pink dupatta around her sprightly figure, go to the Red Fort and take care of the sick and the disabled. Phuppho continued her work unabated with the needy—a young girl, studying to be a doctor, full of dreams, hopes, and stars in her eyes, beholding humanity at its worst and witnessing tales of rape, loot, plunder, murder, darkness, and depravity. Phuppho would be there every day—cooking, cleaning, and tending to the sick—within the ramparts of the Red Fort, the seat of Indian, and some may say, Mughal glory. This continued for months, which morphed into years, until the last of the refugees found a home, either in the city, or in God's abode. Unafraid, not heeding the advice of elders, not caring about the threats of violence, and above all, not giving up her dream of becoming a doctor, and having a family—Phuppho continued her noble service. Meanwhile, her entire family left for Pakistan. Her father passed away and was buried in Delhi and she refused to leave his grave. Having never married, she stayed on alone, loyal to his memory and to the idea of a secular nation. It was a dedication spoken of in hushed tones of reverence and awe amongst those who knew her. Over the years, she would earn the title, Begum Sahiba.

In years to come, Begum Sahiba was cheated of her inheritance. Her own lawyer conned her into selling her glorious home to karkhandars—small businessmen. The courtyard that once hosted the greatest poets and philosophers of Delhi, mushairas, and theological debates, slowly became home to goats, and a tannery. The glorious haveli was divided up into and sold as tiny apartments, so cramped and perilous that one would struggle to recognize its former glory. Begum Sahiba never got any money from the sale and lost her home and in an act of great remorse and largesse, her lawyer had won for her the right to live in a corner of her old home. Begum Jamila Khwaja, doyenne and diva of erstwhile Old Delhi, an incredible social worker and patriot, continued to live in a corridor, scarcely bigger than her charpai with all her worldly belongings in a gnarled tin trunk under her narrow single bed, and all her clothes on a peg on the wall above her bed. She would cook a solitary meal over a small electric heater, usually a thin khichdi. Sometimes, she would rummage under her bedclothes for some money for visiting kids, for kebabs from Jawahar Hotel—a restaurant not far from where she lived. She would stitch tiny potlis from scraps of brocade and velvet, edged with silver kinari and hand-made lace. By this time, it was the 1980s, and no one had money to spare for hand-stitched frivolities. The epitome of genteel penury, the paan daan was her only indulgence, and even in her last days, she would painstakingly make an elaborate paan for herself.

She died in the mid-nineties, alone and unsung, haunted by the petty court cases filed against her by her tenants, and her memories. She was buried in an unmarked grave behind the *Times of India* building opposite Khooni Darwaza, a few kilometres away from where she had decided to take huge risks to her life. This is the story of the young girl who broke social dogma and barriers of class and birth to serve the victims of the bloodiest riots in Indian history; the beautiful girl who refused to get married while Delhi burned; the student doctor who gave up a promising career to lead a life of service instead, and the fierce patriot who refused to leave India, even when her entire family left India.

GOA

28

The Potter's Girl and the Divine Cow

Once there lived a potter and his wife. They had a baby girl who was about one-and-a-half years old. One day the potter said to his wife, 'Let's go to the forest to dig mud for pots.'

'Okay,' she said and took out the shovel, picked up the wicker basket, clasped the baby to her hip and followed the potter into the forest to collect mud. Both of them dug a lot of mud, filled the baskets, and raised them to their heads. But the potter's wife could not lift up the baby to her hip. Do you know what she told the potter? 'Give me the baby or the basket!' The potter got upset at this. He said, 'You bring the baby or the basket! If you want, you come; otherwise stay here!'

Saying this, the potter walked away. Meanwhile it was getting dark. The potter's wife could not decide what to do. She thought for a long while. If she did not get the basket of mud, the potter would yell at her when she reached home. Thinking of this she put the baby on the ground near a bush, placed the mud basket on her head, and started for home. The poor baby started crying finding herself alone in the forest. In the meantime, some temple cows were passing through the forest. They heard the baby and went looking for it. Among the cows there was one which was nursing her calves. She made the baby drink her milk. When the baby had drank till she was full, she became quiet and started playing. The cows were relieved and went back to their sheds.

The next morning, the cows came looking for the baby. The cow gave her some milk. This continued for sometime and the child started to grow up, healthy and strong. After a while, the baby also started moving around with the cows every day. Two to three years passed in this manner. The cows then took the baby and put her in the temple cowshed.

When the child was about ten years old, a giant saw the child playing outside the cowshed. He thought of making a crispy meal out of her. He ran after the child to catch her, but the child got frightened on seeing the giant and ran into the shed and locked the door. The angry giant started pushing the door of the cowshed.

'Bai! Bai! Open the door,' the giant pleaded in a woman's voice. Now, there was a God who was watching this. He took pity on the poor child. He hid behind a nearby bush and started speaking to the child, 'No, don't do that, child. The giant may eat you.'

Hearing this, the giant became very angry. He went to the bush and with one kick uprooted it from the ground. The giant then came back to the cowshed and started saying again, 'Bai! Bai! Open the door.'

Nearby, there was a coconut palm. It also pleaded to the child to not open the door. The angry giant was again consumed with rage. With one kick he uprooted the coconut palm. It was becoming dusk now. And it was time for the cows to return to their shed. Planning to come back again the next day, the giant left for his home in the hills. In the evening, when the cows came back they got the smell of the giant. They got frightened and started looking for the child.

Finding the child hiding in the shed, all the cows gathered around her, licking her to show their affection, and asked, 'What happened?' The child told them the entire story. The cows then got angry. 'Tomorrow we will teach that giant a lesson,' they said. The next morning the cows got up and hid themselves in the shed. None of them went to graze in the forest. The next day, the giant got up early in the morning, washed his face, brushed his teeth, and eagerly made his way to the cowshed.

On reaching the cowshed, he banged on the door saying, 'Bai! Bai! Open the door.' Nearby was a mango tree. She quickly shouted out, 'No, don't do that, child. The giant will eat you.'

When the mango tree said this, the giant in his fury, gave it one kick and uprooted it. Like this he uprooted one tree, then another...then another. One by one the giant uprooted all the trees around the cowshed. Then he thought of breaking down the door of the cowshed. With one kick he smashed the door and went in. As he went in, the cow which had given milk to the child gave the giant the first blow with her horns. After that the next cow, then the next...then the next. In this manner, all the cows struck the giant with their horns and broke his waist, hands, and head, and threw the headless body into the forest.

But the giant had magical powers and soon healed himself and became whole as before. He then swore that he would make his living as a beggar but never come back to that forest and went off to another forest.

After this incident, the child lived happily with the cows and gradually grew into a beautiful young woman. One day, the prince of that kingdom came to that forest to hunt. While wandering in the forest he came across the cowshed. He saw the young woman outside the shed and fell in love with her at first sight.

The prince left his hunting adventure and went back to the palace. He then expressed his wish to marry that woman to his parents. Hearing their son's wish they immediately sent soldiers with a palanquin to bring her to the palace. Soon, the marriage took place with much pomp and splendour and the forest girl lived happily for many years with her prince.

29

The Wicked Mother-in-law

In a village, there lived an old woman who was also very poor. She had a son. After her husband passed away, she raised him up with great difficulty. When the boy grew up, she got him married. She had thought that she would be free to rest and pray once he was married. But that did not happen. After her son's marriage, his responsibility increased. There were more people to feed and his earnings were not sufficient. He would go in search of work, but it was difficult to get work regularly. The day he found some work, his wife would also accompany him.

Days passed and their lot did not improve. Since he could not work regularly in the village, he decided to leave. He bid farewell to his mother and wife and reached the king's court. Seeing his strong and well-built body, the king recruited him as a soldier in his army.

The wife started suffering in his absence. The old woman started troubling her daughter-in-law. She started saying, 'My son left his home and village because of you. We lived together all these years, but with your arrival, Lakshmi has departed.'

The poor daughter-in-law spent her days suffering all the injustice meted out to her by her mother-in-law. After some days she realized that she was pregnant. She thought her sufferings would now be over. But that did not happen. Rather, they increased. She had to work both at home and outside. When she was due to deliver her child, her mother-in-law sent her to the forest to fetch firewood. She handed her a lemon and said, 'You will deliver a child when this lemon gets over. Get the child home only if he is a son; do whatever you want but if she is a girl, don't bring her home. Hearing this, the daughter-in-law cried a lot, but knowing that she could not escape this, she left for the forest, as the mother-in-law sang:

Pains in her stomach
Lady climbs the hill
Lad being born
She can get him home
If newborn baby is a lass
She's to leave her and come
Having the lemon
Lady walks on and on

Climbing the hill, the daughter-in-law sang:

O deity of my mother's side
Be with me in this danger
What am I headed to suffer
Protect me, O my Saviour

She reached a tree, singing, when suddenly she had pains in her stomach. She gave birth to a chubby baby girl. She remembered what her mother-in-law had told her and started crying. She held the newborn baby close to her chest and returned home with a heavy heart, leaving the baby in a cavity of a tree trunk. The mother-in-law was happy seeing her daughter-in-law returning empty-handed. She dreamt of sending her away after a son was born to her the next time.

The daughter-in-law would go to the forest every day to collect firewood and come back after feeding the little girl. When her husband returned home, the wicked mother-in-law poisoned his mind with wicked stories. In a fit of anger, he beat his wife, but she quietly suffered it all.

He left home again after a month or two. She was pregnant again. When she was about to deliver her baby, the mother-in-law gave her some cumin seeds and said, 'Go to the forest, eating these cumin seeds. Get the child home, if you have a son. If she is a girl, leave her and come.' The daughter-in-law left crying. The mother-in-law sang sitting at home:

> *Pains in her stomach*
> *Lady climbs the hill*
> *Lad being born*
> *She can get him home*
> *If the newborn baby is a lass*
> *She's to leave her and come*
> *Having cumin all the way*
> *Lady walks on and on*

The mother-to-be sang as she walked:

> *O deity of my mother's side*
> *Be with me in this danger*
> *What am I headed to suffer*
> *Protect me, O my Saviour*

But no one came to help this time too. This time too, she gave birth to a baby girl. She named her firstborn Limbavati, as she was born while the mother was eating a limbu, lemon, and because the second was born while eating jirem, cumin seeds, she was named Jiravati. Both the girls were kept in a cavity of a tree trunk. As the days passed, the girls grew up. They started asking her many questions about their father. She would reply, 'My dear children, wait for a few more days. I shall tell you everything.'

A few years later, the husband returned home. When his mother made up stories against his wife, saying that his wife had killed her own children, he was enraged. He said, 'Better kill this woman who kills her own children.' Accordingly, he announced to the village, 'The mother who killed her own children will be hanged in the central square of the village.

All are invited to witness.'

The old woman was delighted. The daughter-in-law kept saying that she had not killed her daughters. She pleaded not to hang her. But no one paid her any heed. The next morning, she was brought to the gallows. She climbed the steps to the gallows singing:

O my darling Limbavati
Come to save me from danger
O my darling Jiravati
Come to save me from danger

People listened. There was a huge crowd who had gathered to see mother who had killed her own children. They heard a different voice as they were listening to the killer mother.

King of the Earth our father
Queen of Leisure our mother
Very wicked our grandmother

People turned their heads to see where the voice was coming from. When they saw the two sweet girls singing, they asked: 'Who are you? Where have you come from?' The girls told them the whole story. The husband realized his mistake. He understood that his mother had tortured his wife a lot. He was furious at his mother. When he decided to hang her from the same gallows that were kept ready for his wife, the mother became scared. She fell at the feet of her daughter-in-law and sought forgiveness. The daughter-in-law took pity on her. She saved her mother-in-law, pleading with her husband not to hang his mother, and they all lived happily ever after.

30

1956: A Love Story

In the early 1940s, during World War II, some villages in Goa experienced an outbreak of a smallpox epidemic. Many lost their lives to this incurable disease. It was a difficult time. That year, just before the annual Ganesh Chaturthi festival, Ladu Ghadi the coconut plucker got busy to prepare for the festival, like many others in the neighbourhood. One evening, he saw minor rashes on his shoulders. By next morning, his entire body was covered with rashes, followed by high fever and unbearable body ache. Very soon neighbours came to know that coconut-plucker Ladu has got smallpox. As it was an infectious disease, people were instructed to report all cases to the government. The patients were taken away by Portuguese soldiers to the Reis Magos Jail which was converted into a quarantine centre. Very few were lucky to return from quarantine and Ladu Ghadi wasn't one amongst them.

His wife, Savitri, became a widow at the age of thirty-two. Ladu Ghadi had left two fields, a small hut without clay walls and eight children to feed. Savitri was a strong woman and worked very hard in the fields. She grew sweet potatoes, chillies, onions, and vegetables and sold them in her mother's village in the Siolim market, 13 kilometres away from her village. She had two friends who had met with a similar fate, her Catholic neighbours, Filzu and Filomena, who had also lost their husbands to smallpox.

In 1947, after India gained Independence, many Goan youths began travelling to Bombay in search of work. Times were rough and jobs were difficult to find and above all, wages were abysmally low. Savitri's son, Saju, was bored with his shepherding and farming duties—all of which yielded very little wages. In 1951, he ran away to Mumbai with another friend and got a job at Colaba in the Godrej company. He started out as a labourer but learnt to drive, operate fork-lifts, and push shovels too. Three years went by and he refused to return home. Thus, Savitri borrowed some money from friends and neighbours and travelled to Bombay, by steamer, to bring back her son.

In those times, in Portuguese Goa, it was not easy to get a driver's licence. After three attempts, Saju got his licence and began driving a truck in the then recently started iron-ore mines but was soon bored with his job and often thought of returning to Bombay. Savitri feared that Saju may never return if he left for Bombay again. She planned to get him married. She had heard about sixteen-year-old Indira from her brother, Oxel. On meeting Indira, Savitri made up her mind and soon the marriage took place. Following traditional customs, till the day of the marriage in 1956, the bride and the groom never met each other, but this happy marriage materialized into one of the most memorable stories which is still remembered fondly by many contemporaries.

This was a time when traditional beliefs forbade men and women to express their love in public. However, the story of Saju and Indira was different. Many times, Savitri remarked in jest: 'Azunui bailechea fatlea fudlean dhavta.' Still runs after his wife like a newly-wed husband. Immediately after their marriage, Saju drove a truck for a living. This took him away to various places including, the extreme north in Usgao, Sonshi, Pale, but wherever he went, he took Indira with him. In 1961, when Goa was liberated from the Portuguese, the new Goa to Bombay bus service started. Saju became a bus driver on this route. Till late 1970s, Goa to Bombay road was in an extremely bad condition and during monsoons it became a nightmare for drivers. The road would often be riddled with heavy boulders and stones, uprooted trees, huge potholes and flash floods. Often, buses would remain stranded for two or three days, till help came. In such difficult times, often there would be several days when no news arrived of Saju. Indira would sit in the dev ghar praying with her eyes closed for several hours and eat only after she heard news of her husband's safety.

Returning from his Bombay trip, Saju would park his bus at Mapuca stand and rush home. Indira would be busy in the field below the house making cowdung cakes for fuel. Saju would quickly change into his shorts and run to the field and help her make the cowdung balls—too eager to help and not showing any signs of exhaustion. The aunts in the family would giggle, seeing him doing the job generally done by women in those days, but Saju was least bothered. If Indira was sweeping the courtyard, Saju would take the broom from her and start sweeping, since she had a weak back. The neighbourhood women would feel shy seeing both of them at work. They would smile and run away, hiding behind their sari pallus. Saju loved to clean the fish too—an excuse to help Indira. Indira's love, on the other hand, reflected through the large tika on her forehead. Saju liked to see this tika, the size of a fifty-paisa coin, on Indira's forehead. They would often go around the neighbourhood on Saju's bike. This continued until they were well into their seventies. Twice they had a fall with minor injuries and Saju's son's friends would tease that one day their parents might end up getting serious injuries, but Indira would just smile and say, 'If something happens to us, while we are together, it will be a blessing from Ishwar.'

The two of them never quarrelled, argued or fought, so much so that their love became immortal in the entire neighbourhood and the pair came to be referred to as 'the lovebirds'. When their sons, Digamber and Ramesh got married, initially, the new wives in the house often felt embarrassed to see the old couple sitting in the courtyard, but slowly, like the rest of the neighbourhood, they too got used to it.

Several years later, Ramesh got a job in the Gulf and every departure after a visit would entail a tearful farewell. One day in 2005, Ramesh got the news of the sudden death of his father. The first thought that crossed his mind was, 'When one lovebird dies how will the other one survive? How would my mother look without that large fifty-paisa tika on her forehead?' Saju passed away only a month before their fiftieth wedding anniversary. Perhaps God had other plans and without a warning, the 1956 love story came to a sudden end, but the story is still remembered fondly till today.

GUJARAT

31

Dug-a-dug, Dug-a-dug, Digging

In a small village in Gujarat, there lived a Brahmin with his wife and two children. Misfortune had fallen on the family and their financial conditions worsened with each passing day. The wife urged her husband to be more enterprising and start working, 'Why don't you start some work? Can't you see our children are dying of hunger?' The man replied, 'You are cent per cent right! But I am neither educated nor accomplished. What do I do to earn a livelihood?' The wife decided to use her education and wisdom and confided in her husband, 'I will teach you a profound philosophical verse. All you have to do is to memorize it and recite it in the royal court. I have heard that our king is a patron of knowledge and arts and he might give you some money in return for the wisdom you share with him. But please ensure that you keep reciting the verse all along your journey so that you remember it at the right time.' With this, she shared the precious verse which was sure to change the destiny of her family and bid her husband adieu.

The man started on the long and arduous journey to the royal court. It was a scorching afternoon and soon the man was hungry and exhausted. He stopped by a small pond to have a refreshing bath and to eat the meal that his wife had packed. He cooled himself by swimming in the pond and then opened the small bundle of food and tried to recall the verse, but alas, he could not remember any of it. So engrossed was he in swimming and relishing the meal that he had forgotten the verse. He thought for a long time but could not remember a single word. The verse was forgotten but he could not bear the thought of returning since he was already halfway to the city.

Looking around vaguely for clues, he spotted a moorhen digging the soft earth, foraging for worms. His fatigued mind, eager to retrieve the lost verse, created a new one 'Dug-a-dug, dug-a-dug, digging'. The moorhen, till now oblivious to any human company, suddenly heard a voice in the vicinity and extended its neck to look around. At this, the man instantly composed his second line, 'Stretch-a-neck, stretch-a-neck, watching'. By now, the moorhen had spotted the man. The moorhen crouched to avoid being seen by its potential predator. Looking at the bird, the man came up with his third line, Cramped-up, swamped-up, sitting'. Being disturbed so many times, the moorhen decided to go to a more peaceful spot. It ran over the floating plants and dove into the pond away from the prying human eye. The man captured its movement and composed the last line of his quartet, 'Hot-a-foot, hot-a-foot, running'.

This new verse added an invigorating spring to the man's walk. With sheer joy, he hummed his latest composition all the way to the city:

Dug-a-dug, dug-a-dug, digging,
Stretch-a-neck, stretch-a-neck, watching,
Cramped-up, swamped-up, sitting,
Hot-a-foot, hot-a-foot, running.

Soon, the splendours of the city greeted him. Without wasting any time, he went to the royal court. It was the hour for the king to meet his subjects, and the man armed with his profound verse was granted immediate entry. He bowed to the king and quickly blabbered the lines lest he forget the words again. The king and the courtiers were stunned to hear this strange verse which did not make any sense. Their inability to understand it made it all the more mysterious as they assumed that the verse had a cryptic message in it. The king was determined to decipher the meaning of the verse so he urged the man to spend a few days at the court enjoying the royal hospitality. The king had the verse inscribed on the wall of his bedroom. Every night at midnight, the king would wake up and recite the verse. He hoped that someday he would be able to decipher the verse.

One night, as usual, the king woke up at midnight to recite the verse. Just then a group of thieves sneaked in with the intent of looting the royal treasure. They had just started digging a burrow outside the king's bedroom to get to the royal treasury behind his bedroom, when they heard someone saying, 'Dug-a-dug, dug-a-dug, digging'. One of the thieves peeped through the window to check if the king was awake or sleep talking. The king recited his second line, 'Stretch-a-neck, stretch-a-neck, watching'. The thief thought that the king had spotted him and signalled his companions to stop. As the thieves were huddling together in a dark corner, they heard: 'Cramped-up, swamped-up, sitting'. The thieves decided to flee from the scene before they were caught. They were about to get up, when the king uttered his last line, 'Hot-a-foot, hot-a-foot, running'. The thieves ran for their lives without waiting for a single second.

Now those thieves were actually the guards of the royal palace who, in their greed, had attempted to steal from the royal treasury. Though they were sure that they were not seen, yet the lines that the king had recited were a live commentary of their actions and it petrified them. They decided not to report to duty for a few days until the matter had cooled off. The king, unaware of the impact of his verse, was surprised that none of his guards had turned up for duty. Being concerned about their well-being, he asked the soldiers to call the guards in order to make sure everything was all right. Hearing the king's summons, the guards thought that the king knew about their attempted robbery last night. They were so terrified of the king's fury that as soon as they entered the court, they confessed their crime and begged for forgiveness.

The king was surprised! So finally, he understood the meaning of the profound verse. He praised the Brahmin for his wisdom and foresight and gave him loads of precious gifts. The Brahmin decided that no further explanations were required and walked back home to delight his family.

32

Chamadbhai in the Forest

One cold winter night, Chamadbhai Fatubhai the exorcist of the Rathwa community was returning home. Over the years, he had been visiting many villages, curing people of various ailments, and helping them with their problems by chanting potent prayer songs shaking his head vigorously. Today had been a truly fulfilling day—he had cured Gamji Rathwa of a life-threatening disease. Gamji Rathwa rewarded the exorcist generously by giving him a basketful of gifts— succulent meat of hen and goat, delicately rolled maize dhebras, and freshly made gravy bhaidku. As per the Rathwa tradition, Gamji offered Chamadbhai the alcoholic beverage made from fermented flowers of the mahua tree. In fact, the whole village was invited to join in the ceremonial drinking.

After the revelry, Chamadbhai started walking back to his village. It was two in the morning by the time he reached the dense forest which he had to pass in order to reach his village. Walking in the forest is an everyday thing for us, the forest dwellers, he said to himself and entered the forest. The inebriated state he was in, soothing breeze, and chirping of the nocturnal insects made him terribly sleepy. He neatly bundled up his priciest possessions—a small dhak, leaves of the khakhra tree, and some peacock feathers, and placed them along with the basket filled with goodies in the crevice of a massive tree trunk. He soon fell into a deep slumber.

As soon as human activities cease, the forest come alive with the activities of its inhabitants. Some sing to attract their mates and some hungry ones such as this sow was out looking for food. To the hungry sow, the tree trunk smelled divine. On approaching the tree trunk, she was overjoyed to find a basket filled with raw meat and cooked vegetables. She quietly took away the basket and as soon as she found a safe spot on a hillock a little distance away from the forest, she started gobbling the food.

The sow was still in her feeding frenzy, when the first rays of the sun alighted on earth. With the forest warming up in the morning sun, the monkeys started their morning acrobatics. Screeching and grunting, they came to the mahua tree under which Chamadbhai was sleeping blissfully, unaware of anything around him. The monkeys spotted Chamadbhai's bundle in the crevice of the tree and the few curious ones started rummaging through it. They were fascinated by each item—the small drum, leaves of the khakhra tree, and peacock feathers—they discovered. The monkeys took all the items.

On their way up the hillock, the monkeys met the sow who was now in tremendous pain. The sow asked the leader of the troop: 'Bandar bhai, you travel far and wide, could you tell me how to relieve my terrible stomach ache? I can barely breathe.' The monkeys pointed in the direction of the sleeping Chamadbhai. Yes, they had seen him shake his head vigorously, play his little drum, and dance as he went around the villages curing people. The sow thanked the monkeys and started walking down the hillock towards the forest.

Down in the forest, Chamadbhai finally woke up. In his half-sleepy hangover, he realized that his bundle and basket had vanished! He was not one to give up his hard-earned possessions so easily. After all, he needed his exorcist's tools—feathers, leaves, and drum for his livelihood. All his headshaking, songs, and dance would be so lacklustre without them. He started looking around for clues—a few twisted peacock feathers and some crushed khakhra leaves—pointed to the hillock.

As he was walking up the hillock, he bumped into the sow

who was in great pain. Whimpering, the sow asked, 'Uncle, are you the famed exorcist?' When Chamadbhai nodded, she asked him to cure her of this sudden stomach ache. Without losing time, Chamadbhai broke into an instant song:

> *Ripe-unripe timroo fruits you have had my dear sow*
> *If you ask me to cure you of your pain, then my*
> *answer is a big no.*

The sow instantly started feeling better and as good as before. Thanking the exorcist, she hopped into the forest. As Chamadbhai was about to resume his journey in search of his belongings, he suddenly heard the sound of a drum, 'That's the sound from my dhak. I am sure of the sound of my dhak. I have played it all my life.' From a distance, he saw a monkey playing it rhythmically! 'So, the monkeys are the culprits! But how do I take my belongings from these notorious monkeys?' he ruminated. He knew he had no time to lose. Moving a little further away from the monkeys, he broke one branch from every tree around him. He then took the thickest of the creepers and tied the branches all around him covering every inch of his body. He looked like a tree himself!

Slowly, Chamadbhai started inching step by step towards the spot where the monkeys were loafing around with his belongings. The monkeys were so engrossed in their antics that they took Chamadbhai for a tree. When he reached very close, the monkeys noticed the tree and found it unusual. The tree looked unlike any other tree they had seen; it was part a sagwan tree, part a nilgiri tree, part a kado tree, and part a khakhra tree. In their excitement and wonder, the leader of the troop started playing the dhak very hard. At this the tree started dancing! The tree swaying to their music excited the monkeys even more. They drew closer to the tree and the leader started playing even more vigorously. As the rhythm of the drum became wild so did the dancing of the tree.

Suddenly, Chamadbhai took out a large stick that he had firmly tied onto his back and hit the monkeys with great force. This sudden attack jolted the monkeys and the entire troop fled leaving Chamadbhai's belongings behind.

Chamadbhai quickly picked up his drum and basket and went home.

33

Father's Gift

He silently thanked the gods that all flights to Ahmedabad from Pune were overbooked. He was happy to go to Kalyan, a small town in Maharashtra. He had dropped off his daughter in Pune for the Short Service Board interview. He now had no option but to return to Ahmedabad in a Volvo bus. As soon as the bus reached Kalyan, familiar smells engulfed him. In the darkness of the night, here he was, in modern-day Ulhasnagar watching the light rain. He was transported to 1945 to the old military transit camp and the gushing Kali River from the days of yore. He was a small boy of about eight years old. The ancient Ambernath temple, their imposing government bungalow in Rambaug and the lingering presence of his father.... His father was a judicial magistrate and his role model. The boy tried to be like his father—a miniature version—with his pleated trousers and bush coat stitched from rationed fabric—quite resembling his father's. He even pinned a replica of the silver 'V' for victory brooch worn by his father—an emblem made mandatory for British government officers by Winston Churchill during World War II. He loved it when his father offered to 'educate' him to make him a 'scholar' rather than sending him to school. He savoured the smell of the freshly polished wooden bench where his father would sit on and conduct his judicial proceedings. It was here that the son practised to say the new words he had learned.

One morning, after his father had retired to the judge's chamber, he sat peering through an intricately woven cane barricade, watching the people meeting his father. He saw a toddler with his mother. The woman had an almond-shaped face. Her head was covered with an azure-coloured dupatta. The woman addressed his father, 'Sahib, I am an unwilling plaintiff of the ongoing divorce case. Considering you as my own father, I have a request to make. My father, Kutubuddin Pathan, and my mother-in-law are having ego tussles over my bidai ceremony to my in-laws, now that I have to return after the birth of this child. The tussle has now turned into a court case. I want to confide in you that I want to go back home, to my husband.' Listening attentively my father replied, 'Sister, go back to the waiting area. I will see what can be done.'

Kutubuddin—the name had a musical ring. The boy said aloud: 'KUUUUT TTU BUUU DDDIN.' His father told him that Kutubuddin had single-handedly wrestled and killed a tiger. He got to meet Kutubuddin in person soon at the court, while the proceedings were on. Kutubuddin was a massive man with blue eyes and orange hair. There was commotion in the courtroom during the proceedings, as his father tried his best to settle the case amicably. Throughout, the almond-faced woman sat silently. Later, as he sat with his father in their Ford V8, he heard his father speak aloud to himself: 'Their rigidity will not melt away in the stiffness of the court, I will have to call them home.'

After a few days, when he was playing who-has-the-best-soldier's cigarette case game with the sessional judge's son, Aziz, he saw Kutubuddin and the entire group entering their compound gate. So many people meant so much action. He followed them to the hall. His father was talking in a concerned voice, 'So, do you think, being the judicial magistrate of this place, I am like a father-figure to the residents and all those who come to the town?' Everybody answered in unison: 'Yes.'

Then his father continued, 'As the father of this young lady here, I will conduct the ceremonial ritual of bidai here and now.' The woman's husband fell at my father's feet, saying:

'I have never seen a judge so impartial and affectionate.' He rushed to embrace his child. The frozen hearts melted away. The families became one and left in the car that his father had offered for the bidai ceremony. He jotted in his notebook, 'impartial and affectionate'.

A few days later, he saw a different Kutubuddin. His father had taken a break from reading his stack of files that came every day, tied in a large red cloth. He was explaining the meaning of stoicism by using a verse from the Bhagavad Gita: 'Sukh Dukh Samay Kritva, Labha Labho Jaya Jaya.' (Fight for the sake of duty, treat alike happiness and distress, loss and gain, victory and defeat.) It was then that a group of policemen came to inform about a possible communal flare-up in Shivaji Chowk. The little boy sneaked into his father's car as he rushed for duty late in the night. At Shivaji Chowk, he saw men wearing two types of caps: one group was wearing the kulla cap and the other was wearing the boat-shaped cap. He could hear words such as 'Pathans' and 'Marathas' from the crowd. Their fierce eyes and angry stances told him that they have either fought or are about to fight. Kutubuddin was leading the men with kulla caps: his eyes emitting fire. Before he could see further, he saw his father in the middle of the crowd. His heart skipped a beat. It was dangerous!! He sneaked into the crowd to be with his father. His father's booming voice filled the air, 'So Kutubuddin, what is going on?' He saw that the fire in Kutubuddin's eyes extinguished immediately. 'Attack sahib,' the crowd screamed but Kutubuddin retorted, 'Dare you do that! Sahib is my daughter's father.' He turned to my father, 'Sahib, this is just a get-together,' and looking at the crowd, he asked, 'right, brothers?' That was the look no one says no to. The crowd agreed. His father said in mock anger, 'So gentlemen, now that you have disturbed my sleep, I'd better be compensated with tea and sweets.' Swords were sheathed and smiles followed. Men wearing both types of caps came together to prepare tea for the gathering and to fetch sweets. A riot had turned into merrymaking. After reaching home early that morning, he wrote in his book 'The Power of Stoicism'.

The blaring bus horn interrupted his journey into time. He saw his daughter's message flashing on his mobile phone screen: SELECTED. He took out his father's autobiography from his attaché case and clutched it tightly. He knew what he would give to his soon-to-be army officer daughter.

HARYANA

....

34

Danveer Karna

Karnal, a town in Haryana is named after Karna, one of the major characters in the Mahabharata. Even today, when a young boy is named Karan, it is hoped that he would inherit the qualities that were the essence of the great and glorious Karna.

According to the Mahabharata, many years ago, before the epic battle took place in Kurukshetra, Haryana, a princess named Kunti was granted a divine mantra by the sage Durvasa. He was so pleased with her dedication and devotion that he granted her a mantra by which she could have the power to have any god appear before her and bless her with a son, born in the likeness of the deity she had invoked. Out of curiosity, she recited the mantra and asked for the sun god to appear before her. The sun god blessed her with a son who came to be known as Karna. Karna was born with a set of divine armour—a kavach (armour) and kundal (earrings) which made him invincible. Kunti realized that she had made a mistake as she was not yet married, and the presence of a son would make people cast aspersions on her character. In a desperate bid to save herself from a fall from grace, she placed the beautiful baby in a basket and set it afloat in the Ganga. Adhiraj a charioteer found the baby and raised Karna as his own son.

Kunti was later married to King Pandu of Hastinapur and had five sons popularly known as the Pandavas. These five sons were also born by the invocation of the divine mantra as King Pandu was cursed to die if he mated with any of his two wives. It was a strange twist of fate. Meanwhile,

Karna grew up to be a strong and handsome young man and an accomplished warrior. In his eager desire to master the Brahmastra, he disguised himself as a Brahmin so that he could learn from the great teacher, Parshuram. Parshuram only taught Brahmins and took to teaching Karna as he did not know his true identity. One day, however, he discovered that Karna was a Kshatriya and cursed him for betraying his trust and said that he would forget all that he had learnt from him at the most crucial juncture in his life. Thus, began the endless ordeal of Karna. The benevolence of Karna came to light when before the battle of Kurukshetra, Lord Indra came disguised as a Brahmin and asked Karna to give him his kavach and kundal. Lord Indra was Arjun's divine father as he was born to Kunti with blessings from Lord Indra. Thus, Indra wanted to protect his son and he feared that due to the divine powers vested in the kavach and kundal, Karna would defeat the mighty Arjun. Karna offered both to Lord Indra without a second thought as he believed in performing charity towards a Brahmin and considered it a pious duty of man. Lord Indra was so pleased with Karna's generosity that he granted him a boon that he could use his divine weapon Shakti against any enemy, but only once. The battle of Kurukshetra spelt doom for Karna through Parshuram's curse. Karna forgot the Brahmastra mantra during the battle. To make matters worse, the wheels of Karna's chariot got stuck in the soft mushy earth and he could not move his chariot at all.

Karna's life was filled with tragic circumstances, but he never wavered from his belief that generosity, compassion, and kindness are the driving forces of this world. He took life as it came and never accepted defeat. Even though he was a greater warrior than Arjun, life never gave him a fair chance. He was rejected over a matrimonial alliance by Draupadi, as he belonged to a lower caste. Draupadi later married the five Pandava brothers. Karna never lost heart even in the darkest times of his life. The Mahabharata clearly demonstrates that not only was he a great warrior but also a man who held generosity and benevolence as the greatest virtues of life. That is why he is also known as Danveer Karna or benevolent Karna and a number of songs, verses, and stories that permeate life in Haryana revolve around him.

An Old War Folk Song

An incident from World War I has been made memorable through folk songs and oral traditions of Haryana. Once, during the war, an entire regiment—the sixth Jat regiment perished in a counterattack by the Germans. This act of bravery came to be immortalized through a folk song:

German ney gola marya, jaa phuvya amber mein,
Gardatain sipahi bhajay, roti chodd gaye langar mein
Rey un viraan ka key jivay, jinkey balam chey number
mein.
The Germans bombed the skies with a vehemance.
The soldiers eating in the mess were taken aback by
the suddenness.
Martyrs were those Jat husbands who were in sixth
(regiment),
No cavalry fighting the madness.

Among folk songs, several similar examples can be found, which helps to trace lost history of various sacrosanct incidents—which are otherwise not mentioned in books.

Kalpana Chawla

Kalpana was an ordinary girl from Karnal. As a little girl, she dreamed of the mystery of the cosmos, the sky dotted with constellations, and other heavenly bodies. This stirred in her a longing to understand the cosmos which lay undiscovered. Kalpana Chawla acquired the habit of holding on to her dreams and never giving up from her father, Banarasi Lal Chawla, who strove to give his family the best he could. Her mother, Sanjyothi, was her support and biggest cheerleader. There is a beautiful story that narrates how Kalpana chose her name herself from the names suggested by her aunt because Kalpana means 'imagination'. This ordinary girl from Karnal empowered with her imagination and creativity did something that not only made her state proud but also added a feather to the nation's cap. She became the first woman of Indian origin to leave her footprints in space.

Kalpana's journey towards her dreams was not an easy one. Her fascination for watching stars at night and her delight at seeing planes from the Kunjpura Flying Club making patterns in the expanse of the sky left no doubt in her mind that she wanted to become an astronaut and explore the realm of heavenly bodies. She is said to have asked her teacher in school: 'How can people be divided into classes, sects, and religions, when they all look alike from the sky?' This innocent question gives an insight into her beautiful heart and mind. There is another instance where her mathematics teacher was explaining the concept of null sets and gave the example that Indian women astronauts are the example of a classic null set as they have never been on a mission to space. Kalpana, with her positivity and inclination to astronomy, was quick to add that the status of women astronauts might change in the near future. The polite young girl had barely known at the time that she herself would become the iconic and legendary Indian woman to reach space! After a lot of struggle, she managed to get admission in aeronautical engineering at the prestigious Punjab Engineering College in Chandigarh. Needless to say, she was the only woman in her class. The rest, as they say, is history.

Kalpana had a diverse range of interests ranging from karate to reading to immersing her tired senses in classic rock and Sufi music, but her primary passion always remained the inherent desire to touch the skies. With grit and determination, she acquired a seat in master's degree in Aerospace Engineering at the University of Texas in the United States. She met the love of her life, Jean-Pierre Harrison, there. He was a flying instructor, and he became her greatest strength when she married him in 1983. The marriage was an alliance between equals in every sense of the term.

Kalpana had an illustrious career as an astronaut and in November 1996, she was assigned the role of mission specialist and prime robotic arm operator on space shuttle STS-87. In 2003, she was selected for her second voyage into space. This time, fate played a cruel role as the Columbia Space Shuttle exploded on its entry back into earth, killing all seven crew members. The University of Texas dedicated a Kalpana Chawla Memorial at the College of Engineering Arlington in 2010. Kalpana's memory will forever be etched among the stars and even though she is not here, her memory lives on.

In her last email to the students of Punjab Engineering College, Kalpana wrote: 'The path from dreams to success does exist. May you have the vision to find it, the courage to get onto it, and the perseverance to follow it.'

HIMACHAL PRADESH

....

37

The Himalayan Mystery: Shikari Devi

This is the story of the temple of Mata Shikari Devi in Himachal Pradesh. The temple does not have a roof. It is surrounded by stone walls on four sides, and the idols of local deities such as Kamrunaag, Chamunda Mata, Lord Parshuram, and others, are placed within these stone walls. Numerous attempts to install a roof on the top of the temple have failed. Sometimes the roof is blown away by a windstorm or sometimes a heavy bout of rainfall destroys the roof. So, the local people have stopped any further attempts to put a roof on the temple. Some village elders believe that Shikari Mata likes to live in consonance with nature and does not allow anything to be put over her head.

The hilltop where the temple is located is accessible to devotees for around six months of the year. Rest of the year, the area faces either heavy rain or snowfall and it makes the region inaccessible. The incident that leaves people baffled is that the area where the Shikari Devi temple is located, experiences two or three feet of snowfall at most times. The temple gets completely surrounded by snow, however, the idols of Shikari Mata along with those of local deities, placed inside are never covered by snow. The snow that falls on them melts within minutes.

An incident from the Mahabharata is connected to the origin of this temple. Long ago, when the game of gambling was being played between the Pandavas and the Kauravas, the Pandavas went into a state of hallucination and the cycle of time stopped for a moment. Suddenly, a woman appeared in front of them and persuaded them to stop gambling. However, as destiny would have it, the Pandavas could not avoid playing the game. As predicted, the Pandavas lost the game and were exiled, forsaking their palace, kingdom, and all the comforts of life. During their exile, while wandering, they arrived at this specific point and resided here for some time. One day, Arjuna, one of the five Pandava brothers, saw a beautiful deer. His four brothers saw it too. A supreme and highly skilled archer, Arjuna went on a relentless spree to hunt down the deer. Despite all his efforts, he failed to kill the deer. The Pandavas thought that it was a magical deer or may be a figment of their imagination. Suddenly, there was lightning and thunder in the sky. A voice spoke from the sky. The voice reminded the Pandavas that she had forewarned them, too, but they had ignored and had to bear the consequences. The repentant Pandavas prayed for forgiveness from the goddess. The goddess Navdurga who resided in the mountain ordered them to build her a temple. The Pandavas had a statue of the goddess made and placed it on the mountaintop, thereby establishing the temple. The goddess blessed them with victory, prosperity, and well being. Since the goddess was found in the form of a mystic deer whom the Pandavas wished to hunt, she came to be referred to as Shikari Devi. Many years later, the goddess once again came to bless the Pandava brothers. This was during the battle of Kurukshetra. During the battle, at one point of time, the Pandava brothers were faced with a challenging situation at the hands of the skilful warrior, Bhishma Pitamah. Bhishma was unstoppable and mass carnage occurred in the battleground. Arjuna was deeply discouraged. He lost hope and suddenly Goddess Durga, in the form of Shikari Mata, appeared and motivated Arjuna. She told him to follow the instructions of Lord Krishna whom she referred to as Narayana. She blessed him with victory against evil in the epic battle which she said is to be fought in every yuga or era.

38

Scandal Point

In Shimla, there is an area where the Ridge and Mall Road converges known as Scandal Point. It is located on the western side of Shimla. The region is famous for its oral folk tale about Maharaja Bhupinder Singh of Patiala, and the young daughter of the viceroy of India, Lord Curzon.

The young, beautiful, and hazel-eyed daughter of the viceroy could charm her way into any man's heart. She happened to come across Maharaja Bhupinder Singh somewhere. His masculine persona and royal bearing bewitched her. Similarly, the maharaja was also under the spell of her enchanting beauty. Being the daughter of the viceroy also added an appealing aura to her personality.

One day, in the summer of 1892, the viceroy's daughter was strolling on Mall Road. In those days, Mall Road was out of bounds for Indians. But that day, a young, dark, stout man wearing a shining armour appeared on Mall Road riding a horse. The calm atmosphere was disturbed by the galloping sound of the horse's hooves. The horse halted in front of the girl. The sun was behind the figure that stood in front of the girl and so she could not see the face.

The young daughter of Lord Curzon was staring at the horse rider, who had an invincible aura. She was standing at the intersection point of the Ridge and the Mall Road. The horse rider peered into the eyes of the young girl. This rider was Maharaja Bhupinder Singh of Patiala. Suddenly, he bend down and pulled the young girl towards him. He lifted her with his strong arms, placed her in front of him on his horse and sped away, before the guards could get into action.

The elopement of Bhupinder Singh and the daughter of Lord Curzon became one of the biggest scandals in the history of the British Raj. As a consequence, the British banished the maharaja from Shimla. The maharaja, on the other hand, remained unscathed and established a parallel summer retreat in the picturesque hill station of Chail, located of 45 kilometres away from Shimla.

The area where Mall Road and the Ridge converges and where this incident occurred subsequently came to be known as Scandal Point.

39

Pahadi Gandhi: Baba Kanshi Ram

During pre-Independence times, Himachal Pradesh was at the forefront of many nationalist movements. One of the legendary crusaders against British rule was Baba Kanshi Ram. He was born in the remote village of Dadasiba in Dehra tehsil of Kangra district in erstwhile Punjab (now Himachal Pradesh) on 11 July 1882. When he was seven years old, Baba Kanshi Ram was married to Saraswati Devi, who was five years old at that time. He lost his parents when he was thirteen and had to give up his studies. He was fond of music and literature and wrote poetry in the Pahadi dialect; however, to sustain himself, he moved to Lahore to earn a living. Here he got an opportunity to meet the great freedom fighters of the time, including Lala Lajpat Rai, Lala Har Dayal, Sardar Ajit Singh, and Maulvi Barquet Ali. Lahore imparted vision to his thoughts and wings to his poetry. Regular interactions with celebrated poets of the time, including Sufi Amba Prasad and Lal Chand Falak, who composed the patriotic number 'Pagri Sambhal Jatta' turned out to be the turning point of his life.

In 1905, Kangra was hit by a massive earthquake. The young Baba Kanshi Ram joined the team of Congress workers led by Lala Lajpat Rai to help those affected by the disaster. When the Jallianwala Bagh massacre happened in 1919, Baba Kanshi Ram was in Amritsar. This massacre filled him with deep pain and anguish, and he decided to fight against the British colonial rulers. As a consequence of his involvement with freedom fighters, Baba Kanshi Ram was sentenced to two years of rigorous imprisonment on 26 January 1920. Upon his release from jail, he returned to his native place in Kangra, along with Lala Lajpat Rai, to spread the message of freedom against the British rule. His activities landed him in jail as a political prisoner eleven times in a period of nine years. The grim news of the execution of freedom fighters Bhagat Singh, Sukhdev, and Rajguru had an enormous impact on Baba Kanshi Ram and he took a solemn vow to wear only black clothes, till India gained independence. This black dress code made people call him 'Shiaposh General' (the general in black). Sarojini Naidu conferred on him the title 'Bulbul-e-Pahar' when she heard his soul-stirring poems in his melodious voice in a public meeting in Una in Himachal Pradesh. His literary disposition was also noticed by Jawaharlal Nehru at a political meeting of the Congress party in 1937 at Garhdiwala in Hoshiarpur. Nehru addressed him as 'Pahadi Gandhi'. Thus, he came to be known and addressed by this sobriquet. He kept fighting the British wearing black clothes until his death on 15 October 1943. In remembrance of his literary work and contributions as a freedom fighter, on 23 April 1984, the then prime minister of India, Indira Gandhi, released a special commemorative postage stamp in his honour at Jawalamukhi in Kangra district of Himachal Pradesh.

JAMMU AND KASHMIR

40

Heemal and Nagrai

Once upon a time, when most of the valley of Kashmir was a big waterbody, there lived a poor Brahmin by the name of Soda Ram. He was unhappy on account of the continuous nagging by his wife and one day brought a snake inside a bag to kill his wife. Soda Ram had found the snake slithering near a spring as he was on his way to the king's palace, to ask for alms. Upon opening the bag, both husband and wife saw a beautiful baby boy sitting inside. It was Nagrai—the lord of the serpents—who ruled the netherworld with his many wives. Now that Nagrai was reborn into the family of Soda Ram, he became the apple of their eye and gradually grew up into a handsome young man. Soda Ram's fortune slowly improved as well. In no time, he became a prominent and wealthy Brahmin.

At the same time, Princess Heemal, the daughter of a Brahmin king was also growing up in the same region. Every day she would arrive at a spring that was heavily guarded to bathe. Nagrai started to visit the spring too disguised as a snake. He continued frequenting every day—till one day, Heemal and Nagrai met each other, fell in love, and decided to marry.

Though the city celebrated the happy marriage, the serpent queens were anxious to have their king return. The queens hatched a devious plan and accordingly, one of them assumed the form of a cobbler woman. She went to Heemal and asked her the true caste of her husband. Though Heemal knew that Nagrai was the son of a Brahmin, yet, the words of the disguised snake queen made her doubt. The disguised snake queen also advised Heemal to instruct Nagrai to take a test. The snake queen said, 'Ask him to plunge into an ocean of milk. His body will sink if he is a true Brahmin and his body will float on the surface if he is a low-caste cobbler.'

Accordingly, Heemal asked Nagrai to take the test. Nagrai understood the interference of the snake queens and cautioned Heemal not to force him to take the test, and if she insisted she would repent later. However, Heemal was adamant. So, Nagrai dived into the ocean of milk and the snake queens, who were lying in wait, started pulling him down. As he was gradually sinking, Nagrai asked Heemal if she was convinced about the purity of his caste now. But, Heemal remained adamant. Finally, by the time Nagrai's body except his forehead was immersed in milk, Heemal woke up as if from a trance and tried to pull him out by his hair. Alas, Nagrai sank and Heemal was left with only a tuft of hair in her hands.

Distraught with grief, Heemal donated all her possessions and wandered through the woods in deep anguish and sorrow. One day, an old man and his daughter came asking for alms and food. They narrated an astonishing story of a spring that they had encountered in their travels. Near this spring, at midnight, they saw a number of servants come out. They cleaned the place and cooked a large meal for many guests, including a prince. After the feast was over, they returned to the spring; only the prince stayed back for a little while longer and kept some food near a tree saying, 'This is for my unlucky Heemal.' This story surprised Heemal and she understood that it might connect her to Nagrai. She asked the directions to the spring and donated her remaining jewels to the old man.

On reaching the spot, Heemal too witnessed the same incident and immediately recognized Nagrai and pleaded with him to take her to the netherworld. Nagrai was anxious and feared for Heemal's life and finally decided to turn her into a pebble, so that she could lie in the water with Nagrai. However, the serpent queens were shrewd enough to smell human flesh and blood in the water. They spared her life and assured that Heemal could be turned back into a human but she would be relegated to the position of a kitchen maid and will not receive the honours of a queen. Satisfied with the fact that she would get to stay close to her beloved, Heemal agreed. One day, Heemal warmed milk for the serpent children and poured them into bowls to cool. However, the children mistakenly gulped down the hot milk. They sadly burned down and perished. The angry serpent queens stung Heemal and she died immediately. Extremely grief-stricken, Nagrai could not bring himself to cremate Heemal; instead, he embalmed her body and kept it near the spring. He came every day to worship her. This incident was noted by a wandering holy man who brought Heemal back to life with his magical powers and took her home, where the son of the holy man expressed his desire to marry her.

Meanwhile, on finding the embalmed body missing, Nagrai kept searching for Heemal and finally located her sleeping inside a hut. He coiled next to her but was suddenly killed by the owner of the house who saw a snake on the bed. Heemal was woken up by the cries of Nagrai as he succumbed to his death. Heemal was heartbroken. She cremated Nagrai and threw herself on the burning pyre. The holy man was greatly saddened at the unfortunate death of Heemal and Nagrai. One day, as he sat meditating, he overheard two birds talking about the deep love and sacrifice of Heemal and Nagrai. The female bird asked her mate if they could ever regain human form and the male replied, 'Yes, surely, if someone puts their ashes into the spring.' The holy man understood that it was Lord Shiva and Goddess Parvati advising him, disguised as the two birds. Accordingly, the holy man collected the ashes from the pyre and threw them into the spring. As soon as the ashes were fully immersed, Heemal and Nagrai came to life in human form and they lived happily ever after.

41

The Only Son

King Harnaam lived with his queen, Sonamaal, and their seven daughters in Rajapuri, the capital of his kingdom. He was a noble king, God-fearing, and popular with his subjects. Well-respected for delivering justice and punishing criminals, King Harnaam was equally keen to preserve the flora and fauna of his kingdom. Drinking water was made available to birds on troughs placed on perches and ponds and wells were dug for making water available to the people.

His subjects were happy as their king was a just ruler. However, the royal couple longed for a son who would become the heir to the throne. They prayed at temples, gave to charity, and sought blessings of saints and holy men. As the king aged, he became increasingly sad for not having been blessed with a son. The queen continued to pray fervently for a little prince. One day, she found a holy man, a jogi, in her courtyard. He had long, black, curly hair rolling down to his shoulders. His body was smeared with ashes, he wore earrings, and his eyes were captivating. He wore padukas—wooden slippers; his voice attracted her attention in total devotion and submission.

The jogi came close to the queen with his begging bowl and asked her for alms in the name of God. The queen offered a precious set of stones and sought the boon of a son. She also shared with him that in one of her recent dreams, she had seen a jogi like him who told her that her wish would be fulfilled in nine months. The jogi gave the royal couple a patient hearing and told them that he would give them a son on the condition that the child had to be returned to him after twelve years. The king and queen promised to abide by the wish of the jogi and on hearing their consent, the jogi walked a few steps but before vanishing, told them to name their son, Akanandun, the only son.

Nine months later, the royal couple was blessed with a son. He became the darling of everyone. With time, everybody was happy to see him grow up into a handsome, strong, and intelligent boy. Twelve years passed and one day, the jogi returned to claim Akanandun.

The queen begged the jogi to accept any gifts that he could name, in return for her son. 'Promises need to be fulfilled,' declared the jogi and he refused to listen to the pleadings of the royal couple. He called Akanandun by name and the prince presented himself before the jogi. The jogi removed the ornaments and clothes from the boy's body, bathed him in warm water, and asked for a butcher's knife to kill the boy. Everybody cried in terror. The jogi also called upon the seven sisters of Akanandun and asked them to catch the limbs of their only brother. The jogi threatened the royal couple of more trouble for the non-fulfilment of their promise.

The jogi passed the knife to the king and asked him to behead the boy. Who would ever kill his son? But the king, having no other choice, cut the throat of his son and wept along with all those who were present. People were beating their chests in grief, hitting each other, shouting and crying in pain. The jogi resumed the task and severed the limbs of the boy, washed all his body parts, and put the pieces in a big earthen vessel. Hell broke loose but few could dare stop the jogi as the king had fulfilled his promise and returned the boy to him. He put oil in the earthenware and starting cooking. The queen protested but to no avail. The jogi directed her to start cooking and put seven pieces of flesh in seven bowls of soup. 'Four are for females, one for the king, one for me and one for Akanandun,' the jogi declared.

As all set to have their soup, the jogi asked the queen to go upstairs and call for Akanandun. The bereaved and crying queen declared that she cannot have the soup and call for Akanandun, whose loss she has faced. The jogi retorted, 'I am not what you see, oh queen, I keep changing my appearances.' She went upstairs and called for Akanandun, who replied, 'I am coming, Mother,' and suddenly, the queen found Akanandun standing before her. She held him in a tight embrace and found that the jogi had disappeared and so had the seven bowls of soup. The royal couple lived with Akanandun and their daughters happily thereafter.

42

The Forgotten Hero: Maqbool Sherwani

On 15 August 1947, India gained Independence from the British. Pakistan came into existence a day earlier. At that time, Jammu and Kashmir, a Muslim majority state, was an independent state ruled by Maharaja Hari Singh, a Hindu Dogra king. He had not been able to make up his mind on whether to join India or Pakistan, or remain an independent state.

Pakistan assumed that the maharaja would opt to accede to Pakistan because of religious commonality of majority population and geographical proximity. As the maharaja was debating which of the two new nations to join, Pakistan sent tribesmen and Pashtuns supported by their army to occupy Kashmir by aggression in early October 1947. This forced the maharaja to seek accession to India on 27 October 1947 and request for military help to secure his state.

By the time the Instrument of Accession was signed between Maharaja Hari Singh and India, infiltrators had reached Baramulla, about 30 miles from Srinagar. These infiltrators were called Kabalis. As they moved towards Baramulla, they wreaked havoc enroute looting, raping, and murdering, and demanding zar (cash), zewar (jewellery), and zanana (women); even the nuns and nurses in Baramulla were not spared. The heroic story of Maqbool Sherwani, a nineteen-year-old young man came to the forefront in this tumultuous time. He was of a secular outlook and a devout follower of Sheikh Mohammad Abdullah, who did not support the two-nation theory of Mohammed Ali Jinnah, the founder of Pakistan. During one of the visits of Jinnah to Baramulla, Maqbool had even disrupted his rally.

On seeing the raiders enter Baramulla on 22 October 1947, Maqbool Sherwani decided to frustrate their onslaught and buy time until the arrival of the Indian forces. He misguided the infiltrators to take wrong routes and roads, making them lose a couple of days. The raiders faced other troubles as well. They squabbled over the spoils even as they faced severe resistance from a group of over hundred soldiers who were already stationed in Kashmir and kept the tribal raiders engaged in a guerrilla-type operation under the leadership of Brigadier Rajinder Singh.

Maqbool had a motorbike and began to misguide the amir of Kabali raiders on routes to the Srinagar aerodome. The amir was keen on locating details, including, finding the shortest possible route to the aerodome in Srinagar, extract the location of Sheikh Mohammad Abdullah in order to capture him and also to find the location of the Indian troops near Shalateng. Maqbool frustrated all their efforts, thereby gaining time for the arrival of the Indian troops. When the amir finally realized about the delay, it was too late as the Indian army had already arrived. The amir declared Maqbool a traitor and punished him with death in a barbaric way. He was nailed to a cross and fired upon multiple times. The body was kept on display for a couple of days to strike terror in the hearts of all, until it was brought down by the Indian army upon their arrival. He was later buried in Juma Masjid on 7 November 1947.

Had Maqbool not frustrated the tribals and made his supreme sacrifice, Kashmir could have fallen into the hands of the raiders and the war would have further intensified. It is through the sacrifices of people like him and his leader, Sheikh Mohammad Abdullah, that secularism and plurality survived. However, regrettably, Maqbool is not a legend much remembered today, apart from an ode in the book entitled *Death of a Hero: Epitaph for Maqbool Sherwani* by Mulk Raj Anand.

JHARKHAND

The Shepherd and the Tiger

This is the story of a shepherd. One day when the shepherd was grazing his goats in the forest, he saw a lohtan—a magical lizard. He caught it and just as he was about to kill it, when the lohtan requested him to spare his life. The little lohtan also added that it would like to serve him forever and also help him whenever there was a need. The shepherd laughed at the small life and its larger-than-life thinking and if there was any possibility of such a tiny creature ever helping him out, but nevertheless, he did not kill the lohtan and took it home in the evening. The next day, when the shepherd went to graze his goats in the forest, he took the lohtan along with him. After reaching the forest, the shepherd lay down under a tree and the lohtan kept a vigilant watch on the goats from the top of a tree. The shepherd soon went off to sleep.

After some time, a tiger came out of a bush and rushed towards the goats. The lohtan told the tiger, 'You are threatening my goats! Let me come down, I'll teach you a lesson!' Listening to this, the tiger replied 'Oh! You brave one! Come down the tree, I will gulp you down!' The lohtan jumped from the tree and went towards the tiger and challenged him, 'Gulp me? Is it? Let me see how you eat me!' As soon as the tiger opened his mouth to gobble up the lohtan, it jumped directly into his month and the tiger gobbled it alive. Upon reaching the stomach of the tiger, the lohtan started to jump around. Thereafter, the tiger started feeling very uncomfortable and began to writhe in pain. Listening to the helpless cries and shouting of the tiger, the shepherd woke up and on seeing the condition of the tiger, he started to laugh out loud. Now the tiger started to plead, 'Oh brother, I am dying of pain and you are laughing. Please help me. A lohtan is creating nuisance inside my stomach. Please take it out from my stomach. I will hunt a deer for you every day.'

The shepherd cleverly replied, 'Okay! Open your mouth!'

The tiger opened his mouth and the lohtan came out of his stomach as soon as the shepherd called it. Now, as per his promise, the tiger killed a deer and brought it to the shepherd and told him, 'Let bygones be bygones! But don't mention this incident to anyone, otherwise I will kill you and eat you up!' After that the tiger went away and the happy shepherd also returned home with fresh deer meat, his goats, and the lohtan. Over the next three days, the tiger hunted a deer every day and presented it to the shepherd. When many villagers asked the shepherd how he had managed to hunt a deer every day, the clever shepherd stayed silent as he was scared of the tiger's threat.

A few days later, when the shepherd was playing with his friends, he suddenly remembered the incident of the tiger and the lohtan and started to laugh. His friends started pestering him to share the reason behind the mirth. The shepherd replied, 'No, brothers, I cannot tell you and if I do, the tiger will kill me.' Upon this, his friends replied, 'How can anyone kill you as long as we are here with you? We will save you, but first tell us about the incident.'

The shepherd narrated the incident of the tiger and the lohtan. Meanwhile, the tiger was also on the lookout as to when the shepherd would mention the incident and he would kill him. The tiger was, thus, stalking the shepherd. So as soon as the shepherd finished his story, the tiger came running, lifted the shepherd and started to run as fast as he could. Now, there was a small tin-box filled with pebbles in the shepherd's pocket. As the tiger ran, the pebbles jingled and clattered. This frightened the tiger and he asked, 'What is this sound?' The shepherd replied, 'It is the sound of the same lohtan which had entered your stomach. It is feeling suffocated and so it is jumping around to come out of a box in my pocket.' Listening to this, the tiger became nervous and said, 'No, no! Don't let the lohtan out! It is a very naughty creature.' The shepherd replied, 'Okay! If you leave me alone, I will not allow the lohtan to come out; however, if you do not leave me, it will definitely come out. Now, you have to decide.' Out of fear, the tiger let go of the shepherd and quickly fled into the forest. Free at last, the shepherd returned home, safe and sound.

44

The Clever Fox

In the olden days, there once lived a tiger. One day, he was accidentally trapped under a big, fallen tree. Even though he tried hard, he could not get out from under the tree. Just then a traveller was passing by. The tiger addressed him and said, 'Dear friend. Please help me. Free me from this agony. I will not eat you. Please do not be afraid.' The man replied, 'It is hard to believe you. Technically, you are an enemy of the human race. How can I believe you?' The tiger swore that he would not harm the man and being convinced by the tiger's sweet words, the man rolled away the big tree and freed the tiger.

As soon as the tiger was out, he stretched his body and told the man, 'Now I am going to make you my food.' The man reminded him of his promise. The tiger replied, 'I am hungry. And necessity has no rule. I am going to eat you.' The man had an idea and requested that the dispute be settled by a third party. Thus, they went in search of someone who would decide the matter. Soon, they came upon an ox and the man narrated the whole story to the ox.

After listening to the man, the ox said: 'You human beings are very bad animals. You torture us by twisting our tails, hitting us with sticks, and making us work hard when we are young. When we grow old you do not give us food and throw us out of your house. My decision is in favour of the tiger.'

The tiger said, 'Now the decision has been made. Allow me to eat you.'

The man replied after thinking for a while, 'Don't get impatient! We should go to a wiser person for the decision.'

The tiger agreed and they went to meet a fox. The fox was very busy. It said, 'I am returning after conveying a message to the king about a very long and difficult journey. Let me drink water at my home and then I will listen to you.'

Saying this, the fox went inside his den. The fox returned after some time and listening to the whole story said, 'The whole story is concocted.' The man said that the story is a true story, and the tiger confirmed the story. Then the fox replied, 'I think both of you are making a fool of me. Show me the fallen tree.' They went to the place where the tree was lying. Casting some doubts after seeing the tree, the fox said, 'If possible, you have to show me the exact situation as it was earlier, including the position of the tiger.' Listening to this, the man lifted the tree trunk with much difficulty and the tiger crawled under the trunk; the man then let go of his hold and the tiger was once again caught under the tree as before. The fox told the tiger, 'Now you show me by freeing yourself.' The tiger struggled but could not move even a bit. Then the fox told the man, 'Now look for a strong stick and kill this ungrateful fellow,' and the man killed the tiger with a stick.

45

The Story of the Tana Bhagats

The Indian freedom struggle, spanning more than a century, has many stories which are not known to the world, but speak of significant historical events from specific regions. Such a story is that of the Tana Bhagats of Jharkhand. Their history is still reflected in present times across the region.

After World War I, the demand for complete independence had spread across almost all of India. In the present-day state of Jharkhand, so many stories of struggle against British atrocities are on record.

In the early 1920s, some Mundas of Ranchi (present-day Khunoti district), inspired by the story of Bhagwan Birsa Munda, decided to unite and defy the British rule. They decided to make their life disciplined by taking an oath to inculcate various habits into their daily life such as abstaining from the consumption of alcohol, ban on hunting, to stop eating outside their homes, to maintain complete cleanliness, and to wear only white-coloured clothes, and so on.

It was also the time when Mahatma Gandhi was working for the independence of the nation. A few of the representatives of this group, who called themselves Bhagats, went to meet Mahatma Gandhi in Gujarat. They were greatly influenced by his way of life and took it upon themselves to not tell lies, use only Indian-made things and to consider the Indian national flag as their only God and worship it henceforth.

In the history of the freedom movement, they came to be known as the Tana Bhagats of Chota Nagpur. Today, they are several thousands in number and they still reside in the districts of Ranchi and Khunti in Jharkhand. Even in present times they still maintain the same vows taken several decades ago and follow the Gandhian principles as their way of life, such as, following the principles of truthfulness, non-violence, and respecting and worshipping the Indian national flag. They follow naturopathic medicines in place of mainstream western medicines. One can also notice them in plain white clothes and turbans in the regions of Khunti and Bero (of Ranchi). They still remain an inspiration for several Indians.

KARNATAKA

46

The Story of the Magical Mango

Early one morning, Mabala Swami woke up. He had something on his mind. It was the day he was going to get the 'Muttu Mavina Hannu'—the magical mango. So, he dressed in white kurta-pyjamas, draped a cloth around his head, took an umbrella in his hand, and set out of the house. He came down from the attic, bending his head, so that he did not bump his head on the low doorway. He stepped out onto the courtyard where he saw the sweeper girl at work. Mabala Swami knew that she was a big gossipmonger, so he said to her, 'Don't you dare tell my wife which direction I went. If you do, I will not pay you a whole year's salary, understood?' After this warning, Mabala Swami confidently took the path that led into a dense forest where no one dared to venture.

On his way, he met some cowherd women. They called out to Mabala Swami, 'We know where you are going. No one ever goes there, and no one ever returns from there. No one has ever been able to bring back the magical mango. Please don't go. It's an impossible task, please don't try this impossible task,' they requested him.

But Mabala Swami didn't listen to the women and he kept walking towards the dense forest. As they were determined to save his life, the women thought of a way out. They were women who roamed the earth and knew some handy magic. They called out to Mabala Swami again and gave him four magical stones. They told him, 'Go if you must, but don't go without any tricks like a fool. Here are four stones. One of the stones can make the mighty snake, Nagappa, fall asleep.

Since Nagappa is always guarding the mango tree, once he falls asleep, you can pluck the mango. They pointed to the second stone and said, 'The second stone must be used to wake Nagappa from sleep. The other two stones will do your bidding. You can use them whenever necessary.'

Mabala Swami started walking towards the dense forest with four magical stones. When he entered the forest, he saw a mighty mango tree and the huge five-hooded snake, Nagappa, guarding the tree. He threw the first magical stone and just as the cowherd women had promised, Nagappa went to sleep. He quickly went towards the mango tree, climbed it, plucked a mango from the tree, and climbed down the tree. As he started walking away from the mango tree, he threw the second magical stone to wake up the snake from his sleep. Nagappa woke up and looked around. He could smell the fresh scent of plucked mango from the tree. He knew someone had plucked a mango from his tree. Nagappa quickly climbed the mango tree, reached the top and put down his tail on the tallest branch and stood up straight and tall to look around.

At a distance, Nagappa spotted Mabala Swami in white clothes, looking like a shining white stork's feather. Mabala Swami had already reached halfway to his home. A furious Nagappa swiftly started moving, making a tremendous hissing sound. Mabala Swami became aware that the snake had woken up and was coming after him. He quickly threw the third stone to create boulders and thorns in the way of Nagappa to slow him down.

But Nagappa was very fast. He soon caught up with Mabala Swami and was about to attack him with his five-hooded head, when Mabala Swami threw the fourth stone and bid the stone to make a river. This river is called Gangavali, now in Uttara Kannada region where the Halakki tribes live. Mabala Swami also bid the stone to get him a magical boat to row to the other side of the river and a magical sword as well. He started rowing the boat across the Gangavali River. Undeterred, Nagappa put his tail deep in the ground and lifted his hood over the water and started moving towards Mabali Swami. When Nagappa was about to attack him, Mabala Swami chopped his four hoods with the magical sword and left only one hood to keep him alive. When both of them reached the shore, Mabala Swami requested Nagappa saying, 'Guarding the mango tree is not your job, O snake! You are supposed to stay in a termite mound. I am now going to create a termite mound for you on the shore and you can stay there forever.' He further added, 'Once a year, all the villagers will come and offer you milk on Naga Panchami and they will worship and honour you.' Mabala Swami then created a termite mound and henceforth, Nagappa started living in the termite mound. Mabala Swami left the mango in the river and the mango floated away in the waters of Gangavali.

Later that day, Mabala Swami's wife and his sister came to the river to wash away menstrual blood from their bodies. As they were bathing, they saw a beautiful, juicy mango floating in the river. They both wanted the mango.

'How do we catch the mango?'

The wife suggested they trap the mango with her sari pallu. They managed to catch the mango and started to wonder....

'How to cut the mango?'

The wife suggested cutting it with her nails, but the sister felt it might spoil the mango so perhaps they should use a metal knife instead, but the wife doubted, saying that it might turn black the flesh of the mango. So they decided to cut the mango with cane strips. They reached for a bush and pulled out a cane strip and the wife cut the mango with the sharp edge of the cane.

The wife ate the flesh, and the sister ate the skin of the magical mango. So the magical mango gave the wife a baby boy and the sister a baby girl. The wife threw away the seed

of the mango and from this seed a mango tree grew and bore
many more mangoes. Now there are mango trees everywhere
in the village. This is the story of how the mango tree came
to the village.

47

Kodai and Poovatha: A Strange Relationship

There was once a farmer's wife, Kodai, who was also a devoted daughter-in-law. She followed all her mother-in-law's instructions without complaining.

Every morning Kodai would ask Poovatha, her mother-in-law, how much rice she needed to cook that day. Poovatha would think for a moment and then hold up either two fingers or three—indicating how many measures of rice were required for the day. The understanding between the two women was so deep that the mother-in-law hardly needed to say a word except show her fingers.

One day, Poovatha fell very ill and died soon after. This left Kodai heartbroken. She greatly missed her mother-in-law and felt a little helpless now that there was no one to give her those silent instructions.

Maaran, Kodai's husband, was a farmer and had always felt very pleased with his wife's devotion to his mother. But now when his wife started asking him every morning how much rice she needed to cook that day he was soon fed up.

He thought of a plan to rid himself of this daily pestering. He asked the village potter to make a life-size clay statue of his mother, with one hand holding up two fingers and the other holding up three. When the statue was ready, it was painted and dressed in one of his mother's saris. The farmer brought the statue home and placed it outside the kitchen.

'Amma is back!' Kodai, the innocent young woman, said happily. She returned to her routine of asking Poovatha for instructions. Every morning she looked out of the kitchen

window at the clay figure. If her eyes fell first on the hand
holding up two fingers, she would cook two measures of rice
that day. And if she happened to see the hand holding up three
fingers, she would cook three measures instead.

Maaran was relieved that his wife no longer pestered him
for answers to the same question every day. For a few weeks
he felt at peace, until he realized that his wife was cooking
the same amount of rice she used to cook even though there
was one person less to consume it.

One night, he asked his wife. 'Why do you cook for three
people when there are only two of us?'

'How can you say that?' she protested.

'Amma has come back, by the grace of God. I still serve
her food before I eat. And don't mind me saying so, but her
appetite is much bigger than it used to be. Sometimes very
little food is left for me, but I don't mind that as long as
Amma is satisfied.'

Maaran was enraged. He was a poor man who worked
hard to make a living and here was his wife talking nonsense
and wasting his hard earned money.

'You've gone mad!' he shouted. 'How can a clay figure eat
rice? Get out of my house and take your Amma with you!'

Saying this, he thrust the clay figure into her arms and
threw them out of the house.

But the daughter-in-law had neither gone mad nor was she
telling lies. What had happened was this. Their neighbour's
wife was a clever but unscrupulous woman. She often spied on
their household and had made a hole in the wall between their
houses where the clay statue stood. Every time the daughter-
in-law served food to her clay Amma and went back into the
kitchen, the neighbour's wife would grab the food through the
hole in the wall. The innocent daughter-in-law never realized
that the food she so lovingly cooked and served for her Amma
every day was being stolen, right under her nose!

Helpless and terrified, poor Kodai wandered through the dark night, clutching her clay Amma for comfort. She had hardly ever been out of the house, let alone at such late hours of the night. Soon she came to a forest, and seeking shelter, climbed up a large tree. Trying to hide herself between two branches, she held onto the clay figure and tried to sleep.

Soon, a gang of robbers happened to come that way. They had just robbed a jeweller's house. Carrying large bursting sacks of loot, they stopped under that very tree to divide the loot. The young woman woke up when she heard voices below. In the light of their burning torches, she saw big, burly men armed with daggers. The poor woman nearly fainted with fright.

As she desperately debated if she should climb higher to save herself, the clay figure slipped from her trembling hands. Down it went, crashing through branches and leaves startling sleeping birds, and landed in front of the robbers with a loud crash!

'Bhoot! Bhoot!' yelled the terrified thieves and ran for their lives.

The daughter-in-law was equally alarmed. She fainted on a branch and came to her senses only at daybreak. She immediately began searching for her clay Amma and found her lying in three pieces on a huge pile of gold and silver coins and ornaments which the robbers had left behind.

She picked up the clay pieces carefully, hoping that her husband would be able to put them back together. She also picked up a few gold ornaments, thanked her Amma for them, and walked home.

As soon as she knocked on the door, her husband opened it. He was relieved to see that his wife had come to no harm. When she told him all that had happened, he hurried to the forest with her and brought back the rest of the robbers' loot. He was richer now than he had ever imagined.

The next day he told his wife to borrow a pair of scales

from their neighbour's wife so that they could weigh their treasure.

'But don't tell her anything about it,' he said before leaving the house to work in his fields.

The neighbour's wife was as inquisitive as she was greedy. She pestered Kodai with questions till she divulged the whole story. 'So now we have a lot of gold and silver,' she said.

The neighbour's wife was green with envy. That very day she told her husband to get a similar clay statue made. 'If that poor fool can use a clay figure to scare away robbers and get their loot, so can I!'

When the statue was ready, she carried it to the forest, climbed the same tree and waited. Night had fallen and soon enough the robbers returned with loot. As they divided it among themselves, she threw the clay statue down on them as hard as she could. The robbers fled in alarm a second time, but this time they didn't go far. They hid and watched to find out who and which bhoot it was that had driven them away and perhaps stolen their earlier loot.

The neighbour's wife came down from the tree. She was busy gathering gold and silver when the furious robbers surrounded her. They spared her life because she was a woman, but they tied her tightly to the tree and left her to the mercy of wild animals.

The following morning, her husband found her half dead with pain and fear. The clay statue lay in pieces around her. There were no signs of any treasure. The robbers had taken away everything.

48

Saalumarada Thimmakka

Saalumarada Thimmakka was one of the six children of the late Chikkarangayya and Vijayamma in Kakkenalli of Gubbi, Hosalli taluk, in Karnataka. Being poor, Thimmakka's father used to work in the agricultural fields in a nearby village and her mother used to work in the houses of rich landlords—cleaning grains, washing utensils, and doing other sundry jobs. Thimmakka's job was to collect firewood and sometimes muttukada, sal leaves, from the forest. She would often collect these and sell them in Gubbi village which was 3 kilometres away. Muttukada leaves were and still are sewn together to make plates to serve food. Life trudged on with the regular ups and downs. Soon, one day, Thimmakka's parents felt that she was of marriageable age and decided to get her married.

The marriage was finalized with Chikkaiah from Hulikal, who owned an agricultural land of 4 acres. At her in-laws', Thimmakka lived with her husband, mother-in-law, and brother-in-law. Thimmakka worked hard in the agricultural fields of her in-laws and was initially happy; however, problems started to crop up soon as years went by and she did not conceive. Five years went by and people started to gossip about the couple. With time, the problems escalated. People started to harass them to capture their agricultural fields since they had no heir. The couple had no option but to complain to the police. By this time, Thimmakka was already into her twentieth year of marriage and without a child. To avoid further harassment, the couple decided to build a separate house and move away from their family. Situation grew grim with each passing day for Thimmakka. Even Chikkaiah would often taunt and insult her. This would hurt her immensely.

Solitary, spending their days and nights in despair, the couple finally decided upon a solution. They thought of finding solace in Mother Nature and of planting trees and tending to them just as they would take care of children. Thus, the couple took upon themselves to shower all their love on nature, which got reflected in the verdant stretch between Kadur and Hulikal, where the couple started their innovative journey of planting trees—around eight decades ago. However, it did not happen overnight. Banyan trees were available in plenty near their village and they grafted the saplings from these trees. Ten saplings were grafted in the first year and they planted these near the neighbouring village of Kudoor. These ten saplings were nurtured and the couple watched them grow. Once these ten plants took roots, the couple planted fifteen more saplings in the next year and twenty in the year after that. Thus, it continued for nearly ten years and today, 385 strong trees stand as a testimony of their selfless efforts, along a four-kilometre stretch between Hulikal and Kudoor village, near her husband's hometown in Tumakuru district. The entire avenue is a sight to behold, with the wide and strong branches of the trees spreading to form a green canopy.

According to Thimmakka, there are two varieties of trees: goni alla and chittaru alla. Though the verdant avenue does paint a picturesque view today, it was not an easy challenge for the couple. They had to nurture the saplings very carefully. They had to get water from a pond, 3 kilometres away, which was called Thopayya Kalyani. They had to protect the young trees and the tender leaves from being eaten by cows and goats by strapping a protector using firewood sticks and making a circular stand around each sapling. According to Thimmakka, they were overjoyed to witness the young, green leaves sprout from each young tree. The couple would water and nurture them very early in the morning, before anybody was up, and leave for their day's work at a nearby quarry in Nagenahalli. They had to reach the quarry before the day became hot and humid. Working at this quarry one day, Thimmakka lost one of her eyes in an accident.

In due course of time, the request of the couple to the village chairman to grant them a piece of land met with a positive response. Recognizing the couple's good works, the director of Watershed Development Programme, K. V. Sarvesh, helped to have a pond dug in Thimmakka's land and gave her the technical training to manage it. In 1991, Chikkaiah fell ill and passed away, but Thimmakka continued her work for the village and the environment.

Thimmakka has received more than 300 awards and citations for her hard work. She was awarded the Padma Shri (2019), Nadoja Award by Hampi University (2010), and the National Citizen Award (1995) by the then prime minister of India, H. D. Deve Gowda, amongst other awards. Thimmakka is more famously called Saalu Marada Thimakka—named after the rows of trees, which have become very famous.

KERALA

49

The Tale of the Brave Lady

Unniyarcha's father, Kannappa Chekavar, was allied to a famous Chekavar family. He was a master in Kalaripayattu and had won forty-one duels and owned four martial art training schools, popularly known as kalaris. He lived in his ancestral home, Puthuram House, which was linked to a group of legendary fighters. Unniyarcha was the only daughter of Kannappa Chekavar. She had two brothers, Aromal Chekavar and Unnikannan, both of whom were well-versed in sword fight. She spent her childhood with her two brothers and a cousin named Chandu. Chandu was an orphan. He lost his parents soon after his birth. Kannappa Chekavar, his maternal uncle, brought him to Puthuram House and brought him up as his own child. Kannappa Chekavar was very affectionate towards his sister's son, and trained him in sword fight.

At the age of seven, Unniyarcha started practising sword fight at her father's kalari. Her brother, Aromal, and her cousin, Chandu, helped her to master the art of Kalaripayattu. She excelled in using the flexible sword, urumi, and proved her competence in martial arts in her teens. Unniyarcha's feminine charm and generosity was propagated by many travelling bards in Kerala.

Chandu was deeply in love with Unniyarcha and desired to marry her as 'cousin marriage' was a customary practice among the Hindus at that period of time. But Unniyarcha considered Chandu as her elder brother and enjoyed his love and companionship. Her father also showed special attention to Chandu. Unniyarcha's elder brother, Aromal, did not like his father's favouritism towards Chandu. He despised Chandu and was cynical about his words and deeds. When Unniyarcha completed her training and turned fourteen, her family decided to look for a groom for her. Her cousin daringly professed his wish to marry her. But nobody in the family supported his wish except her father. Aromal Chekavar openly exposed his aversion and displeasure about Chandu's proposal. It led to an enduring enmity between Aromal and Chandu. Finally, Unniyarcha married Kunhiraman, a martial art trainer. After her marriage, she went to her husband's home and as was customary, she took her husband's family name and was called Attumanamel Unniyarcha. Chandu, who lost his dreams, left his uncle's home in despair.

During Unniyarcha's stay at Kunhiraman's home, an interesting incident accidently occurred to prove her courage. One fine day, Unniyarcha heard about an auspicious local festival that was happening at Allimalarkavu, a famous temple far away from her home. She wished to participate in that temple festival but Kunhiraman's parents did not give her permission to go there as they were afraid of the misogynist ruffians at Nadapuram market. Somehow, Unniyarcha convinced her husband and he finally agreed to go with her to the temple. When the couple reached the market, a gang of armed hooligans surrounded them. Kunhiraman, though he was a martial art trainer, started shivering. To his surprise, Unniyarcha challenged the hooligans and told them that she was born in Puthuram House, the birthplace of many legendary fighters. She fought with the armed ruffians and wounded them with her urumi. The wounded ruffians ran away and reported the incident to their gang leader. He, along with other gang members, came to the market and fought with Unniyarcha. She bravely fought and defeated all of them. Later, the gang leader realized the truth that they had fought against the daughter of a renowned sword fighter. He begged her forgiveness and offered her gold ornaments and valuables as a reward to pacify her. Instead of receiving his gifts, she ordered him to stop attacking the women who were travelling alone through Nadapuram market. Unniyarcha's daring intervention put an end to hooliganism in that area and her bravery saved the lives of many helpless women.

Another mysterious incident in Unniyarcha's life was the unexpected visit of Chandu in her sleeping chamber. One midnight, Chandu covertly entered her sleeping chamber hid under her bed. When she saw him, she was furious and shouted at him. Chandu tried to console her. But in anger, she threw a brass vessel at him and insulted him by calling him a traitor. Chandu was deeply hurt and his discontent flared up.

Unniyarcha's life moved to a new phase with the untimely death of Aromal. Aromal was fixed to fight with Aringodar for settling a conflict between two brothers. Aringodar was a maestro of sword fight and the master of eighteen kalaris. Unfortunately, Unniyarcha's father deputed Chandu as Aromal's first assistant in the fight with Aringodar. Aringodar, the trickiest fighter, persuaded Chandu to make a flawed sword for Aromal. In the duel, Aromal bravely attacked Aringodar with the defective sword and killed him. After the tiresome fight, Aromal slept keeping his head on Chandu's lap. Chandu planned to take revenge on Aromal. He stabbed him with the sharp edge of a brass lamp and killed him. After Aromal's brutal murder, Unniyarcha came back to her own family. Her only aim now was to kill Chandu. She vowed that she would tie her hair only after the assassination of Chandu the traitor. She took charge of her father's kalari and intensively trained her son, Aromalunni, along with Aromal's son, Kannappanunni. Later, both of them fought with Chandu, cut his head, and gave it as a gift to the brave Unniyarcha.

50

The Tale of the Lady with the Ruby Anklet

Kaveripoompattinam (Poompuhar) was a famous port city of the Chola kingdom ruled by King Karikala. There lived a rich merchant who had a son named Kovalan. He was very handsome and was adept in art and music. When he grew up, he joined his father's business and became a rich merchant like his father. He was married off to Kannagi, a rich merchant's daughter. She was a sincere, beautiful young lady and was obedient and dutiful towards her husband. She loved her husband deeply and was considered an embodiment of chastity by family members and relatives. The happiness of the couple, however, was short-lived as Kovalan fell in love with a courtesan named Madhavi. Kovalan was so deeply in love with Madhavi that he left his ideal wife and his family, and started a new life with Madhavi in her home. Madhavi's greedy mother took advantage of her daughter's fortune and shrewdly planned to grab all the properties Kovalan had inherited. Gradually, he lost all his assets and became a destitute. As Kovalan lost his riches, Madhavi started to distance herself from him. One night, Kovalan heard Madhavi singing a song which reminded him of his dutiful wife, Kannagi. He became desperate and suspicious about Madhavi's deeds and finally he decided to leave her forever.

Kovalan returned empty-handed but was warmly received by his loving wife. She sold all her belongings to pay off his debts. The only valuable she kept was a pair of precious ruby anklets. They decided to go to the city of Madurai, a business centre and the capital of the Pandya kingdom, to start a new life. They went on foot and reached a village near Madurai. Here, they decided that Kannagi would stay in the village under the care of a village woman. Before Kovalan left for Madurai, Kannagi gave him one of her precious ruby anklets to exchange it for money. When Kovalan reached the city, he went to a goldsmith to weigh the value of his wife's precious ruby anklet.

Meanwhile, the priceless anklet of the queen of Madurai was stolen and the king's soldiers were looking for it. The anklet had been stolen by the king's goldsmith. Alas, Kovalan also approached the same goldsmith to measure the value of his anklet. The goldsmith was a dishonest man. He noticed the similarity between Kovalan's anklet and the one he had stolen from the queen. He reported to the king that Kovalan had stolen the queen's anklet. The king believed the goldsmith and ordered his soldiers to behead Kovalan without any trial. Thus, Kovalan was killed and the stolen anklet was returned to the queen.

When Kannagi heard about the great misfortune her husband had met with, she rushed to the king's court like a wild wind with one anklet in her hand. She confronted the king for slaying her innocent husband. The king replied that Kovalan had stolen the queen's anklet and as punishment, he was beheaded. Kannagi refuted the king by showing him one of the pair of ruby anklets. The queen's stolen anklet was made of pearls, though it looked exactly like that of Kannagi's. In anger and to prove her statement, she hurled the anklet on the ground. It shattered into tiny pieces of ruby all over the floor. The king realized his mistake. He was speechless as he could not repay the widow for the pain and loss he had caused her. In her anger, Kannagi cursed the king and tore off her left breast, and burned down the entire city of Madurai with the power of her chastity.

Kannagi went to the Chera kingdom in Kerala and reached

a place called Attukal. There she appeared in the form of a small girl and requested an old man who was sitting on the banks of a stream to help her cross the stream. He was surprised to see the small girl and tried to take her to his home. But she vanished suddenly. Later she appeared in his dream and demanded that he build a temple in his grove which had been marked with three golden lines. He built a temple dedicated to Goddess Attukal Devi, the divine form of Kannagi. It is also believed that Kannagi reached Kodungallur, the capital of the Chera kingdom and received salvation at the Sree Kurumba Temple.

51

The Revival Story of Navara Rice

The story of navara rice from Kerala dates back to more than 2,000 years ago. It has been mentioned in Ayurveda for its health benefits. The crop was on the verge of becoming extinct but through the tireless efforts of P. Narayanan Unny, navara rice has managed to survive till today. Narayanan Unny's twelve-acre farm is a testament of his work towards the revival of navara rice, making it available across the nation and establishing its name across different parts of the world. A deep red in colour, navara rice is used traditionally in treating arthritis. It is also in high demand during the Malayalam month of Karkidakam for Ayurvedic rejuvenation treatments.

Located in the rice belt of Kerala, Narayanan Unny's farm is situated in Karukamani, under Peruvemba Panchayat at Chittur in Palakkad. The farm is 125 years old and dates back to three generations of the family. Unny remembers his father cultivating navara rice during the 1960s, along with the famous Palakkad red rice. However, these efforts were not consistent due to several reasons. Navara rice, being a short duration crop, had low productivity and there was hardly any awareness about the rice even among the locals, thus there was no demand in the market. Coupled with this, there were severe limitations about the productivity per acre of a farmer after the introduction of the Land Ceiling Act of the 1960s, which stated that a family can only own six acres of paddy land for cultivation. This proved to be too small to produce enough for sustaining a family, thus, producing a crop which had no market in those times was a challenge. The production in those days was mostly for domestic consumption just enough to sustain a family.

The story of navara rice changed in the last few decades. In 1994, when Unny's father passed away, he left his computer business and took over the family business. However, the beginning was rough. The price of rice was stipulated very low in the market, which hardly provided any profit to the rice farmers, while the cost of production was extremely high. The farmers were facing real challenges to make ends meet. Unny was even told that taking up farming was a negative proposition, but he did not lose hope nor give up. He decided to concentrate on both red rice as well as navara rice.

When Unny started out, pure navara rice seeds were unavailable. So his first task was to purify the seeds. Over the next three years, Unny purified the seeds and then started cultivation work. To maintain the organic touch, Unny did not use pesticides. Today, Narayanan Unny's farm not only produces navara rice, but also boasts of a collective agricultural output of seventy-two different kinds of crops, including medicinal plants, fruits, spices, vegetables, including green leafy ones, different types of creepers and flowers. The farm received an organic certification and by 2006, the entire farm was certified organic by India, European Union, and the United States Department of Agriculture (USDA). In 2004, Naryanan Unny applied for a Geographical Indication (GI) tag, and in 2007, navara rice received a GI tag. This GI tag was immensely helpful and created a benchmark in Indian history as it became the first agricultural product through a farmer-led initiative to receive a GI tag.

Unny's efforts have also been reflected across his participation in 171 workshops, seminars, presentations, and discussions from 2006 to 2019 in India and abroad. At these events, Unny highlighted the health benefits of navara rice, and the most recent one was his participation at the 2019 National

Biodiversity Expo, organized by the Kerala State Biodiversity Board. Recently, Narayanan Unny was also awarded the Anirudh Bhargava–INTACH National Environmental Award, 2019, for his pioneering work which has not only regenerated a priceless heirloom grain, but opened up possibilities of restoring financial sustainability to rice farmers in Kerala. Narayanan Unny's efforts have also inspired a lot of farmers' collective initiatives in the region and many people have followed his example to increase the production in their respective farmlands.

LADAKH

52

Tsi-zo Lha-wang and Shing-zo Lha-wang

Once, there lived a great wood craftsman, Tsi-zo Lha-wang, and a famous painter, Shing-zo Lha-wang who were well known in the region for their respective crafts. The king was also aware of their great artworks. One day, Shing-zo Lha-wang hatched a nasty plan against the wood craftsman which would have him permanently eliminated from the kingdom. Shing-zo Lha-wang appeared at the king's court and declared that he had recently paid a visit to heaven and had met the king's father there. On hearing about his father, the king became emotional and asked, 'What do you know about my father? How is he keeping? Is he doing well?' Shing-zo Lha-wang replied, 'Your father is doing fine. He is also having a good time in heaven. You would be very pleased to know that he has built a great temple there and now he needs a good carpenter to help with the construction of statues and sculptures for the temple. Thus, he is looking for a good carpenter or a wood craftsman who can help him in heaven,' and thus saying, he handed the king a parchment scroll on which these requests were written in the form of a letter. The handwriting resembled the king's father and upon reading the scroll, the king became more emotional. Shing-zo Lha-wang was a clever person as he was a painter and had also mastered the art of calligraphy. Thus, he could easily emulate the handwriting of the king's father. The king, on the other hand, got fooled easily and started to think about possible ways in which he could help his deceased father in heaven. Suddenly, he remembered the best craftsman he had in his kingdom, Tsi-zo Lha-wang, and immediately declared to make arrangements to have him sent to heaven. But it was easier said than done as heaven seemed far away and all the people sat thinking of possible ways. At this point, Shing-zo Lha-wang proposed to send Tsi-zo Lha-wang to heaven on a horse of smoke. This also meant that Tsi-zo Lha-wang would be put on a pyre and thus would meet his death.

Tsi-zo Lha-wang, on the other hand, upon hearing this was terrified at first and then he cleverly thought of an idea to outwit the cunning Shing-zo Lha-wang. He approached the king and proposed, 'I am extremely fortunate that I have been chosen for this noble work and I would be more than happy to do it, however, I would like to perform the work and ascend to heaven from an open-air field, chosen by myself.' The king readily agreed. Thus, an open-air field was chosen, and an auspicious day and time was ascertained for sending Tsi-zo Lha-wang to heaven. A platform was constructed, on which a pyre would be lit to form a horse of smoke. In the meantime, the clever Tsi-zo Lha-wang dug an underground tunnel from his home to the base of the platform in the open-air field. It was large enough to have him walk across the tunnel from one end to the other. Nobody knew what was happening as Tsi-zo Lha-wang was very careful in his planning.

Finally, on the appointed day, a large, wooden throne was placed on the platform in the open-air field. Tsi-zo Lha-wang was made to sit on the throne. The king arrived in pomp and splendour, along with his courtiers and musicians. Everybody was in a celebratory mood and all the people from the kingdom gathered to see this significant event. Amidst much merriment, the pyre was lit and as the smoke started to rise up, blocking the view of the spectators, Tsi-zo Lha-wang slowly slipped down into the tunnel below the wooden platform. He then ran and hid in his house. Nobody suspected that Tsi-zo Lha-wang had escaped, except Shing-zo Lha-wang, who wondered why Tsi-zo Lha-wang did not utter a single sound at being set on fire. On the other hand, everyone was praising Tsi-zo Lha-wang for performing the brave act, while he sat comfortably in his house.

Tsi-zo Lha-wang stayed in his house for a month and ate the choicest of food and drank milk and became plump. Staying away from the grime and dust of the roads and the harsh rays of the sun, his skin started to glow. Finally, one morning, after a month, he took a ladder and climbed to the roof of the king's palace. Thereby, from the roof, he jumped down and landed in the middle of the king's inner courtyard. Everybody came rushing to see him and they all thought that he had landed onto the king's court, directly from heaven. He was invited to meet the king and upon meeting His Highness, he proposed, 'Your father is very happy and doing very well in heaven. He was also very happy with my work; however, he still needs one important thing from our kingdom. He needs a very good painter to finish his work.' At this, the king immediately thought of Shing-zo Lha-wang and said, 'Of course, I would never disappoint my father. Just as I had sent you to help him, I will send Shing-zo Lha-wang to him as well.' Thus, he ordered a second pyre to be built for Shing-zo Lha-wang, who could not understand how Tsi-zo Lha-wang had escaped. The poor painter, who was not as cunning as Tsi-zo Lha-wang thus lost his life.

53

The Wish-fulfilling Well

Once upon a time, in a village in Ladakh, there lived a farmer and his daughter. They had a small well in their house compound, but this was not an ordinary well, for it granted wishes. The father and daughter were not greedy and only wished for necessary things from the well. One day, they felt that it would be an honour to invite the king over for a feast. Thus, they invited the king and he arrived along with many of his courtiers. The father and daughter spread out a lavish feast as they wished for the choicest of dishes from the well. The king enjoyed the meal but wondered about the extravagant meal, complete with dishes that were not available in his kingdom. On being asked, the simpleton farmer told the king about his wish-fulfilling well. The king was very surprised and complimented his host and returned to his palace, but all the while, he kept thinking about the unusual feast.

Finally, one day, the greedy king sent his soldiers with a proposition to the farmer. They approached the father and daughter and stated that the king wanted to have their well transferred to his palace compound. The farmer became terrified; however, his daughter stayed calm and thought of a way to find a solution to the problem. She told the soldiers to speak to the king and demand a similar well to be placed in their house, if the king was to take away their well. She even compared the well to an exchange gift of an elephant. 'If the king takes an elephant, he has to return one as well,' she mentioned. 'In a similar manner, he should also return a well to our compound,' she added. The soldiers went back to the king and conveyed the message from the clever daughter. The king and his courtiers listened to this carefully and everyone was in awe of the brilliant request made by the daughter. However, the greed of the king had the better of him and he expressed a desire to nevertheless get the well, at whatever cost. This behaviour seemed unethical to his courtiers and they all became angry at the king and his foolish decision.

54

The Ice Man of India

Asmall, trickling stream running through a garden near his house in Leh, led to a great discovery in the cold mountains of Ladakh. This is the story of Chewang Norphel, also known as the Ice Man of India, for creating artificial glaciers, to aid agriculture, amidst the failing ecological health of the region.

'In the last four to five decades, this region of Ladakh has been suffering greatly due to global warming and climate changes,' says Norphel. According to him, this change has adversely affected agriculture, primarily due to lack of water. 'The sowing season in Ladakh is between April and May. Earlier, there used to be heavy snowfall during the winter months and by the time of the sowing season and after that in June, there used to be enough water for agriculture. However, with the effects of global warming, the water from the glaciers almost dries up by June. This is very harmful for the cash crops in the region,' further explains Norphel.

With a short summer season, water is essential in the region for the brief time of agriculture, especially during the sowing period of the cash crops. At the time, when Norphel was working at the Rural Development Department of Jammu and Kashmir in Ladakh as a civil engineer, he conceived the idea of making artificial glaciers, which was inspired by Norphel's close observation of a garden near his house. He says, 'I noticed a small waterbody in a garden near my house, which had accumulated water that flowed freely from a running stream nearby. This still water amongst the trees remained in shade and water in this area remained frozen even in the months of

May and June. However, I noticed that the running water of the main stream, from which the trickling water entered the garden, was never frozen. From this, I gathered the idea that it is possible to make water freeze by restricting water flow and started to work on my first glacier.' Thus, the first artificial glacier was made in 1986, with ninety thousand rupees and with help from the Desert Development Agency in Ladakh. Since then and till the time he retired from his post at the Rural Development Department in 1994, Norphel helped to create fifteen artificial glaciers. Norphel's method of working entailed creating diversions in a river and making it enter into a valley and also slowing down the stream by creating and constructing checks. Norphel also constructed these at lower areas so that these glaciers could melt earlier, which also resulted in extending the season of agriculture. The largest of Norphel's glaciers is at Phuktsey village, where a village of 700 people benefits from the glacier. This glacier is 1,000 feet long, 150 feet wide, and 4 feet deep. Most of Norphel's projects have been funded by financial assistance from several state-run programmes, the army, and various national and international NGOs.

Manual labour was provided by the local villagers and Norphel created each glacier as close as possible to villages so that the settlements benefit in several ways. 'These artificial glaciers are low maintenance and very effective. Secondly, they melt faster than regular glaciers, but provide enough to sustain the agricultural season of the summer months. Thirdly, these artificial glaciers also help to alleviate the groundwater level in the area. This is greatly beneficial for year-round woes related to water scarcity.' Thus, Norphel's artificial glaciers created a significant change in the ecology and environment of Ladakh. At present, a retired man, Norphel however feels happy that his work lives on, 'There are at least three NGOs in the region of Ladakh which work on artificial glaciers. I think it is an important work and it is good to see it being continued with earnest effort. At times, they mention my work for the purpose of discussions.'

Norphel's work has been documented across several dailies as well as on audiovisual media, including the documentary, *White Knight*, by noted documentary filmmaker, Aarti Shrivastava. For his remarkable work, Norphel was awarded the Jamnalal Bajaj Award, 2010, and Padma Shri, 2015.

LAKSHADWEEP

The Legend of Pampum Palli of Amini Island

'Farangi kappal' (Portuguese corvettes) arrived in the island of Lakshadweep in small boats with dangerous weapons such as guns. Soon, an episode of loot and plunder started, including molestation of local women. The helplessness of the locals paved the way for further ruthlessness. The locals were no match to the gunpowder used by the Portuguese and a large number of people laid down their lives. Houses as well as mosques were burned down and women were treated mercilessly. The atrocities knew no bounds.

Angry and frustrated with the mayhem and carnage caused by the 'firangis', the people of Amini Island united under the leadership of the qazi and made a plan to end this tyranny. The qazi decided to kill the 'firangis' by poisoning them. As there was no poison available in the island, they decided to bring snake poison from Kozhikode (an ancient port city in Kerala, popularly known as Calicut). Soon, a trading vessel from Kozhikode brought snake poison to the island and the qazi, along with many locals, waited for the enemy to arrive.

When they did arrive in small boats, the qazi and the locals invited them for a feast in the mosque. The invitation was accepted. The food served to the Portuguese was poisoned with the snake poison brought from Kozhikode. They died immediately after consuming the poisoned food. Thus, the islanders took their revenge for the atrocities committed against them.

The mosque in which this last feast was offered came to be known as Pampum Palli—the snake mosque.

The Legend of Farangiya
Aruta Kunnu of Andorth Island

The Portuguese caused mayhem in the island of Lakshadweep. They arrived in small boats to loot and plunder with the help of their guns and molest the women. In order the save themselves from the hands of the Portuguese, many locals thought of various precautionary measures. Many made underground hideouts inside and outside their houses. These hideouts were used as a hiding place for the women and also to secretly store gold. Whenever a person spotted a Portuguese ship in the horizon, he would climb a coconut tree and scream loudly about their arrival. On hearing the same, the islanders would panic and start working immediately to hide their women and gold in the hideouts. Neverthless, despite these measures, the atrocities didn't stop. They continued to kill the men, molest the women, and loot the wealth, and this continued for a long time, till when the locals felt that they could take it no more. A group of people decided to end this tyranny by risking their own lives and they made a plan. The next time the Portuguese arrived on the island, instead of running away to their homes, a few people welcomed and invited them to a special treat. The Portuguese went with these people to the interiors of the island. When they reached, the islanders surrounded them with knifes and attacked them. The men panicked and tried to run but the angry islanders caught them. Many Portuguese men were killed on a hill and buried there. This hill is located in a small village called Keechery of Androth Island and the hill is known as Farangiya Aruta Kunnu.

Ali Manikfan: A Traditional Scientist and a Genius

As environmentalists the world over struggle to find a solution against the high rate of deterioration, it is the efforts of several unsung heroes that make every effort worthwhile. Such is the story of Muradu Guanduvar Ali Manikfan. Born in Minicoy, Lakshadweep, in 1938, Ali Manikfan is a man of many talents and is well known for his diligent work across the disciplines of marine biology, ecology, cosmology, shipbuilding, agriculture, and linguistic studies.

Initially, Ali Manikfan worked as a teacher in 1956 and later became a clerk for the Amin of Minicoy Island (Amin was the chief civil officer of the island in those days). Later, in 1960, Ali Manikfan joined the Central Marine Research Institute as a lab boy. His love for nature and a keen sense of observation led him to significant discoveries in the field of marine biology. He played a pivotal role in the identification and classification of over 400 marine species through his extensive journeys in the sea. The museum at Mandapam Regional Centre of Central Marine Fisheries Research Institute still preserves the significant contributions made by Ali Manikfan towards marine biology. Dr Santhappan Jones, a well-known marine biologist, had made specific reference to Ali Manikfan and his significant contributions in his book, *Fishes of the Laccadive Archipelago*. Ali Manikfan discovered a new species of fish which was unknown till 1968. This species of fish was named *Abudefduf Manikfani* after its discoverer. His contribution towards traditional knowledge related to farming is also interesting. During his stay in Tamil Nadu, he had discovered a scientific farming method named 'Do nothing farm'. This unique method can fruitfully convert a barren land to a farm full of vegetation without disturbing the natural order and without using any harmful chemicals, pesticides, and fertilizers or artificial methods of irrigation.

The childhood days of Ali Manikfan had their own challenges. Unfortunately, he could not receive conventional education beyond the eighth standard. His parents sent him to Kannur (in Kerala) to pursue his education after five years of homeschooling, but he soon returned home as he was convinced by the idea that nothing could teach him better than Mother Nature. Thus, he continued his education through a keen sense of observation and by mastering traditional knowledge. His fascination with learning languages turned him into an expert linguist. This gift helped him master fifteen languages, including both Indian as well as foreign languages. His love for nature often used to encourage him to spend a lot of time at the observatory of Minicoy and he learned to fly hydrogen balloons to study the weather.

It is noteworthy that Ali Manikfan's traditional knowledge helped in acquiring knowledge about engineering and automobiles as well. He designed windmills to produce electricity for domestic use. He also successfully built a roller-driven moped-motorcycle out of a single bicycle and travelled to Delhi from Tamil Nadu with his son. He also obtained a patent in India for making mopeds. His knowledge of engineering further came into assistance in 1981 when the British explorer, historian, and writer, Timothy Severin, wanted to build a replica of the ships in the stories of *The Adventures of Sinbad the Sailor*. Though Severin searched long and far, he was unable to find a suitable engineer who could help him through traditional methods. Finally, at the recommendation of Dr Santhappan Jones, he approached Ali Manikfan for the task. Ali Manikfan and a team of thirty-one carpenters carried out the work in line with ancient Maldivian naval architectural specifications at Muscat in the Sultanate of Oman and completed the task to perfection. This ship was named *Sohar* and Severin and his team travelled in it from Oman to China. At present, the vessel is preserved in a museum at Oman.

As an octogenarian at present, Ali Manikfan spends his days with his near and dear ones, but he continues to encourage the younger generation with his thoughts through discussions. He was conferred with the prestigious Padma Shri Award in 2021 for his innovative methods in grassroot innovations in Lakshadweep.

MADHYA PRADESH

58

The Chudail Who Stayed Back

The story goes back a long time to a town where lived a sahukar. He maintained a shop and worked there. During the afternoons, he would come back to rest for a while and again return to his shop in the early hours of the evening. Now, where the sahukar lived, there was a baoli nearby. That baoli was never seen to run dry, even across several dry months. There was a neem tree close to the baoli. One afternoon, when the sahukar had come home for his daily siesta, he noticed a lady sitting under the neem tree. On looking closely, the sahukar heard the lady call out to him in a nasal tone, 'Why don't you come down here and sit next to me?' She pleaded a few times more. She was also waving to him to come and join her under the neem tree. The sahukar finally accepted the invitation and went towards the neem tree. Upon reaching, the sahukar suddenly looked at the feet of the lady and discovered that her feet were pointed the other way and the ankles were facing the opposite direction. The sahukar immediately knew that the lady was a chudail and was trying to lure him. Nevertheless, the sahukar didn't feel or express any fear. He kept visiting the chudail almost every day and this continued for four days. Finally, on the fifth day, the chudail asked the sahukar to marry her. He was a little confused and told the chudail, 'I will answer you in sometime.' He then went to seek help from a village elder, who advised him that in order to make a housewife of the chudail, he should snatch the chunri of the chudail and put it under a mortar. This should make her stay within the household and she will not be able to escape.

Listening to the sage advice, the sahukar approached the
chudail. Upon reaching her, when the chudail asked, 'So, have
you thought about your answer?' Without saying anything, the
sahukar snatched the chunri of the chudail and ran as fast as
he could and put it under the mortar. He then turned to the
chudail and said, 'Yes, I am ready to marry you.' The chudail
knew what the sahukar had done and realized that she was
trapped. She stayed and married the sahukar. In due course,
the couple was blessed with four kids. Years passed by and
the kids grew up. Slowly, it was time for the eldest son to get
married. Just days before the marriage, the chudail approached
the sahukar and said, 'Now that I am your wife with four kids
and the eldest is about to get married, you know I will not
leave. Please release my chunri from under the mortar.' The
sahukar agreed this time and released the chunri from under
the mortar and handed it over to the chudail. Immediately, the
chudail danced in a circle and vanished forever. She was not
to be seen or heard, again.

59

The Story of Shaligram and the Butcher

Once upon a time, Lord Vishnu had a massive fight with the demon Jalandhar, and was unable to defeat him. Finally, Vishnu realized the reason for the strength of Jalandhar. Vrinda, the wife of Jalandhar, was leading an austere life of penance and praying for Jalandhar's immortality. Vishnu conceived a plan. He disguised himself as Jalandhar, went to his wife, and distracted her from her meditation. He also killed Jalandhar through deception. When Vrinda found out the truth, she was furious and cursed Vishnu to become a stone. Thus, Lord Vishnu was turned into a shaligram, black stone.

The story of shaligram and its importance is also seen across the ages. There is another story associated with the shaligram from the time of Emperor Akbar in India during the sixteenth century and the time of the poet, Tulsidas.

'Mano toh patthar, nahin toh bhagwan.' If you don't have faith it is a mere stone, else it is God.

Lord Vishnu continued to live as a shaligram. When the Mughals came to India, life and society changed, but the significance of the shaligram continued. During this period, there lived a butcher. He was very dedicated and hard-working. He cared for nothing else but his work. He was too poor to afford a proper range of weights and kept a lovely smooth black stone for months together to use as a weight. Since he was not a Hindu, he had no clue that this black stone was a shaligram and was a divine symbol. A Hindu priest used to pass by his shop every morning. One day, he noticed the shaligram. He was shocked and shouted, 'Hey! You! How could you do that? You've got no sense! Don't you know that the stone you're using as a weight for your meat is no ordinary stone?'

The butcher was perplexed and asked, 'Then, what is it?'

'It is our Lord Shaligram, Lord Vishnu!'

The butcher smiled, and said, 'You are a scholar and a sophisticated man, maybe you know better. I am a poor man, and this is the only way I have learnt to earn a living from my father. I am poor and am not able to save up enough money to buy a suitable weight. I found this stone and it is apt for the usual piece of meat which I sell during the day.'

The priest was already furious about finding the shaligram amongst meat pieces and when he found that the butcher was about to pick it up again to continue to weigh the meat, he yelled, 'Don't you touch that again! Give it to me at once. Our Lord Shaligram must be kept in a clean and pure environment, in a place of worship.'

He took away the shaligram from the butcher and placed it in the alcove of his small temple. In the morning, the priest entered his temple and started giving the holy bath to each of the deities, one by one. The moment he tried to lift the small shaligram, he could not do so. He kept trying, but it did not move an inch. While he was struggling with it, he was startled by a ray of light coming from the shaligram. Within a few seconds, it reflected an image on the wall and this image began to speak, 'Oh pujari, it seems you're just not ignorant but foolhardy too! Love and dedication are foremost for me. Even if you put together hours to worship me, you can never reward me with these, like the butcher. Please take me back to the butcher's shop! It's there that I am loved and respected most!'

The pujari was bewildered. All his life, he had waited for this day, when the Lord would appear in front of him. The voice of the Lord turned sonorous and continued to address the priest. 'The dear butcher picks me up with love and affection at least a thousand times a day, and puts me back with utmost care because it values me more than anyone else does, so I would rather be with the butcher than in a temple.'

The priest had no choice but to return the shaligram to the butcher with a heavy heart.

60

The Story of a Teacher

'I will take her responsibility,' a sonorous voice echoed in the corridor of the college. This man was barely forty years old. It was not a joke to take the responsibility of a twenty-three-year old female student from the college, especially when no one from the family of this girl was ready to shoulder any responsibility. Swarna belonged to the Himalayas in the north. She was lean, thin, and very beautiful. Her skin dazzled like the full moon! She had big, black eyes and thick, long, black hair and anybody could be enamoured by her beauty! Vibrant but volatile and wavering! Nobody could stop her from jumping off the tall thick walls of the hostel fence. Swarna had many boyfriends from one of the reputed engineering colleges of the state in the same city. She was very friendly with them and without the permission of her hostel warden would spend nights out of her hostel mingling with these friends. Despite several warnings, she remained undeterred. Warden, teachers, and friends had given up on her.

Finally, her expulsion was definite and her parents were summoned from her native town. But...that sonorous voice of the teacher was heard again and this time he roared... 'If students who are a little bit off the track are expelled from schools and colleges then they will be thrown and pushed back to the same world that had spoilt them, once again they will be floundering about in the muddy waters of a hypocritical society!' He continued, 'it is our duty to help them to be on track once again!'

The principal, the colleagues of the teacher, and even the

guardians of Swarna refused to allow her to continue her studies in the college. They argued that her consideration might encourage other girls to flout the rules. It wasn't just this girl, but that year unfortunately, the entire batch of students had rebellious young girls and boys! It was a trying situation for the principal and the teachers and everybody was disturbed by the severe situation, however, the teacher was different. His teaching methods were different from the rest and he was fast gaining popularity over the past few years for his depth of knowledge, dedication, and compassion for his students. This teacher took up the responsibility of the troublesome girl and also asked the principal to make him the in-charge of that particular batch. The teacher started his duties. This was not only limited to classroom teachings alone, but continued even after class hours. Discussions and conversations continued with the students and they in turn, started to reciprocate with conversations from the heart. His compassion, dedication, and vision worked and gradually, everyone noticed a marked difference amongst the students of the batch. They were seen, busy writing, narrating, or could be heard engaging in meaningful discussions. For the college authorities, it was a pleasant surprise and they liked the change. Little did the college or even the teacher realize that the change will go a long way and transform several of the students. This rebellious batch produced some of the most promising, talented, and sensitive writers, artists, teachers, government administrative officers and BSF (Border Security Force) personnel.

There was a considerable change in Swarna's behaviour as well. Composed and poised, she was now ready to listen and work on what she was told, but the teacher constantly felt that something was missing. Though Swarna was quite understanding in comparison to previous times yet, the teacher could perceive an emptiness in her eyes and felt that Swarna could never open up completely. It was as if Swarna was holding something back. The teacher found this unnerving, considering Swarna's young age. He was determined to find a solution. One day, he confided in his wife for advice and a possible solution and they reached a conclusion that they need to speak to the parents of the child and she seemed to have experienced a disturbed past. The parents were summoned, but they turned up after several months. The teacher got to know that Swarna had lost both her parents when she was young and she was raised in a joint family. A family, with too many uncles—the siblings of her father. One of her uncles and his wife showed up, but the teacher found that they seemed elusive of their responsibilities.

Months later, the tragedy unfolded as Swarna herself confided in the teacher and his wife. During one of her conversations Swarna, mentioned that she was repeatedly sexually abused and raped by her uncles in the joint family. Consequently, she became pregnant when she was around fourteen or fifteen years old and gave birth to a child. The baby was left in an orphanage and after her school, Swarna was sent to the hostel for her further studies.

That year and the following year, Swarna topped her class in graduation. She finished her graduation, completed a B.Ed degree, and found a teaching job. The teacher continued his work with further motivation. He was also a poet and a writer, a sensitive human being and a loving father to his five children. He had gradually lost touch with Swarna, but years later, he received a letter from Europe. It was from Swarna. He read it aloud in front of his family. Swarna wrote that she was happy and married to a wonderful man and settled in Europe.

MAHARASHTRA

61

The Copper-tiled House

In Sattad mohalla, there lived the virtuous and saintly Juran Koli. Beyond the fort walls lies the village of Koliwada, where Juran is the leader of the Kolis. Fair and just like a scimitar, Juran wields his authority as the Patel of the panchayat.

One day, Juran Patel and the Wadia were sitting and gossiping on the veranda of Juran's house, when suddenly the carriage of H. E. the Governor passed by. The Parsi rose and made profound salutations. Juran, however, remained stolidly seated and showed no signs of recognition. 'Who is this worthy Koli?' enquired the governor of the Wadia and the latter replied, 'He is the special favourite of Lakshmi, for he spreads his gold daily to dry, measuring them with the phara. His cellars bulge with wealth, his riches are beyond compare,' and, he continued, 'many coat the soles of their shoes with wax and trample over his hoard, but the pile of wealth never dries, never is he short of money; he goes on drying his gold and silver in full measure and never misses a coin, for Lakshmi always fills his cellars. He is in truth a real mine of riches.' The governor, in wonder, turned towards Juran Patel and asked him how much wealth he possessed, and the Patel answered, 'Take away as much as you can by measure and by cartload.'

And straightaway, the carts were collected. They stretched in an unbroken line from Sattad mohalla to the Fort in Mumbai. The governor, amazed at so much wealth, cried, 'Only express the wish and I will make you a zamindar.' But the Patel declined the honour, and added, 'My Lord, take away as much as you will, I only ask your permission to roof my house with silver tiles.' The governor demurred and suggested the use of copper tiles instead. 'Henceforth, it shall be the privilege of your family to use five copper tiles. This will make you famous, songs will be sung in your honour. Your name, O Koli Patel, will be more widely known than the beating of a battaki.'

Though he is dead, the name of Juran Patel is known throughout India. His fame has become legendary. This ballad[11], in his honour, was composed by Antone, son of Dhondu. Let us sing it, and let Enas (Ignatius, son of Antone) decorated with pearls and diamonds, with the banner in his hands and pipe in his mouth, make you merry.

CHORUS

Once upon a time, two friends, Variya and Zuran Patel were chatting in Zuran's courtyard,
Speeding away went the governor's carriage, says the singing bard.
Variya got up with joint hands to wish the mighty governor,
But Zuran Patel, not moving an inch, kept sitting without a care.
Dharmodaataa the Governor, questioned Variya, who is the Koli gentleman?
Variya said, Oh Lord, this person has Goddess Laxmi, living in his abode.
He dries his money in the sun, and uses shovel to count it, Oh Lord.
He stores his wealth in the big warehouse, with blessings of the god.

---

[11]The ballad or 'powada' was sung in praise of Zurin Patel. That is why, the word 'ser' might men 'sher' (as in Urdu) or it might mean chorus, which is sung by a group and the main portion is sung by the lead singer. Dharmodaataa might be the poet and the singer might have been Dhondu Tanya Antony, as mentioned in the last stanza.

CHORUS

Many men put wax on the sole of their shoe
And walk on the money that is drying.
But the money remains with him, Oh Lord, despite
people trying.
Variya told the Governor, Zuran was truly a gold mine.
Dharmodaataa the Governor said to Zuran, Oh You
wealthy man,
Tell me how much wealth you have?
Tell me if you can.
Patel said, feel free to take, as much as you want.
Fill the carts and carry with you, it wouldn't make a
difference at all.

CHORUS

The Governor lined up the carts and Patel filled them
with money.
The Governor said, 'Ask anything in return, I will
grant you a wish.'
Patel said, 'I need nothing, allow me to cover my roof
with silver tiles.'
Dharmodaataa the Governor said, 'Oh Patel, You may
use five copper tiles on the roof.
People will sing your praises forever, you fame will
spread all over.'
Dhondu Tanya Antony sings his praise whose brooms
are studded with pearls and gems.
Playing the drums, I sing for you, to amuse you with
my song....

62

Friend

This is a story of a long time ago. There lived a young girl named Saee. At thirteen years of age, she was married off to a man much older than herself. In those days, girls were married as soon as they attained puberty. Thus, little Saee went off to live with her in-laws. However, she found a very different surrounding at her in-laws as her husband was away at work for long hours and Saee was left alone at home. In her parent's home, there were many cousins with whom Saee would talk and play at all times. However, at her in-law's, Saee felt lonely. Her mother-in-law was not a very interactive person. Thus, Saee began to feel very lonely. One day, Saee's mother told her to speak to the lizard in the kitchen. One day Saee spotted a lizard, close to the cooking area in the kitchen. Saee was delighted and began to talk to the lizard. She felt the lizard responded by making sympathetic 'chuckchuk' sounds.

From that day onwards, Saee's life changed. She became much happier as she found someone to talk to. She would pour her heart out and talk to the lizard as if the lizard could hear her and reply to her as well. She would often leave small amounts of milk and kheer for the lizard and would be happy to see the lizard lap it up. A few times, Saee's mother-in-law caught her talking to herself in the kitchen and thought that her daughter-in-law was acting strange. This even encouraged the mother-in-law to keep a close eye on Saee.

Days passed and one day, Saee noticed that the lizard was getting fat and she realized that the lizard was pregnant. 'Oh, there is good news. I am so happy for you,' she said, and she took it upon herself to feed the lizard with food that would nourish an expecting mother. She even did her best to keep her happy and kept speaking to her about the baby that was due to arrive. One day, over one of these conversations, Saee mentioned, 'I believe that you would be blessed with a bonny baby boy. It will be a smiling child and it would be so wonderful,' and Saee felt happy within herself, as if she was having an actual dialogue with another person.

However, soon after, the lizard went missing. Saee thought that the lizard must have gone to her mother's house for her delivery. She thought happily, 'I wonder what the lizard will give birth to—a girl or a boy?' The same night when the lizard went missing, there was a loud knock on the door. Saee's husband opened the door and found a group of people outside, who were taller than regular humans and wore old-fashioned clothes. There were soldiers, performing girls who were dancing, attendants who carried platters full of gifts, including jewellery, fruits, and sweetmeats, and two tall palki-bearers, who carried a decorated palki. The tallest person, who was standing closest to the door bowed in salutation. He had a big moustache and carried a mashaal, torch. He said, 'Greetings! Our queen has been blessed with a son, just as Saee madam had predicted. Our queen has sent us to fetch Saee madam for a ceremony at her palace as she wants to convey her gratitude. Saee madam took good care of her, especially during her pregnancy,' and the tall man stopped as abruptly as he had begun, anticipating an answer.

Saee's husband and mother-in-law stood awestruck and speechless, while an overwhelmed Saee couldn't believe her ears and fainted.

....

63

The Single-handed Legal Battles of Akkatai Teli

When Akkatai Teli decided to fight her first court case in 1990, she knew it was going to be a long haul. Three decades later, she says, 'I will reclaim my remaining half acre land also.' The tedious law process couldn't break her. 'How could it?' she asks. 'If I give up, how will I fight for so many rural women?' She often helps rural women in matters related to court cases. Today, she is a symbol of inspiration in Shirol village and adjoining regions in the Kolhapur district in western Maharashtra.

Akkatai's land dispute case was not like any other open-and-shut case. Her battles started a very long time ago when she was just seven and her mother had passed away. 'My grandmother married me off when I was nine because someone offered her five hundred rupees in return,' she recollects. The late Mahadev, her husband, was an alcoholic and fourteen years older to her. 'He would sell whatever he found in the house to buy alcohol and then beat me and our two daughters,' Akkatai says. Eventually, she left her home with her daughters and started working as a labourer in a tobacco factory in Jaysingpur town. Mahadev passed away in 1989. The agricultural land belonged to him and his brother, Shankar. Akkatai was legally entitled to inherit a share of the land but her mother-in-law, sister-in-law, and brother-in-law sold parts of the land to other people without her permission.

Today, at sixty-six, Akkatai, an illiterate woman from Shirol village, recollects, 'Going to the court was my only option, but I didn't even know what legal documents were required.' After visiting several government offices, she collected the required documents over a year. In 1990, she filed her first case against her mother-in-law and the person to whom the 23 guntha (0.57 acre) land was sold to. 'I couldn't afford the lawyer's fees, so the government lawyers (public prosecutors) would fight my case,' she says.

This case went on for close to five and half years after which the court ordered the defendant to return Akkatai's share in 1996. However, the defendant now filed the case in the District Court at Kolhapur, which went on for another eight years. The Kolhapur court gave a similar verdict in 2004. The defendant now moved to the Mumbai High Court. Within the next two years, the decision came in Akkatai's favour, and that's how she won her first legal battle, and reclaimed her share of the land. 'It wasn't easy. Almost every fortnight I had to go to the court hearing,' she recollects. For this, she had to work at least twelve hours every day as a labourer for which she was paid a pittance. After working for seven years at the tobacco factory, the owner accused her of theft and filed a police complaint. In retaliation, she boldly filed a case in the labour court in Ichalkaranji town. 'The court revoked all the false charges after seven months and ordered the factory owner to employ me again. But I never went there,' she says proudly. For a decade from then on, she became a fruit seller and lived at the margins of survival while paying for her legal battles.

There were times when she was fighting two land dispute cases simultaneously. 'When I was working, my mother-in-law and sister-in-law gave away both my daughters to someone for money. Immediately, I went to the police station and got a search warrant issued,' she recounts. Her mother-in-law continued troubling Akkatai. She mortgaged a half acre land to a rich farmer for a sum of ₹15,000 in 1989 for ten years. 'How could she do it without my written signature and permission?' This was the second case which Akkatai fought for a decade in the Jaysingpur court. 'I won the case. The rich farmer didn't even ask for the mortgage sum and vacated the land within a year,' she says with a wide grin. Her third case turned out to be the most challenging. 'The person who illegally bought the land would bring his men and police to my home at two in the night. They would threaten me, and the police would force me to come to the police station,' she narrates. As a measure of self-defence, she kept a sickle with her. 'Once that man beat me and I thrashed him with my chappals,' she says laughing. She filed several complaints against this man, but all went unheard. 'I managed to bring the stay order on this property and after a few years, I won back the land. How could someone buy the land when there was a stay order from the court? Isn't that an insult to the law?' she asks.

Akkatai has not kept a record of how much money she has spent on her court cases in the past three decades, but she estimates it to be around ₹3 lakhs. 'A lot of people asked me to withdraw cases, but it was my land and my fight. How could I give up?' Now she cultivates sugarcane on her 1.5-acre land with her younger daughter, Kamal, who is forty-eight years old. Her metal trunk is now filled with several legal documents. 'It's a reminder of what a rural woman can do.'

From the 1980s, Akkatai has been helping a lot of rural women file cases. 'I have now become a support for women. I solve their problems,' she says proudly. Akkatai has also been at the forefront of several farmers' protests. For this, she has travelled to the national capital at least seven times. 'I am just an illiterate woman. But I am never going to give up,' she says.

MANIPUR

64

Henjunaha and Lairoulembi

Many years ago, in a village in the kingdom of Moirang, there lived a brave and handsome young man called Henjunaha. He was the son of Langlenhanba, a skilled carpenter. As a token of appreciation for his skill in making boats, King Phan Phan Polenhanba, the first king of Moirang, gave Langlenhanba a kangjei. Now, this kangjei was not an ordinary stick. It had magical powers to protect the owner from evil spirits. However, Langlenhanba met with an untimely death when he was attacked by evil spirits while looking for wood in the forest. Henjunaha was a little boy when his father died and he was brought up by his widowed mother, Khoidom.

After the death of her husband, Khoidom did not allow Henjunaha to go to the forest. However, as Henjunaha grew up, he persuaded her to allow him to go to the forest with his friends so that he could start taking care of his family.

One early morning, Henjunaha was out on a boat with his friend cruising along the Laihalli River when they saw the beautiful Lairoulembi and her friends bathing on the riverbank. Henjunaha and Lairoulembi could not take their eyes away from each other. It was love at first sight. However, the girls left before Henjunaha and Lairoulembi could introduce themselves to each other.

The next day, filled with the desire to know more about the beautiful girl, Henjunaha and his friend came to a place where girls from the nearby village would come to gather flowers to be offered to Thangjing, the guardian deity of Moirang. They waited hoping that Lairoulembi and her friends would

also come there. Lairoulembi and her friends finally came and
Henjunaha and his friend introduced themselves to the girls and
expressed their feelings. To their delight, they came to know that
the feeling was mutual and thus, they began to meet regularly.
However, as Henjunaha was poor and Lairoulembi belonged to
a rich and powerful family in Moirang, her parents opposed
their friendship. But Henjunaha and Lairoulembi continued
to meet and vowed in the name of God Thangjing that they
would be lovers not just in this life but in all their lifetimes.

One day, Khoijuhongbi, Lairoulembi's mother, caught them
meeting again. Lairoulembi confronted her mother saying that
she loved Henjunaha and wanted to be with him. Outraged,
Khoijuhongbi slapped her daughter. Filled with sadness and
rage, Lairouembi cried her heart out and decided to elope
with Henjunaha. She asked him to come and take her from
her house late at night on the first Saturday of Lamta (the
months of March–April).

The first Saturday of the month of Lamta is considered
to be an ominous day. On this day, the evil spirits called
sharoi-ngarois feast at night and decide the fate of the mortal
beings for the coming year. Elderly women of the locality offer
flowers, vegetables, and other items on the roads to the sharoi-
ngarois to ward off any misfortunes. People do not venture
out and stay in the safety of their homes on this fearful day.
Henjunaha's mother warned him not to go out on this day.
However, fuelled by the desire to meet Lairoulembi and to
keep his promise, Henjunaha sneaked out of his house late at
night carrying his father's kangjei with him.

On his way to his beloved Lairoulembi he came upon a
road where a feast was being held. He did not realize that this
was the feast of the sharoi-ngarois. So, he sat down in front
of an empty plaintain leaf waiting for his share of food that
was being served. But when he saw pieces of human fingers
and toes on his plate, he was appalled. In utter amazement he

looked at those sitting near him and saw that their feet were not touching the ground. At that moment, he remembered his mother's words and realized that he was amongst the sharoi-ngarois. He stood up and ran as fast as he could to Lairoulembi's house, waving his kangjei to the flesh-hungry evil spirits who were following him.

Meanwhile, Lairoulembi was anxiously waiting for Henjunaha on the veranda of her house. Since he did not come for a long time, she thought he would not come and went inside her room.

A while later, Henjunaha reached Lairoulembi's house with the sharoi-ngarois right behind him. He jumped over the bamboo gate but his kangjei got stuck on the gate. Without the kangjei on him, he was defenceless against the sharoi-ngarois. They overpowered Henjunaha, and he fell down dead with a loud thud outside Lairoulembi's house. She rushed out at the sound and saw the lifeless body of her lover. Grief-stricken, she took her own life with a knife.

65

Galngam: The Thadou Kuki Idol

The Kuki is a warrior tribe in Manipur. Many years ago, deep in the mountains of Northeast India, there lived a peace-loving community called the Thadous, the most loved clan amongst the Kukis. Many moons have passed since the days of the exploits of the Kukis, but the adventures of one Thadou Tahchapa still mesmerize every soul. Galngam was a legendary warrior, wizard, lover, and most of all a 'thug'.

Galngam was introduced to the art of witchcraft at a tender age by his grandfather, who was one of the best wizards of all times. Legend has it that Galngam's grandfather had a life-giving walking stick which had mysteriously vanished along with him.

One day, Galngam befriended Hangsai a werewolf from the faraway land of Scandinavia in northern Europe. The incredible friendship between Galngam the wizard and Hangsai the werewolf was based on heir abilities to do extraordinary tasks as they were equal in almost every trait. The apex of their jolcha[12] was when Galngam journeyed to the mountainous land of the Super Canine, lead by his jol, friend, Hangsai. This was the first time a human had visited the Super Canine, a community of wolves.

Galngam's motive behind his visit was to gather as many cosmic spells secretly preserved by the Super Canine. Hangsai, on the other hand, took all precautions to protect his friend in the world of the canines. To control the thirst for human blood of his wolf friends, Hangsai did every possible cover-

---

[12]deep friendship.

up for Galngam and also took precautions to not transform himself into a predator during his friend's visit. The 'thug' from the real world was introduced to the pack in the world of the Super Canine by Hangsai as one of the most revered wizards from the mortal world. Hangsai himself was no less a great wizard.

In the land of the Super Canine, while Galngam was enjoying all the comforts and reputation created by his jol, Hangsai, he came across the legendary khipi tree. This magical tree does not grow on the land of the mortals and was full of different types of khichang or red beads of pearl. Tempted to seize all the red pearls, Galngam asked Hangsai if he could take a few as a souvenir. Being a guest of the village, Hangsai could not deny such a request and told Galnam, 'You can take some, but not the gigantic one on the top.'

However, a thug will always be a thug, so Galngam started plucking the magical beads and at the same time tried to find a way to get to the most precious one at the top of the tree. To get this precious pearl, he devised a master plan. He hung his bow on the topmost branch of the tree in such a manner that it would seem as if he had done so unintentionally. He got hold of this hanging bow and started to shake the branch as hard as possible—bringing down the gigantic red pearl— along with several other pearls. Hangsai was furious at this but could do nothing and finally helped to gather the red pearls for his friend. It is with these red pearls that the khivui or the magical necklace of red pearls of the Thadou women came into existence. This adventure followed by many such adventures in the world of the Super Canine made Galngam famous in the mortal world.

Finally, when Galngam returned to earth, he was revered as a legendary wizard. There was lot of excitement in the village after his return and a homecoming ceremony was held with much pomp and splendour. It was for the first time that the people of the village saw an incredible bamboo container which hung from Galngam's belt. This was Galngam's canteen and within it was an unlimited stock of freshly cooked meat for the entire village. There was more excitement as Galngam chopped his walking stick for firewood to cook for the whole village a grand feast which was to be held as part of his homecoming ceremony.

Galngam's legends and exploits spread throughout the mortal world. Tales of his wizardry and romance with the most beautiful maiden in the entire land are still believed to be true to this day but that's just a small part of this legendary wizard's life.

66

Chungkham Rani: The Creator of Rani Phi

The famous Rani phi, a special innaphi (traditional stole or shawl of the Meitei women) was created especially by Chungkham Rani, an extraordinary weaver, designer, and entrepreneur. The gossamer silk shawl with beautiful patterns is popular among the womenfolk of Manipur and is worn during weddings and various other ceremonies.

One day, Thoibi, the wife of an engineer from Kwakeithel in Imphal came to meet Chungkham Rani. She had brought some fine silk threads from Bangalore. She said that she wanted to wear a phi (cloth) woven with those silk threads and asked Chungkham Rani if she could weave her one. Chungkham Rani was fascinated by the idea and wanted to experiment with fine silk threads. She wove a beautiful silk sarong with the traditional namthang khuthat design.

Having gained some confidence, Chungkham Rani then wove the first set of silk innaphis for the wives of some engineers. She only made five pieces as she was not sure how the womenfolk would receive her new innaphis. This new innaphi became quite popular and they came to be known as engineer phi, an apt name implying the exclusiveness and opulence of the phi and its wearer. This innaphi became so popular that Chungkham Rani alone could not handle the demand and she had to hire and teach other weavers to produce it. It eventually came to be known as Rani phi (cloth created by Rani). Rani not only wove the traditional designs but introduced diverse motifs onto this new phi. Some of these new designs included a peacock, pair of swans, lotus, shirui lily (*lilium mackliniae*), rose, china rose, orchids, deer eating grasses, pheasant, ginger lily, frangipani, and so on.

Chungkham Rani was born on 1 March 1932 at Wangkhei Lourembam Leikai in Imphal, an area traditionally known for weaving the Wangkhei phi, one of the innaphis of Meitei women. Her father was Chungkham Tolen Singh, a farmer and a carpenter by profession and her mother was Chungkham Ongbi Thambal Devi, a skilled weaver. She was the youngest of eleven siblings (seven sisters and four brothers).

When Rani was around eight years old, World War II (locally known as Japan lan or war) had struck Imphal and Rani and her family fled to a village called Tingri in Manipur. She started learning to weave from her mother. She was about eleven years at that time. Right from a very young age, Rani was quite skilled in many other handicraft activities such as knitting, crocheting, embroidery, and dyeing threads.

At around fourteen years of age, Rani got married to Wangkheimayum Iboyaima. However, her marriage was short-lived. Her husband died of cancer in 1961, and she became a childless widow when she was barely thirty years old. Despite being advised by many to remarry, she refused to do so, and returned to her maternal home where she continued to weave the traditional innaphis.

The innaphis she wove were of the finest quality. At that time, only the traditional designs such as the namthang khuthat (worn only by the royal family), leina (floral design reserved for royal families), and salai mayek (design depicting the different clans of Meitei society) were woven. The traditional patterns of the innaphis were beautiful and complicated, yet she was not quite satisfied with merely weaving the same patterns. She was inspired by the beauty of nature and she imagined how beautiful it would be to weave them onto the innaphis, just like the clothes with beautiful designs manufactured outside the state. She took a bold step and began experimenting with her creative ideas using new threads, patterns, and designs.

Chungkham Rani had become quite a popular weaver by 1960s. In 1975, the Rani Handloom Industries was established producing the finest handwoven clothes in Manipur. Chungkham Rani also worked towards imparting her skills to the younger generation by developing a new scheme called Learning cum Earning Scheme and she trained over 1,000 young women through this scheme.

Rani represented Manipur in various national and international trade fairs. Acknowledging her skills and outstanding contribution to the textile industry, Chungkham Rani has been honoured with various awards and accolades such as the state award for Master Craftsmen (1979–80), National Certificate of Merit (1990), and the Shilpa Bhushan.

Chungkham Rani passed away on 15 March 2012, leaving behind an indelible mark on the history and culture of Manipur.

MEGHALAYA

67

Two Orphans

Once upon a time, in a village in Meghalaya, there lived a brother and his sister. They were orphans. One day, the chief of the village called for a community hunt and decreed that all able-bodied men should take part in it. The boy who had now grown up into a young man had no one to leave his sister with and so he took her along with him. On and on the young man walked carrying his sister on his back, following the men as they went deeper and deeper into the forest. At last, he stopped as he could no longer carry his sister. He put her down under the shade of a banyan tree. He then joined the hunting party. After the hunt, the young man came back to the spot where he had left his sister and upon arriving, he heard a voice calling him. When he looked up, he saw his sister sitting high up on one of the branches of the banyan tree.

'Come down and let us go home. I have come to fetch you,' he said.

'Dear brother,' she said, 'tonight you go away. Come back tomorrow. I shall go back home with you.'

'Are you sure?' he asked.

His sister replied, 'Yes, indeed.'

The young man went away, but it so happened that he forgot all about his sister. After a year had gone by, one morning, he suddenly remembered his sister and hastened to spot where he had left her. When he arrived at the tree, he could not see any sign of his sister. She saw him from the thick foliage of the tree but kept quiet. After a long time, her brother went away.

One day, the chief and his men were hunting in the vicinity when he sighted the girl who had grown into a beautiful woman.

'There,' cried the chief, 'that is the one for me. I must have her as my wife.'

But the woman refused his offer. The chief, not to be put off, renewed his entreaties.

Finally, the woman said, 'Dear chief, if you want to make me your mate, you have to do one thing.'

'Yes, yes, anything!' replied the besotted man.

The woman sang:

Dear chief, O sweet chief,
Weave me a fan of gold
And I will follow you,
Will be your wife
Will bear you children,
O dear chief.

The man immediately started weaving a fan of gold and when the task was done, he went up to the tree and said, 'Fair woman, here, look at this, the fan of gold your little heart desired. Take it!'

The woman then sang:

O dear chief, sweet chief
Weave me a sleeping mat.
So that we can rest together,
When I live with you,
To be your wife,
To bear you children.

The chief quickly set about weaving a mat, a task he promptly completed. With the mat in his hand, he stood under the banyan tree and said to the woman, 'Dearest one, look, this is the sleeping mat you wanted. Now, come down and let us go away to my house.'

The woman then exclaimed:

Ado! O dear chief,
I see it, the mat of gold,
Please, I want a bed,
a bed so I can sleep in.

In haste the chief made a bed. 'Now, look here I have made a bed,' said he, 'I beseech you, come down the tree.'
The woman sang:

Ado! Dear chief,
Yes, I see the bed you made,
Please could you make me
A bed of silver, please?

The chief set about making a bed of silver and when it was done said, 'Hei! Here, the very thing you wanted.'
The woman sang:

Ado the bed of silver, true!
Could you, dear one, make
Me a pair of gold earrings?
Forthwith I shall come with you.

The chief made a pair of beautiful earrings and showed it to the woman on the tree saying, 'Here, a fine pair of gold earrings. Now come, come with me and let us go.'
The woman sang:

Ado! What a lovely pair of earrings.
Indeed
They will adorn my ears
Dear one, please bear up.

The poor man camped at the foot of the tree going without food and drink. After a long time, the woman took pity on him and she sang:

> *Much have you endured,*
> *My chief. Come now,*
> *Up this tree to be with me.*
> *Come up here, please come.*

The man, in haste, started to climb up the tree but found that he could not reach her as the tree was very tall.

The woman sang:

> *Ah, my darling chief,*
> *You lack the skill of the monkey, the squirrel.*
> *Here, I am sending down*
> *sap of the tree*
> *to help you climb to me.*

The chief took the sap collected in a bamboo vessel and smeared it on his hands and feet, and started to climb up the tree. Up he went, until he reached the branch where the young woman sat. There, together, they feasted on the food the young woman had promised.

When they had finished eating the sumptuous meal the chief said, 'Now, my love, let us go.'

The woman sang:

> *Sweet chief, this one night*
> *You go alone.*

The next day, the woman sang:

> *I shall come with you, yes,*
> *build me a house of gold*
> *I shall care for you, yes,*
> *build me a house of silver.*

The poor man was greatly saddened and said, 'Alas, a house of gold or silver I cannot build for you. I do not possess such fabulous wealth. But I shall care for you all the same.'

The young woman smiled and said, 'Dear one, go home

now and sleep. When you wake up, the first thing you should do is rinse your mouth and wash your face. Then look around you and see what you shall see.'

The chief went home and slept. When he woke up, he saw that his thatched dwelling had turned into a house of gold and silver.

The woman sang:

Yes, today is the day,
when I come to you,
I shall follow you and
Yes, live with you.

And she went with the chief and lived with him. But her husband could see that there was still something that bothered his wife. He asked her and she sang:

Could you make a shata-wood, a carving exactly in my
likeness?
Have it placed in the village square so that it is seen
by all and sundry.

The chief carved the shata-wood in the likeness of the girl and she sang pointing to a prominent spot in the village plaza:

My dear husband, place the shata on that spot.

On that very day, the girl's brother came, where the shata-wood stood, and he wept. People started gathering at the village square and soon the chief's household came to know about the commotion at that place.

Said the young woman to her husband, 'I hear that there is a strange man at the village plaza weeping like a baby. Pray, let me go and see what ails him.'

The woman went to the village square and saw that the man who was weeping copious tears was none other than her brother! She called out to him and the man, through his tears, saw his sister. They ran towards each other and one on either side of the shata-wood, holding each other close, fell down dead.

Grapmangtata: Funeral Song

Grapmangtata or funeral song is especially performed during Chugan and Saram Chaa ceremony of the Atong, Gara Ganching, and Matchidual sub-tribes of the Garo, who reside in the southern parts of the Garo Hills in Meghalaya. Chugan is a post-funeral ceremony, while Saram Chaa is a post-harvest festival. This particular oral poetry is performed by a mourner, who is a female relative of the deceased. The lyrics of the grapmangtata are divided into three parts:

1. Rama Aganata or A Path Shown to the Spirit: Garos believe that the spirit of the dead person journey to the eternal abode of the spirit called Balpakram—the place where the spirits of those who pass away, travel to settle down permanently. While travelling he or she may face unforeseen dangers on the way, especially Nawang, an evil spirit who devours souls of men on their way to purgatory. Therefore, for these reasons, mourners show a path by singing a song for safe journey by sitting in front of the body of the deceased.

> O.... Alas!
> At the seven crossroads,
> At the seven pathways,
> That day Guangpa[13],
> With outstretched hands holding onto something,
> He was whiling time, my Mother,

---

[13]An evil spirit.

O.... Alas!
Opening his mouth wide,

He is waiting there,
Leave this one,
Take this one,
Give it to Guangpa,
O.... Alas!
Throw it over to Nawangpa[14],
Raising dust with his feet,
Oh, while the search goes on,

Oh, among the grasses,
Oh, while looking around,
Throw it over to the left side,
Go through the right way,
O.... Alas!
Once you cross that place,
There is a land of lazy ghosts,
A place of landless Nangdu[15],
Ignorant of sunrises,
Plays on the flute endlessly,
And whiles away time,
Regardless of night falling,
Beat on the drums,
And whiles away time.
If you rest there,
If you pause there for a while,
More[16] will then take you as a slave,

---

[14]An evil spirit, who devours souls of the dead on their way to purgatory.
[15]A village, supposed to be somewhere in the southeastern parts of Garo Hills.
[16]Land of spirit. Garos believe that the human soul journeys through this place and stays for sometime, before reaching its final destination.

Mangra[17] will force you to work,
Do not rest there,

Maintain your dignity, O Mother,

Go straight forward,
The land of More;
Should be escaped from quickly,
As also the main pathway of Mangra,
As you leave those places,
The More bachelors,
Holding paddles in their hands,
And manoeuvring them in their arms,
Hanging on a raft of bamboo roof,
Come, which way you want to go.
Take this with you,
This is for your boat fare,
Here, pick it up,
Travel fare for you, O Mother,
As you cross that place,
And arrive at the place called More kera onram[18]
A place called Mangra matchu karam[19],
Put your basket down and rest,
Rest your feet,
At the place called More kera onram,
In the spot called Matchu boldak karam[20],
While you are taking rest,
Maintain your decorum, O Mother,
As you set out from this place,

---

[17]The name of a spirit.
[18]The place where the spirit puts the basket.
[19]A place where the spirit ties the bull.
[20]The spirits of dead people go to their permanent resting place at Balpakram, they would take rest in this very place and tie the bulls on the boldak tree.

Thousands of Mangra,
Ten thousands of More,
Baring their long, pointed teeth,
May be waiting there,
They are talking exposing their long teeth,
They might laugh at you, O Mother,
Tell them the name of your clan,
Tell about your ancestors, O Mother,
Once you reach beyond that place,
Once you left it behind,
More will never come back, they say!
Mangra never return, they say!
With thousand Mores,
Walking hand in hand,
With ten thousand Mangras,
Holding on to each other's hips,

Thus, they did while away time,
And settled in the land,
And made the streams their own.

2. Debra Stita or Tying the Cloth: Tying a cloth on the back of the mourner is a sign of respect towards the loved one, who is no more with the family. The mortal remains of the deceased, kept inside an earthen pot, is taken out and tied on the back of the mourner, who is a female and close relative of the deceased person.

O.... Alas!
Balarasong[21], two brothers,
O.... Alas!
Balarasong, uncle and nephew,
From beneath the four strata of the earth,

---

[21]Two brothers who were the first to get the clothes and sell in the markets.

From the fathoms of deep water,
With just one whistle,
They got it in their hand,
With just one clap,
Their eyes beheld,
That the one in the eastern market,
Shown hanging,
In the marketplace of Noepa[22]
Draped around and displayed,
Norinik[23] the damsel,
Secured in her hand,
Nochinik[24] the younger sister,
There she herself saw.
O.... Alas!
Norinik the maiden,
The pretty one is holding on to,
Clasping what came into her hand,
Nochinik the younger sister,
Who saw with her eyes,
Oh dear, holding in her hands,
Somewhere you are being,
Till More roams around alone,
Till Mangra flees,
And secured at the back,
Fastened with a cloth,
Well supported at the waist,
Tying you up on my back,
Oh, dear!
Mother, don't you forget your clan,
Don't you forget your siblings,
It may not be a beautiful homestead,

---

[22]Owner of the market where different types of clothes are sold.
[23]A maiden.
[24]Younger sister of Norinik.

But home it is, of your children,
It may not be attractive,
But it's been beautified by your children,
Oh, dear!
Look here,
As one is about to enter from under the eaves,

Where the swallows make their homes,
Where rain drips from the eaves,
If you pause there for a while,
It would not bode well for you!
Eaves may frighten you,
Door may play with your vision, Mother,
Don't you tremble out of fright,
Don't let your body be shaken,
Don't you succumb to illusions,
As you take time to enter,
Beneath the expansive beams,
The big lizard may be lying in wait,
To frighten with its big teeth,
Even the side door of the house,
Might mimic you and mock you,

There at the side of the wall,
Might appear a black spider,
And tease your vision, O Mother,
Come, stop and take rest,
What is there for you?

To feel embarrassed, O Mother!
A stool made of bolong[25] tree,
Smoothened with great finesse,
A big round woven cane stool,
Especially kept for you,

---

[25]A genus of a big and tall tree (*Cyathocalyx martabanicus*).

If you feel hot and perspire,
Rest for a while, mother,
If you wish to pause and rest,
Do as you wish, Mother,
Oh, dear!
Should you feel hungry,
Should you thirst for water,
There is prepared for you, Mother,
Neither unclean rice nor impure water,
A choice elongated rice,
Soft and palatable, O Mother,
This you shall eat, Mother,
Such as this you drink,
O Mother!

3. Miksuata or Washing the Face: Cleanliness is part of life
in Garo society and it is extended to the last rites too. After
death, the Garo washes the body of the deceased with chubitchi,
the best rice beer, before the final journey. This is done by a
close female relative, while she continuously sings a song, till
the work is completed.

O.... Alas!
In the murky waters of More,
If you lean on the soles of your feet,
You'll be infected with the smell of gibbon,
Say so to More,
In the black waters of Mangra,
If you wash your hair,
Foul smell of monkey dung clings to you,
Report thus, Mother.
Aiao...o...o!
In the cool waters of More,
If you lean on the soles of your feet,
It's as if one gets a whiff,

Of the cooked fragrant rice,
In the cool waters of Mangra,
If you wash your hair,
You'd feel the sweet fragrance,
And sweet fragrance of the damsel,
Would feel your nose.
O.... Alas!
Let me comb and untangle,
Your hair with rori[26] comb, Mother,
And bathe you with soap made by banggal[27],
Oh, dear!
With the fine-toothed rori comb,
Let me comb your hair, Mother,
Leaving out not a single curly hair,

Without a single grey hair,
Let me comb till your hair become straight,
O Mother,
Oh, dear!
This is the best oil sold by banggal,
Let me apply to your scalp,
And also, on your body, O Mother,
Although peddled by banggal,
And rori came to the threshold to sell,
I am the one bathing you,
See, I am washing your face,
O.... Alas!
When you spend time with thousand More,
When you are with ten thousand Mangra
May sweet fragrance emanate from you,
May you exude sweetness like that of a damsel.

---

[26] A non-Garo, a foreigner.
[27] A non-Garo, a foreigner

69

The Skull of U Syiem Syad Lukhmi

Long ago, Chief Syad Lukhmi ruled over a territory to the east of Nonglyngdoh, a community of villages in present-day Ri-Bhoi district of Meghalaya. His rival was Wan Marin, the chief of Nonglyngdoh who had, as his confidants, two brothers named U Wan and U Ksha Sangot. The two brothers were renowned warriors in the area. They were also known for their expertise in erecting megaliths of significant sizes to commemorate events and episodes of the community. Before Sajer, a religious ceremony that marks the beginning of the agricultural calendar, Syad Lukhmi ordered the people of Nonglyngdoh to clear the grounds for the ceremony. In reality, he had no jurisdiction over Nonglyngdoh but this order was given to provoke chief Wan Marin and thus give chief Syad Lukhmi reasons to attack and annex this adjoining territory which he so coveted.

However, the people of Nonglyngdoh saw through his plans and went along with him. Chief Syad Lukhmi was immensely pleased to see that the people of Nonglyngdoh paid him obeisance, went a step further by plotting to have the two warrior brothers, U Wan and U Ksha Sangot, killed. After the successful performance of the Sajer rituals, he invited the people of Nonglyngdoh to a feast. He gave instructions to his people to generously serve rice beer so that the two brothers would be easy prey in their inebriated state.

On the day of the community dance, that is the third day of the Sajer ceremony, the people of Nonglyngdoh participated in the festivities and returned to their villages at night. U Wan and U Ksha Sangot stayed back with the men of Chief Syad Lukhmi. The brothers feigned drunkenness as more and more rice beer were poured into their jhoh or bamboo cups. Later, Syad Lukhmi joined the drinking party and a bawdy singing session commenced. The chief ordered for more drinks to be brought.

Before dawn, Syad Lukhmi left on a pre-arranged signal which would cue his men to fall upon the two brothers and kill them. Sensing something amiss, U Ksha Sangot excused himself to relieve himself and discreetly followed the chief. At some distance away from the place of revelry, he eased out his sword and confronted the chief. A fierce combat ensued and U Ksha managed to strike the first blow and slashed the chief's thigh. But Syad Lukhmi was an equally good swordsman and returned a wounding strike to Ksha who fell to the ground. Just then U Wan who had managed to escape the drunken men of the chief intervened and Syad Lukhmi, seeing that he was no match for both the brothers, turned away and fled into the black night. Following in hot pursuit, the two brothers finally ran the chief to the ground, and U Wan, with a single stroke, took his head.

The brothers carried the bloody trophy to their own chief who received them with honour. The chief, as was the custom, offered the brothers the choice of three gifts—gold and silver, land, and paddy fields. As was the custom again, no offering could be made to the gods unless the two warriors have made a choice of the gifts. Only then could the head of the enemy be displayed on a wooden spike at the altar near the eastern and western gates of the village.

The brothers declined the gifts offered and only asked for the head of Syad Lukhmi. The chief of Nonglyngdoh generously gave in to their request and personally carried the decapitated head to the ancestral house of the brothers. Ka It, their sister did not want to keep the head on display in her house, and so the brothers carried it to the house of Tung, their other sister. Thus, U Wan and U Ksha got what they wanted—Chief Syad Lukhmi's head. The skull was later adorned with reeds and constitutes a special annual offering to the clan deities of Wan and Ksha. The skull is now with a certain family belonging to the clan of the two brothers in Nonglyngdoh and even today, is a worship symbol.

MIZORAM

70

Thangchhawli

Long ago there lived a poor widow. She had a beautiful daughter named Thangchhawli. Their house was often frequented by young men, who came to court Thangchhawli. One day, mother and daughter went out to work in their farmland. This was very far away and was lying uncultivated for some time. Around noon, Thangchhawli became very thirsty so her mother said, 'Chemte,[28] go down to the little stream at the edge of the farm and see if there is any water.'

Thangchhawli followed her mother's instructions. But the stream was completely dry. Suddenly, she saw some water in the hollow of a tree and she quenched her thirst. Quite unknown to her, this water belonged to a keimi, tiger-person. When she went back to her mother, she said, 'Mother, the stream was dry but since I was very thirsty, I drank water which I found in the hollow of a tree.'

Soon, Thangchhawli's face began to change. Her skin became striped and long, sharp talons grew on her hands and a thick tail sprouted behind her. Her mother lamented, 'Chemte, what a terrible disaster, the water you drank must have belonged to a tiger-person!'

After a while, Thangchhawli turned back into a human again, but her mother advised, 'You must keep this a secret.'

For some time, they did manage to guard the secret closely; however, one night, when their house was full of Thangchhawli's boyfriends, the secret was revealed. The men were lying casually

---

[28]A term of endearment for a young child.

all over the floor after a meal. Thangchhawli and her mother tended to the kitchen fire. When Thangchhawli was certain that all the men had gone off to sleep, she gradually whispered to her mother, 'Mother, I am hungry.'

Her mother said, 'Go and eat the leftover rice on the shelf.' Thangchhawli said, 'I'm not hungry for rice.'

'Go eat the goat that's tied outside the front door.'

'I'm not hungry for goat meat.'

'Go eat the sow below the house.'

'I'm not hungry for pig meat.'

'All right, go out to the edge of the forest and feed on the cow we keep there.'

But Thangchhawli refused again, saying, 'I'm not hungry for cow meat.'

Her mother was worried, she looked around at the young men fast asleep on the floor and seeing the youngest one, sleeping by the furthest wall, told her daughter, 'All right, go to the youngest boy over there and feed on him.'

However, the young man was not asleep, and had been listening all along to the conversation between the mother and her daughter. Filled with great fear, he woke his companions saying, 'Get up, get up, I have a terrible stomach ache,' and pretended to be racked with abdominal pain.

So, his friends carried him to the zawlbuk, dormitory for bachelors, and there, he told them what he had overheard. 'I was only pretending to be in pain because while you were all fast asleep, I heard the girl tell her mother how hungry she was. But to everything that her mother told her to eat, she would say she was not hungry for that. Finally, the mother told her, "Go feed on the youngest boy", and I was so frightened, I woke all of you.'

The eldest of the men said, 'Tomorrow night, we shall call on her again and find out the truth. We must all secretly carry a rock and a stick of firewood.'

So, the next evening, the young men went to Thangchhawli's house. Unnoticed by the girl and her mother, they dropped their rocks into the pot of pig swill cooking over the fire, and hid their firewood sticks under their puan, the traditional woven cloth. Then they stretched out on the floor and pretended to fall asleep.

After a while, the pig swill was cooked and Thangchhawli got up to remove the pot from the fire. But the rocks the young men had secretly dropped into the pot, made it very heavy and she was unable to lift the pot. As she drew all her strength, her supernatural tiger-powers took over her mortal form and she was able to easily pick up the heavy pot and remove it from the fire.

At this, all the young men jumped up and cried, 'This is a tiger-person. No ordinary woman could have lifted that pot!' Arming themselves with their sticks of firewood, they got ready to beat Thangchhawli to death.

Her mother intervened, 'Alas, we can hide our secret no longer. Forgive us!' She then told the young men the sad story of how the misfortune had befallen her daughter. But the young men said, 'However sorry we feel for you about this situation, your daughter can no longer continue to live in this village.'

And so, the poor mother and her daughter had to part ways. Being no longer allowed to live with human beings, Thangchhawli was told to live in the jungle and her mother watched her leave, weeping bitterly.

Because of her reluctance to leave her mother, Thangchhawli moved around the outskirts of the village for several days. She often brought choice pieces of wild animals she had caught and left them at her mother's doorstep.

One night she brought the hind leg of a domestic cattle and her mother told her, 'Chemte, you know I've told you not to prey on domestic animals. If you keep doing it, huntsmen will soon shoot you. Go far away from here for your own safety.'

Thangchhawli replied sadly, 'Mother, it breaks my heart to leave you forever.'

Her mother told her, 'You must go. But be careful wherever you go.'

So Thangchhawli went away deep into the jungle where she later married a tiger and had children with him. When she left her home, she was wearing a thihna, a traditional Mizo necklace. It is said that her offsprings could be identified by their necks. To this day, whenever Mizo elders come across tigers with white markings on their necks, they refer to them as Thangchhawli's descendants.

71

Chiasung and Manghan

A long time ago, there lived two lovers. Both were known for their good looks and they lived in adjacent villages in Pawi country. The girl was called Chiasung and the boy, Manghan. It was a long journey between the two villages, but Manghan the enthusiastic, young lover would often make his way to the neighbouring village to court Chiasung.

The two wanted to be together and the time came when Manghan finally asked for Chiasung's hand in marriage. Chiasung's parents readily agreed, and the young couple happily made their way together to Manghan's village. To celebrate the marriage, a big feast was held in the groom's village. Every family member attended except the new bride, Chiasung, who was instructed to remain indoors. So, Chiasung remained at home accompanied by her half-witted sister-in-law.

Chiasung was instructed by her husband not to attend the feast or even witness any part of the festivities and so, being an obedient woman, Chiasung stayed back. As the feast progressed outside, Chiasung's sister-in-law offered her a sour drink. As soon as she tasted it, Chiasung despised it, but noticed that her sister-in-law was relishing it.

To her horror, Chiasung soon found that the sour drink had been prepared by soaking a dead body in water. To this horrific revelation was added Chiasung's curiosity about the feast which she was forbidden to attend. She soon found out a short while thereafter that a similar feast would be held soon. Once again, Chiasung was instructed to stay at home, but she followed her sister-in-law, who went to join the feast.

Chiasung hid as the sister-in-law went ahead and joined the festivities. She was greatly shocked at what she saw. To her horror, Chiasung saw that everyone gradually turned into tigers. She was so shocked to witness this phenomenon that she forgot to stay hidden, and her husband suddenly noticed her. He came rushing but Chiasung was quick and managed to run away before he could reach her.

When she reached home, Chiasung decided to leave for her parents' home, but realized that she had to do it discreetly. Thus, when Manghan entered the house to enquire why she was out at night, Chiasung replied that she had gone to keep some items at the outskirts of the village for safekeeping. Manghan did not suspect her and returned back to the festivities.

As soon as he was gone, Chiasung quickly left for her parents' house. When Manghan returned home, he found that Chiasung was missing. He set out in pursuit. By that time, Chiasung had already reached her parents' home and had narrated all that she had witnessed at her in-law's place. In the meantime, Manghan reached her home. He pleaded and begged her to return with him and tried his best to win her back, but Chiasung had made up her mind. She convinced her father to drive him away.

A few days later, Chiasung's father saw a large tiger sleeping in their garden. He quickly took out his bow and arrow and killed the sleeping tiger. The tiger was none other than Manghan, who was lying there as he wanted to be close to his beloved. Manghan's family was informed of his death. They came to mourn and grieve over the tiger's dead body. His aunt searched for wounds on his body and wept profusely, mentioning that their family members always met with unnatural death. The aunt found a deep cut on the tiger's body and sealed it with wax.

A tiger's head is considered a great trophy for a warrior and Manghan's head was also hung as a trophy by Chiasung's father on his wall, but Manghan's soul kept pleading with Chiasung to be buried like a man. This was finally done with great respect by Chiasung for the love they had once shared.

72

Kaptluangi and Rema

The sun was setting, and many families were already sitting down for their evening meal. Rema and his friends were still out playing, oblivious of the fading light cast by the setting sun. Their play was broken by his mother, Pi Kaptluangi's sharp call, 'Mate,[29] come home, we're about to eat.' Hearing this, Rema turned around and ran towards his house.

Rema and his mother lived in Zodai, a small village of about eighty houses, located at a short distance from the capital town of Aizawl. There were few and infrequent visitors to this village because it was hidden in the mountains and there were no proper roads connecting the village.

With the outbreak of the rambuai,[30] this little village in the mountains with its surrounding forests and stormy brooks had become a haven for the hnam sipai,[31] who had gone underground. They were often spotted donning cowboy hats, guns across their shoulders, seeking food and other necessities from the villages. Their forays into the village street always garnered an audience not just of children, but adults too, who understood the grimness of their shared situation. This created a tense air in the otherwise sleepy village of Zodai where nights were always more uneasy than the days.

---

[29]A term of endearment often used by parents for their children.

[30]The twenty years of disturbance when the underground Mizo National Front (MNF) army was at war with the Indian government over the issue of independence.

[31]Literally translated as 'nation's' soldiers', a term used by locals to refer to personnel of the underground MNF army.

The proximity of hnam sipai camps quickly led to patrols by the vai[32] soldiers. The elders spoke in hushed tones. There was an anxiety suspending in the air and a fear that something would flare up soon. The nights were the most fearful. Most people were afraid to keep the fires in their hearths alive at night or even step out of their houses to go visiting friends and neighbours.

Rema sat beside his mother next to the dying fire, as she tried to explain the disturbing circumstances to her son, who was still probably too young to understand. Rema's father, Pu Rinsanga, had left home a couple of months ago to join the hnam sipai and ever since they hadn't heard of him. Pi Kaptluangi anxiously waited for news of her husband. She was also too scared to ask the hnam sipai who came to their village. Even though Rema knew his father had left home on some mission, he was too young to understand the gravity of the situation and his mother was left to suffer alone. He was happy to be with his mother and was often unaware of his father's absence.

That night, at around eleven o'clock, as the leng haw ar, roosters, let out their last crows reminding the suitors that it was time to go home, the air was thick with unexplained tension. Pi Kaptluangi woke up from a deep sleep to go to the toilet. She looked a while at her sleeping son before stepping out of the house. The darkness around her added to the tension and an inexplicable fear caught her as she quickly made her way back. On her bed, she found it hard to go back to sleep and thoughts of her husband haunted her. She remembered how they had said goodbye. Tears welled up in her eyes. She let out small cries but quickly pulled the quilt over her mouth, lest she wake up the sleeping child next to her.

While she was still trying to control her emotions, she heard

---

[32]A term for outsiders or even people from other parts of India.

a loud shout of panic in the distance which made her sit up on her bed. Curious, she peeped through a small hole in the wall and was shocked to see a massive fire, some distance from their house. One of the houses was on fire and people were running all around in panic and fear. In the midst of all this, she also heard the vai soldiers mumbling. Since all the houses were made of wood and bamboo with thatched roofs, she knew it wouldn't be long before each and every house caught fire. This thought brought a sudden wakefulness, and she grabbed her sleeping son from the bed and prepared to rush outside with him. However, in panic, as she was preparing to step down from their elevated house, she missed a step, stumbling into the hole in the leikapui[33] and one of her legs got stuck. She could barely move. She cried for help as Rema woke up in fear. But the entire village was in chaos with people crying, shouting, and running amok. The house next door was on fire and the flames were already edging towards their house. Knowing she could not break free in time, she prodded her son, 'Son, run, run, just run as fast as you can. I can't get up, so don't worry about me. Just keep running.' She pushed Rema out of harm's way just as the flames caught up. Rema somehow found his way to safety even as his mother stuck in the leikapui was consumed by the fire, as she cried, 'Rema Pa, how I miss you.'

Before morning broke, the once quiet but happy village of Zodai with its eighty houses had turned to ashes. The cause of the fire remained unknown, but it was alleged that the fire was a result of the tension between the two armed forces. The village was now unrecognizable. Dead animals, burnt houses, and stench of death and fire greeted the few brave men who came back to take stock the following morning. Most of the

---

[33] A veranda constructed with wood/bamboo connecting the wooden steps and the main house in elevated houses.

villagers, including women and children, had been able to run to the nearby forest for safety and there were no other human lives lost, but the charred body of Rema's mother was found which reminded them of the life that once was in Zodai village.

NAGALAND

73

Songmo and her Tree-lover

Long ago, there lived in Changsang Mongku, a rich man
named Namang Bheshang who had a beautiful daughter
named Nayung Songmo. Every man in the village approached
her father for her hand in marriage. But each proposal was
turned down by Nayung Songmo for she had given her heart
to a young man, whose identity she did not know. Namang
Bheshang believed that his daughter would one day make a
fair choice for herself, but was worried about this secret lover,
who would turn up to court his daughter every night and
leave at the crack of dawn. Nobody knew about his identity.
Even Nayung Songmo tried to look for him in the village in
the morning, but all in vain. Finally, one day, she decided to
tell her father about him and said, 'Abou, a fine young man
comes to my bedside every night. He appears to me wearing
a black shawl; he stays the night and leaves the following
morning. He refuses to tell me where he comes from or what
his name is, and though I have tried, I have failed in all my
attempts to know anything about him.' Namang Bheshang
listened keenly to what his daughter narrated. Pondering over
it for a while, he said, 'Take this aolak[34]. Tie it to the end
of his shawl. Do it just as he wakes up to leave without his
notice. Go and look for it during the day and I'm sure you
will find him in no time.' She did as she was told and tied
the aolak to the tassels of her lover's shawl just as the young

---

[34]Wind chime made from the *Rhus semialata*, a deciduous tree found in the
Northeast.

man was leaving at the break of dawn. The next morning, Nayung Songmo went in search of the aolak but there was no sign of it anywhere. Tired of searching, she gave up all hope and finally headed back home. Just as she was walking past the massive jongnyu, banyan, tree that grew in front of her house, its leaves rustled. Nayung Songmo looked up and to her surprise, there was the aolak fluttering in the breeze high up! Nayung Songmo immediately called her father.

When Namang Bheshang saw the wind chime hanging from the very top of the banyan tree, he knew it was impossible for any man to have climbed up that high and tie it. He understood then that the young man was none other than the spirit of the banyan tree appearing to his daughter as a young man. Nayung Songmo's father was extremely furious. He could not bear the thought that it was the tree spirit who was the lover of his beautiful daughter. So, he sent out word for all the strong men in the village to assemble. Within no time, the young men from all the tribes living in Changsang Mongku gathered under the jongnyu tree and decided to cut it down. Next to the tree was a large boulder on which the young men began to sharpen their axes in turn.

Nayung Songmo stood watching the men swing their axes up and down on the tree. Her father then sternly ordered her into the house and bolted the door. The men took turns and worked steadily, chanting a work song. They felled and felled but the tree did not give way. Instead, it made a strange kee... kee...kee creaking noise. Nevertheless, the men kept cutting but the tree did not even slightly budge. The tree only kept swaying, making a strange sound, its wood creaking but just not breaking. Nayung Songmo, with a heavy heart, heard all the sounds the tree was making and suddenly she wished to see the tree. She made a chink in the matted bamboo wall bigger and put her eye to it. At that very moment, a splinter flew through the air into the tiny gap in the wall and hit Nayung

Songmo's eye, just as the tree gave way falling to the ground with a thunderous crash.

The men then cut up the tree trunk into portions and groups of each tribe carried away their portions, chanting as they went their respective ways. And in this way, except for the Chang, all the other tribes of men moved on from Changsang, made new settlements elsewhere and started living according to their own ways. Now in the jungles of Changsang Mongku, some distance away from Hakchang village, a deep depression remains where the massive banyan tree once stood. A large sandstone boulder also lies nearby bearing grove marks of the axes they sharpened. Nayung Songmo died the very instant her handsome lover, the tree spirit, also died. To this day, a folk song of Songmo and her tree-lover is sung by the Changs. And since she was killed, blinded in a most unnatural way, in every generation, a child is said to be born blind in the Kangshou clan to which Nayung Songmo belonged.

74

A Tale of Two Brothers

Once upon a time in a village, there lived two brothers. As they grew up and as fate would have it, the younger brother became very prosperous. On the other hand, the elder brother was not so lucky and led a poor life. The rich younger brother was always surrounded by several friends and they enjoyed great feasts together. In the process of having such a luxurious lifestyle, the younger brother grew more and more distant from the elder brother and even began to ignore him. Thus, the elder brother became sad as he often thought of his brother. One day the younger brother sat thinking, 'Do I have real friends or are these people only friendly with me simply because I am rich?' This thought bothered him for a long time and he decided to test it himself. He thought of a plan and accordingly, called over his best friend, whom he thought was closest to him and would help him in his times of need. He told his friend, 'Akhum, come over and we will go to the forest to feast on some scrumptious sherithi[35] fruits.'

The friend came over and both of them set off for the forest. Once they arrived at a sherithi tree, they climbed up and happily started to munch on the sweet fruits. Ripe sherithi fruits are blood red in colour and very juicy. Soon, as planned, the younger brother, while they were still up on the tree eating the fruit, started to smear the juice of the ripe sherithi all over his body. Then he pretended to fall from the tree to the ground and called out to his friend for help. His friend

---

[35]*Carallia brachiata.*

climbed down and was aghast to see him covered with blood. The younger brother pretended to have been badly wounded and helpless. However, instead of helping him, the friend told him that he will quickly go the village and bring his elder brother. (In the olden days it was taboo to touch or attend to accident victims as it was believed that the same would befall the person too). Thus, he ran to the village and went directly to the elder brother's house to inform him. The elder brother came hurriedly to the forest and was shocked to see his brother covered with blood. He promptly attended to his brother and said to him, 'Ango ntia nstio.' (Younger brother who doesn't know anything.) Saying so, as he was about to lift and carry his brother home, the younger brother got up and said, 'Brother, don't worry, I am not hurt, and this is not blood but the juice of sherithi that I had smeared on my body. I was just trying to test my friends whether they truly love me or my wealth. I am extremely sorry for the way I have behaved all these years. I have come to understand the true value and importance of family.' Having realized his mistake, the younger brother hugged his elder brother, and they went home happily.

75

The Spear Cry Out
Narrative of a Naga Archaeologist

At an archival exhibition at the Naga Hornbill Festival held in Kohima, an important bulletin was on display that read *Highlander*. It appeared to be an old but informative official biannual research bulletin of the Department of Art and Culture (formerly Department of Cultural Research and State Museum, Government of Nagaland). Flipping through the pages of one of the volumes of *Highlander* (Vol. 2, No.1) published in 1974, the author stumbled upon an article titled 'Recent Prehistoric Discoveries in Nagaland: A Survey' by Vikuosa Nienu whose contribution to archaeology in Nagaland remains significant till today.

Prior to the studies and research of Vikuosa Nienu, no archaeological investigation had ever been conducted in Nagaland, that too, at a time when the political situation in Nagaland was tense, making field archaeology problematic and challenging. The discipline of archaeology in Nagaland owes much to Vikuosa Nienu in introducing the cultural–historical approach, processual and behavioural archaeology in the region. All this was possible from his exposure as a student at the University of California, Berkeley, and the Grasshopper Pueblo Field School during the early 1970s. To the present generation of archaeologists from the Northeast, Vikuosa Nienu's contribution to the region's prehistory is an unfamiliar one. But for those who knew him, he was often considered as a man preoccupied by his own idiosyncratic ideas. Elders of many villages still narrate accounts of his early excavations in the area. Nienu's association with the villages he visited, the keen observations he made, and the insights he drew to identify archaeological sites from the people's cultural memories demonstrate his true spirit and training in anthropology. Barring colonial reports of ground stone tools and others, his report on the discovery of an archaeological site at Chungliyimti stands as the first pioneering effort.

Vikuosa Nienu was born in New Phek on 2 February 1942, but his parents later moved to Sohomi village between 1946 and 1947 to start a new church. Vikuosa Nienu grew up and was engaged variously with education and culture services of Nagaland, before he was sent to New Delhi to learn about field archaeology. Here, he received his first field training and a gold medal from his post-graduate diploma in archaeology (1969–71) at the School of Archaeology, New Delhi. He was fortunate to receive his training from stalwarts such as B. B. Lal and B. K. Thapar. Upon his return to Nagaland, Nienu was appointed as the Investigator of Cultural Research and Officer-in-charge of Archaeology at the Department of Art and Culture, a post he held until July 1974. He then left for the United States in September 1974 to pursue further studies at the University of California, Berkeley. He obtained two master's degree and a PhD from UC Berkeley.

Over a personal conversation with the author on 3 February 2016, Nienu described his academic experience upon his arrival in the US:

> By the time I arrived in the US in 1974, the concept of New Archaeology, often identified as American Archaeology, was making giant strides, leading traditional historical archaeology of recording, cataloguing, photographing, describing, fixing timelines of, and preserving the findings to a rigorous scientific approach to studying and solving/explaining the discoveries. The principal theorist was Lewis Binford in the US. At the same time, in England, David

L. Clarke was making headway whose major contribution was a rigorous application of General Systems Theory. In the US, a few important learning centres had already emerged in the forefront, namely the University of New Mexico (Binford's), the University of Arizona (Longacre, etc.), and particularly at UC Berkeley, headed by Desmond Clarke and Glynn Isaac. I was fortunate to be exposed to both the worlds of 'traditional' archaeology and 'New Archaeology'.... This was a giant step in the field of archaeological studies, generally, but more so personally that made a tremendous impact in my profession as an archaeologist.

At UC Berkeley, he was trained under the tutelage of John Desmond Clark and Glynn Isaac, both Britons, and considered stalwarts in Old World prehistoric archaeology, while George F. Dales, a leading expert on Harappan studies who led the South Asian Archaeology at UC Berkeley was his research supervisor. He also got to work in Arizona in 1975 to participate in the excavation at Grasshopper Pueblo, an Apache Native American site, where the excavation was directed by William Longacre and Jefferson Reid of the University of Arizona Archaeological Field School. Within two years of completing his studies at UC Berkeley, Nienu was about to return to Nagaland and conduct a major research project sponsored by the National Science Foundation (USA), but the proposed project was derailed because the political situation prevailing at the time was extremely dangerous, restricting movements in Nagaland and surrounding regions. Nienu's accounts of the fieldwork, over a personal communication with the author in 2014, reveals the conditions under which the work was carried out at that time, 'Even while our digs were in progress at Mimi cave site, war broke out between a particular insurgent group and the Indian armed forces, a couple of miles away from the cave site, forcing us to flee and this incident was not an exception.

It happened frequently, disrupting our field schedules and our field objectives.... The undesirable political situation in Nagaland took a nosedive the years following and continued unabated for the decades to come. This undesirable turn of events, especially having to abandon my pet project, funded by the National Science Foundation, disappointed no less which led me to seek employment outside of my profession where compensation was much more lucrative than in the academic fields, and have continued since.'

In later years, however, after his return to Nagaland, Nienu left archaeology. He joined the US Chamber of Commerce as a representative (1984–85) and was hired by a company named AMCOR, Petaluma, CA, where he became the district manager (1985–95) and later became the regional director, Genutech, Capitola, CA (2000–02) and thereafter the director, marketing and sales, Berkeley Daily Planet, Berkeley, CA (2003–04). He also taught briefly at the Golden Gate Seminary Department of Intercultural Studies (1994–96) and Department of History, Patten University (1995–96) as adjunct professor. Even though retired, he still serves as an ENERGTEC consultant, while at the same time he is also a member of the American Association for the Advancement of Science (AAA). He taught at a number of universities, at their requests, but taught subjects other than archaeology, except at UC Berkeley where he was visiting scholar of ethnoarchaeology since 2013. At other institutions, he mainly taught World Religion and Anthropology, Cross-cultural Communications, and Multicultural Studies.

ODISHA

76

Stories of the Osakothi Ritual in Ganjam

On their way to heaven, the five Pandava brothers rested for a while on the veranda of a Brahmin's house in the kingdom of Avanti. The house had a sad history—all newborn children born in this house did not survive past the first night. When the Pandava brothers heard of this they were sympathetic. It so happened that at the time they were staying in the Brahmin's house, a child was expected to be born. The kind Pandavas were ready to do anything in their power to save the newborn baby. Arjuna erected a kothi and a chammundia, a temporary shelter, with arrows. This shelter prevented Yama the god of death from entering the house. At night, a messenger of Yama arrived but could not enter the house. Consequently, an agreement was made with Yama—whosoever observes this osa, ritual fasting, will bear sons, and all subsequent newborns will live.

In no time the news spread throughout Avanti. A sweeper woman by the name of Shriya Chandaluni heard it too while she was sweeping the streets near the palace. The king of Avanti had ninety-nine queens. One day, one of the queens expressed her displeasure to the king, after she had met Shriya the first thing in the morning. Meeting an untouchable woman at the morning hour was thought of as an unfortunate event which would bring ill luck. Shriya, too, thought it was inauspicious to have seen the face of the queen because she was an antakudi, a barren woman.

The queen was motivated by revenge and demanded the king that all the seven children of Shriya be killed. After listening to the queen, the king sent out seven paikas, warriors, to kill the children. The paikas took away Shriya's five sons to the forest and killed them. The devastated Shriya went to the forest in search of her sons. Seeing them dead, she cried out loud. Shriya was helpless and could not do anything to save her children from the wrath of the queen.

At that time, Shiva and Parvati were wandering in the forest. They heard Shriya and comforted her. They asked her to observe osa by erecting a chammundia. She replied that she could only build a chammundia if her sons were alive. Shiva then asked her to look away. As Shriya turned her head away from Shiva, he sprinkled water on the dead bodies and her sons came back to life. The sons embraced their mother and paid obesieance to Shiva and Paravati. Meanwhile, the king had been watching everything that had been happening. He also performed osakothi and soon each of his ninety-nine queens bore sons.

77

Origins of the Dongria Kondhs

Once upon a time the earth was heavily populated. There was not enough land for cultivation and space for people to live in. As there was no scope to lead a healthy life, people complained to their king, Dharam Devata the sun god. Dharam Devata immediately set up a committee to discuss a plan. They agreed upon an idea to destroy the entire universe and all living creatures in it and create a new one in its place.

An antelope, which was soon to give birth, heard this conversation. At the same time, there lived a brother, Duku, and his sister, Dumbe. One day, as Duku was returning home after an unsuccessful hunt, he spotted an antelope. As he was about to shoot, he heard a scream, a human voice emitting from the antelope's mouth. It was the kid in the antelope's womb that was talking to Duku.

'Killing my mother is an easy thing for you to do. But know this, this creation, of which you are a part, will be soon be destroyed. I overheard Dharam Devata's plan to destroy everything and create a new world. The earth will tremble, and all the hills, mountains, trees, crops, houses, and people will be destroyed. Nobody will be able to survive the wrath of Dharam Devata.'

On hearing this, Duku shook with fear. He asked the antelope if there was a way to survive the destruction. The animal replied, 'Make a boat with wood of the simuli tree. When the floods come the boat will stay afloat. Take enough food with you to last for a long time.'

Duku rushed back home and narrated his experience to

Dumbe. Without wasting any time, he made a boat, and Duku and Dumbe started sailing to an unknown world. The disaster hit, but the siblings were safe, thanks to the antelope's advice. They heard loud blasts, the rush of flooding rivers, screams and death cries, the rumble of falling trees and crashing rocks. They could only imagine the catastrophe that had taken place around them.

No creature survived except Duku and Dumbe. The gods and goddesses realized that there was no one left to worship them or offer sacrifices to them. They took the matter to Dharam Devata. After hearing their complaints, Dharam Devata pulled some hairs from his body and created a crow and gave life to it. The crow was sent in search of human beings. It flew far and wide and finally spotted Duke and Dumbe. They made their way to the court of Dharam Devata where they explained how they had managed to escape the destruction.

Dharam Devata listened patiently and discussed with his courtiers and finally decided to request the brother and sister to procreate. But Duku and Dumbe did not agree to the idea as they considered it sinful. Then there was another plan. The smallpox goddess, Maa Budhi, was sent to inflict Duku with smallpox and Dumbe with measles. The goddess followed the gods' instructions and inflicted the siblings with the scarring diseases. When they were cured, both Duku and Dumbe looked different and could not recognize each other. They became sexually attracted to each other. From their procreation were born the first Dongrias.

At the time when the Dongrias originated, there was no Niyamgiri. The earth was devoid of any mountains and hills. Dharam Devata called a meeting to which all the gods, goddesses, and the Dongria representatives were invited. He wanted a king to be elected to rule on earth, one who would take care of the well being of the Dongrias and bring happiness and prosperity.

To select the right king, Dharam Devata called for a cucumber and a pumpkin for the test. He placed the vegetables before the assembled gathering and called each aspiring candidate to guess the exact number of seeds in each vegetable and the number of seeds that would germinate. It was a difficult task indeed and all the candidates failed to give the right answers.

At that time, Biribija ruled in the neighbouring kingdom. He had seven sons, but the youngest one was despised by his brothers and father. Though Biribija disliked his youngest son, he admired his judiciousness and intelligence.

When they heard Dharam Devata's invitation, Biribija's six sons went to Dharam Devata's court to try their luck. The youngest son, however, followed his brothers secretly. At the king's court when the six elder brothers failed the test, the youngest brother, who was sitting amongst the common people, stood up.

As he cleared his throat to present his answer, his brothers began to mock him. Unaffected by his brothers' taunts, the youngest brother answered, 'There are 180 immature seeds in each vegetable.'

To verify his claim, the gods sitting in the court directed him to cut open the vegetables and count the seeds. He was proved right. Dharam Devata was delighted and made youngest brother the king and named him Niyamraja. The Dongrias were also satisfied as they finally got a king to look after their welfare.

Dharam Devata instructed Niyamraja on how to manage political affairs and encouraged him to associate with his people in a friendly manner and to give their welfare the highest priority.

Niyamraja took Sita Penu the goddess of wealth along with him to the Dongria kingdom. Dharam Devata had offered Niyamraja five different kinds of seeds to cultivate on earth. Since Niyamraja wanted to present his people with an even greater variety, Dharam Devata requested all other hill gods to supply him with the best seeds available in their kingdoms. Thus, Niyamraja's wish was fulfilled.

But when Niyamraja came to earth, he did not find any hills. His wish was fulfilled as hills and mountains of various shapes and sizes begin to emerge. He maintained himself in the form of a great hill. The Dongrias had already begun to regard him as king of the hills. Thereafter, he enacted laws and principles on how to respond to nature's cycle under all circumstances. From then on, the Dongrias have been following all these instructions and living their lives as Mother Nature's own children. Centuries have passed and unlike their other counterparts, such as the Lanjia Saoras, who have converted to Christianity due to intense missionary activities, the Dongrias' faith in nature and Niyamraja has remained steadfast.

78

From Khasi Cup to World Cup: A Journey of Odisha's Hockey Culture

The Khasi Cup is an important event in the villages of Sundargarh district about 500 kilometres from Bhubaneswar, bordering Jharkhand and Chhattisgarh states. Every morning, in the villages of Sundargarh, young boys and girls step out of their homes with heavy bags on their backs and a spring in their steps. They head to local government schools where besides learning, they get an opportunity to play hockey. All these youngsters have a dream which has been nurtured by the many hockey legends who have originated from the region. Even little children who have barely started going to school know their hockey and want to be like the hockey legend and former captain of the Indian hockey team, Dilip kakeyi (uncle).

In the villages of Sundargarh, a child's first toy is a hockey stick fashioned out of bamboo and just a few inches taller than the owner. An eligible groom is judged not just by the number of bullocks he owns, but also by the goals he scores in a game of hockey. Sometimes, weddings are solemnized in a hockey face-off between the bride's and groom's families.

The biggest event is the Khasi Cup in which a series of games are held, and the winning team receives a goat, which is prepared for the victory feast that is shared by everyone. Without any set rules and having any number of members, ranging from twelve to fifteen, the idea of the Khasi Cup is to encourage young talent. This freestyle and uncoached way of playing hockey have led to the birth of several legendary hockey players over the last several decades, including Dilip Tirkey, Subhadra Pradhan, Lazarus Barla, Jyoti Sunita, Binita Tappo, Ignace Tirkey, and William Xalco. These players provide inspiration for both boys and girls since both genders participate in the games.

The story of the genesis of Odisha's hockey culture, however, begins a century ago in the tribal heartland in Sundargarh district. In the early twentieth century, christian missionaries arrived at several villages of the district to spread their teachings. Along with spreading the good news, they also taught hockey to the young people of the villages. Over the years, Sundargarh has evolved into an important region which has produced several hockey talents. These players have played at both national and international levels. In the villages of Sundargarh, practically everyone is to be found in a hockey field. Traditionally, the non-cultivation months from October to December are considered as the hockey season, which is when tournaments are held regularly where a number of village teams participate enthusiastically.

PONDICHERRY

79

The Creation

In the beginning, there was no land known as Pondicherry, but only the Bay of Bengal. One auspicious day, omnipotent and omnipresent God told the Lord of the Seas to recede a little so that He might have a small piece of land.

'What's that for, my Lord?' enquired the Lord of the Seas.

God replied, 'Human beings are thickly populating this earth. This rampant growth, I am afraid, will only lead to chaos and confusion. I foresee world wars, disaster, and untimely death....' God paused and heaved a sigh.

'I couldn't read your mind, my Lord. One more piece of land will only add to chaos and confusion,' interrupted the Lord of the Seas.

'I have not yet finished what I wanted to say,' continued God. 'Years later, when the entire world is in turmoil, when thugs and ruffians will rule the land, and when violence and hatred will become the order of the day, I want to see all my people in one place where they can live peacefully in harmony. They may converse in different languages but there will not be another Tower of Babel. They will look at one another as brethren and that will be the place where violence and hatred will lose their meaning. Above all, it shall be the place for a great yogi to build his ashram and from there his effulgent message shall radiate to different parts of the world. In short, the land shall be a Sanctuary of Peace.'

The Lord of the Seas beamed and said, 'A noble purpose, my Lord. Certainly, I'll do what you have said, but tell me where?'

'There,' said the Lord of the Universe, pointing to a particular place with his index finger. The Lord of the Seas gave commands. The water receded and gave birth to a landmass, now known as Pondicherry. That was some millions of years ago. And God Himself took personal care in nourishing that piece of land. And this He did to make His dream a reality.

80

Liquor Saves Pondicherry

On 25 May 1740, the main gate of Pondicherry was thrown open and Governor Dumas himself stood at the entrance of the gate to welcome the royal guests. And there entered the widow of Dost Ali Khan, with her daughters, and relations in twenty-two palanquins, followed by 1,500 cavalry, eight elephants, 300 camels, 200 bullock-carts and 2,000 beasts of burden. A few days later, the wife and the son of Chanda Sahib also reached Pondicherry.

Meanwhile, the Marathas occupied Arcot, without any resistance. Safdar Ali made peace with Raghuji Bhonsle and in August 1740, the Marathas recognized him as the new nawab. The whereabouts of Chanda Sahib was unknown to Raghuji, but he knew well that Chanda Sahib's wife and son were under the protection of Governor Dumas. Hence, Raghuji devised a scheme to trap the absconder. As a first step, Raghuji Bhonsle sent an intimidating letter to Governor Dumas and here follows an extract:

> We had consideration for you, and you have acted against us. You have given refuge to the Mughals in the town.... If you wish that we should be friends, you must give up this treasure, these jewels, these horses, these elephants, as well as the wife and the son of Chanda Sahib.... Our ships will arrive in a few days. It will be better for you to terminate the matter quickly....

The dauntless governor refused to surrender his guests. The following extract from his reply shows that he never wavered from asserting his authority, when required:

> As many of the Mughals as have been masters have treated
> the French with friendship, we have given shelter to the
> widow of the late Nawab Dost Ali Khan with all her
> family. Ought we to have shut our gates and leave them
> in the country? Men of honour are incapable of such
> cowardice.... You have written to me to make over to
> your horsemen this lady, her son, and the riches she has
> brought here. You, who are a nobleman full of bravery
> and generosity, what would you think of me if I were
> capable of such baseness? The wife of Chanda Sahib is in
> Pondicherry under the protection of the King of France,
> my master, and all French India would die rather than
> deliver her to you.... You threaten me finally that if I do
> not comply with your demand, you will send your armies
> against me and lead them hither yourself. I am preparing
> myself to the utmost of my ability to receive you well,
> and deserve your esteem, by showing that I have the
> honour of commanding the bravest nation in the world,
> who knows how to defend themselves with intrepidity
> against those who attack them unjustly....

Raghuji Bhonsle was offended. He wrote another letter that
demanded from Dumas not only the delivery of the wife and
the son of Chanda Sahib along with their treasures but also
a huge payment of rupees six crores and an annual tribute.
Dumas remained unperturbed. Raghuji Bhonsle wrote several
intimidating letters but to no avail. The enraged Maratha,
finding that his letters achieved nothing, sent an envoy to caution
Dumas of the impending disaster. Dumas received the envoy
with utmost politeness, showed him the supplies he had stored
up, the guns bristling on the ramparts, the drilled Europeans, the
armed sipahis; he hid, in fact, nothing from him. He then calmly
informed him, that so long as one Frenchman remained alive,

Pondicherry would not be evacuated. The power and resources of Pondicherry and its most daring governor impressed the envoy. When he took his leave, Dumas presented him with ten bottles of liquor labelled Cordials. The envoy handed over the bottles to Raghuji Bhonsle, who, in turn, gave them to his loving wife. She drank the Cordials and soon trouble started brewing. She asked for more. Where to go for more, if not to the governor of Pondicherry? Raghuji hesitated to seek favours from Dumas. Who could avert the fall of a man when there is a pestering woman by his side?

At last, Raghuji Bhonsle was ready for negotiations with Dumas. He withdrew all his demands and declared that he would erase from his memory the thought of Chanda Sahib's wife and son in Pondicherry. Dumas gave Raghuji Bhonsle thirty bottles of Nantes Cordials. Raghuji Bhonsle amicably shook hands with him and went on his way.

81

Know God, Know Peace

Glass windows of shops and houses get broken to smithereens as stones are hurled and hit their targets. The crowd of men and women run amok at the very sight of a foreigner whose look is enough to send a chill down the spine. The secretary of state is informed about this incident, taking place close to the Governor's House in Pondicherry. Policemen helplessly watch the show as they await orders from the higher-ups. The secretary arrives risking his life. The foreigner can neither be arrested nor taken to task for she is mentally deranged. And all that the secretary can think of at that moment is to seek the help of a saviour, Rev. Fr. A. S. Antonisamy.

The reverend reaches the place with a couple of trained nuns. He gives the errant foreigner a bottle of water to drink. As she gulps it down, trying to quench her thirst, the nuns with the help of constables in mufti, tie up her hands together and to the relief of the secretary, take her away to Fraternal Life Home at Ousteri.

The incident happened years ago in Pondicherry and Rev. Fr. Antonisamy became the talk of the town. What did the Father and the nuns do to the errant foreigner? No newspaper ever reported about it, but the author had the opportunity of listening to the entire story from the Father himself, over casual talk, one day.

It took several days for us to bring the foreigner back to shape. Thanks to the helpful doctors of Jawaharlal Institute of Postgraduate Medical Education & Research (JIPMER).

Later we found out that she was an Italian who had lost her mind over the loss of her passport and money. Then we began our frantic efforts to send her back to Italy. As a first step, we contacted the right people and soon heard from an Italian priest belonging to our congregation in Odisha. In his letter addressed to us, he wrote, 'That's my own sister who disappeared long ago. We didn't know her whereabouts for the last nineteen years.'

Today, the Fraternal Life Service Home for the mentally ill at Ousteri has around 700 patients and since the inception of the home in 1983, more than 300 have been treated and given jobs in the home itself. I came to know that the watchman of the home is one of them. Fr. Antonisamy, the founder, further narrated stories about two other patients and how they were treated and sent back home. Achievers are rarely content with what they achieve. They move from one project to another, take all the initiatives, establish it and allow others to continue with the work. Fr. Antonisamy is a real achiever. A multifaceted personality with high ideals, ever since his ordination, he has been a pioneer in various fields, always working towards the welfare of society. He has brightened the lives of many by bringing joy and contentment into many homes, through his multidimensional activities of the Rosary Foundation Centre. No wonder that the former Archbishop of Pondicherry and Cuddalore, Rev. Ambrose said of him, 'His characteristic mark seems to be his insight into the needs and wants of various types of people he desires to elevate to a better tone of human life by offering appropriate spiritual counselling, several practical ways, and means of material betterment.'

The upliftment of the downtrodden being one of his goals, he thoroughly plans and neatly executes it through various schemes. As Executive Director of Pondicherry Multipurpose Social Service Society, Fr. Antonisamy has built it up from scratch into a gigantic organization of social transformation in the Archdiocese, particularly through leadership training, cooperative and non-formal education, and by organizing credit unions among the rural poor. He made the village folk realize that they could not always bank on foreign aids for their welfare and living. In fact, it was he who kick-started the mobilization of their own resources for better utilization for the welfare of the community in each village. Fr. Antonisamy has played an enviable role in starting and nurturing the Holy Redeemer's Finance Corporation, whose main objective is to redeem persons paying exorbitant rates of interest for the money borrowed and to imbibe in them the virtue of saving. Sagodhara Sabha is another creation of his. It aims to give a helping hand to destitute men and women of over sixty years of age, irrespective of caste and religion. It provides food, clothing, shelter, and also money for the poor and the sick.

Pondicherry being a city of peace, all religions live hand-in-hand and Fr. Antonisamy found it easy to start his Inter-Religious Fraternal Life Community, which promotes meaningful dialogue amongst Hindus, Muslims, and Christians. And it is his sincere respect for all religions that brought harmony and peace to Pondicherry on 7 December 1992, the day after the destruction of the Babri Masjid at Ayodhya, thanks to his timely intervention.

Fr. Antonisamy has also been a columnist and a regular contributor to various magazines and journals. He has authored several books, throwing light on Christianity and comparative religions. His words and deeds reflect his philosophy: No God No Peace, Know God Know Peace.

PUNJAB

82

Baba Farid and Beera Bai

Baba Farid was a Sufi saint who lived in Punjab in the twelfth century. One day Baba Farid was meditating under a tree when he was disturbed by the twittering of birds in the branches. Annoyed at this intrusion, Baba Farid cursed the birds, 'What noise! Die ye all!' and immediately the birds fell dead on the ground. Stunned by this, Baba Farid mumbled, 'Oh no, please get up. No problem with your noise, go on.' Immediately, the birds came back to life and flew away. He was fascinated with his newfound power and was filled with a sense of vanity as he thought that he had attained union with God. He started off for home to inform his mother.

On the way as he passed by a village, he felt thirsty. He saw a woman whose name was Beera Bai, drawing bucketful of water from the well and pouring them into a channel nearby. Baba Farid asked for some water, but she said that he would have to wait as she was doing some important work. Baba Farid had no choice, but to wait. However, after some time, he got impatient and said, 'I have been waiting for such a long time, but you are not bothered about my request. You don't have no regard for a thirsty man!'

At this Beera Bai said, 'Baba don't get angry! There are no birds here that you can curse with death. Wait a little and let me finish my work.'

Now, Baba Farid was shocked and wondered how this woman knew about the incident with the birds and if she had divine powers, how did she attain them at such a young age.

He had meditated for thirty-six years and led an austere life to attain the divine powers.

After some time, when Beera Bai finished her work and offered water to Baba Farid, he asked her how she knew about the bird incident and why she was pouring water into the channel. The woman replied that, her sister's house, which was located at some distance away from the well, had caught fire and she was supplying water through the channel so that her sister could put out the fire. If she had stopped supplying the channel with water to attend to Baba, then her sister would have been in trouble. Thus, she did her immediate duty, which to help her sister. She also said that she saw the bird incident with her divine powers which she used sparingly.

On being asked how she attained her divine sight, Beera Bai replied that she attained it by diligently performing her duties as a wife, from the very first day she got married. She narrated an incident from her first night in her marital home. That night as all the family members slept in the same room, she suddenly heard her husband mumble for water. She got up and felt troubled, lest somebody see her and question her why she was up in the middle of the night. However, she decided that it was her duty as a wife to give water to her husband, come what may. Thus, she managed to find her way to the kitchen and got some water for her husband. However, when she returned to the room with a glass of water, her husband was fast asleep. Thus, she kept waiting with the glass at the bedside, should her husband again ask for water. It was nearly dawn. Her husband once again mumbled that he was thirsty and asked for water. Beera Bai immediately handed him the glass of water. The husband was surprised and asked how she managed to give him water immediately at his request. As Beera Bai narrated her story, Baba Farid looked at her kindly and affectionately and said, 'Perhaps that was the moment when God bestowed His grace and blessings on you, granting you the divine sight.'

Baba Farid realized that true meditation and service of God are to be found in doing one's duties and responsibilities with passion and honesty; and not in using the divine power to curse or harm others.

83

The Survivors

The cutting of trees had left the whole place denuded; the peacocks had stopped squawking; rooster feathers littered the ground. Oh! How the rooster would flutter around the old peepul tree the whole day and sleep on its branches at night! Such bright, colourful feathers it had! It was the last rooster that lived on that tree.

Devastation was writ large on the face of this hamlet, yet the residents were not ready to leave the place. Urban development had extended up to the village boundary, and a number of legal notices to vacate the village were slapped on the residents. They didn't have any alternative land; some had their dairy farms here; others had set their business in the nearby town; and the old people had emotional attachment to the land.

Suddenly one morning, a thundering bulldozer made its way into the village. The whole village went into a frenzy. Collecting whatever they could, men and women ran out, hitting their cattle with sticks, opening the poultry sheds, driving out cackling hens and bleating goats. Children, men, young and old, went running, dragging trunks and cots, huffing and puffing, crying and berating.

'Hey! You bloody...woe betide you...trying to destroy us! May the devil take you,' Bhanto Mehri was running, shouting, stumbling, babbling, and driving the goats, hitting them hard with her stick. With her hair tangled and matted, she looked like Kali the goddess of destruction. Another old woman was dragging a cot, while a mooing buffalo was running in circles.

Houses, baskets of chaff, and piles of cowdung cakes were crushed under the wheels of the bulldozer, as if a monstrous storm was gobbling up the whole village.

'They say they will build flats and big showrooms and lay concrete roads.'

At first people tried to block the bulldozer; then they quarrelled and argued, cursed the government, and finally gave up and started taking out their things. Children rambled around listlessly, watching the houses crumble one by one. Overcome by restlessness, they ran after the bulldozer.

'O, look there... Kallu's porch... there it goes!' Bhinda screamed.

'Shut up...you shameless boy,' Kartaro scolded him.

'Look Dhira! Your kitchen...boom-boom...bang bang,' the boys couldn't help bursting into laughter.

The boys competed with each other in running frantically to the next house, to give a helping hand in collecting the goods, and dragging them to the road outside the hamlet. The dogs kept on whining the whole night and the whimpering cats paced round and round the demolished village. The trembling voice of Bhanto could be heard echoing throughout the night; sometimes it seemed as if she was shrieking and wailing; and then laughing and clapping her hands: 'Ha...ha...ha'. A dreadful voice!

At dawn, the contractor and his lumbermen arrived with saws and axes to fell peepul, banyan, and kikar trees. These men were from the same village and had taken up jobs in the town as labourers.

'Hey, don't cut the trees...it will bring ruin,' Bhanto cried, with her arms raised to the sky.

The workers were startled for a moment.

'Why? What's wrong?' the contractor asked angrily.

They looked at each other with surprise, and then began to saw the trees with their axes. Thuk...thuk.

'You...bloody...' one of the lumbermen cursed the hard bark of the tree, and then went on hitting it.

After some time, they turned towards the water pitcher and Kartara said, 'Look, that was my house...that neem tree was planted by my grandmother.'

'Come on, hurry up...' the contractor called out.

'Bloody bastard...!' Kartara said under his breath. Binda and Sheeshu burst out laughing and continued their work.

Small sprightly birds were tumbling in the air, hollering and clamouring around the trees where their nests were hanging on the branches. And inside the nests, the fledglings looked so pitiable, opening and closing their beaks in fear.

'Look, how badly these birds are wailing; what a noise they have created? Oh, my God! What is happening!' Kartara said.

The whole place was filled with broken branches, broken nests buried underneath; crushed fledglings and smashed eggs... and above all, the clamour of the birds.

Children collected some broken nests.

'Taara and others have brought a truck,' someone came panting and announced.

Kallu, Gehlu, and Manna were running around, loading people's luggage onto the truck. People huddled together, discussing the land prices. All eyes were filled with tears as the truck moved away.

A gust of wind passed through the debris and scattered the bright, colourful feathers of the wild cock all around. 'That neem is still left, hurry up now,' the contractor called out to the workers.

Looking at the felled neem tree, the children became sad and quiet. They took out some small neem saplings which had grown under the tree.

'Look Ma, neem saplings! Where should we plant them?' Preeto asked his mother.

'Oh, my God...! We don't have a courtyard any more!'

Preeto was shocked to realize this.

Amaro's old mother and Gehlu's grandmother sat on the debris of a house; covered their faces with shawls and started keening. Nobody knew whether anybody had eaten anything since last night or not. Women and children were trying to rescue their belongings from the rubble.

Overnight, tents appeared on the road outside the village. Women made makeshift hearths with broken bins and prepared meals for their families. Depressed menfolk sat nearby, slurping tea from bowls. The children had caught hold of a stray donkey and tied a broken tin to its tail. Jeeto and Rano brought some newborn kittens who hadn't opened their eyes yet.

'Lo! Where did you find them?'

'Their mother has died...the poor things!'

'Oh...my dear...' Banti's heart melted.

Rano fetched some milk in a saucer; dipped cotton swabs in milk and squeezed the milk into the kittens' mouths.

The boys were thrashing the donkey with sticks and making it run around. The tin behind its tail was rattling giving them a reason to giggle.

'Look at them...enjoying, as if there is a wedding going on!'

'Ho...ho! Look, Kallu has jumped over its back.'

'And that too, facing its tail.'

'Fie on you... You fools...' Everyone burst into laughter.

'Hey! You better blacken its face.' Ambo said loudly.

The tea bowls slipped from the laughing mens' hands. The women broke into a fit of laughter. Revelling, laughing, jumping, and clapping, the boys ran after the donkey.

84

Women Empowerment and the Colours of Phulkari

Rekha Maan is a master crafts designer who, for the past twenty-five years, has been involved in preserving and promoting the languishing art of phulkari, a kind of embroidery particularly famous in the Punjab region of Patiala. Rekha Maan was born in Delhi. She received a post-graduate degree in cutting, tailoring, designing from the YMCA. After she was married to an agriculturist, she came to Patiala. Keen on improving the welfare of women, Rekha Maan turned to the wonderful craft of phulkari. Overcoming hurdles and obstacles, including adjusting to unfamiliar surroundings, cultural differences, among others, she found inspiration from her mother-in-law, who had in-depth knowledge of phulkari art. Later, with the encouragement and support from her husband and children, she embarked on a mission to restore the art of phulkari to its former glory. Defying opposition from relatives and with no adequate funds, she single-handedly set out to fulfil her dream of imparting knowledge and training to the rural women of Patiala and its surrounding areas with an objective to empower them.

Her objectives were clear from the start, namely, women empowerment, preservation of the phulkari craft, socio-economic empowerment of rural artisans, innovative design development—especially handicrafts and industrial development. Dedication, self-motivation, perseverance, and positive attitude kept her going. She took the first step towards achieving these goals in 1995, when she set up the Skill Development Training Centre at village Daru Kuta (Sular) in

Patiala. The centre started with thirty women sitting on mats made from plastic bags, and a teacher who was paid a monthly salary of fifty rupees taught these women the intricacies of this old traditional art form. The workshop was a success, and it attracted much media attention. An article about Rekha Maan in *The Tribune* brought banks and government organizations to her doorstep and since then there has been no looking back.

She has collaborated with the National Bank for Agriculture and Rural Development (NABARD) and Small Industries Development Bank of India (SIDBI) as consultant in their rural entrepreneurship development programmes and women entrepreneurship development programmes. She has conducted a number of need-based training programmes under the Ministry of Minority Affairs as master crafts trainer and worked extensively in the establishment of self-help groups.

In 1997–98, she established the Patiala Handicraft Workshop Cooperative Industrial Society Limited in order to organize her training workshops, as the number of target trainees and teachers were growing. She was invited by the Khadi Village Industries Commission (KVIC), a Government of India institution for its Scheme of Fund for Regeneration of Traditional Industries (SFURTI) to preserve the phulkari. The first SFURTI Patiala Phulkari Cluster report that was submitted to the KVIC by Rekha Maan's Phulkari Cluster was entitled *Mahila Phulkari Shilpkari ke Vikas ka Abhinav Karyakaram.*

Today, about 65,000 women phulkari artisans have received training under Rekha Maan's various programmes. Some of them now work abroad to promote phulkari; some of them are self-employed with their small units, many have become trainers and are making other women empowered and self-reliant. Her products are supplied to big export houses and she owns a company—Kajal International. Her other ventures include the Jan Shri Bima Yojna for 500 artisans, a documentary film on phulkari, exhibitions at international and national levels and running the Common Facility Centre and Rural Hut Showrooms for direct marketing of handicrafts, amongst others. Her work and achievements have been widely reported in the media, both print and electronic, and major television channels.

She is the founder and chairperson of the Patiala Handicraft Limited, Phulkari Cluster Head, Ex-director, Punjab Industry Federation, and proprietor of Kajal International.

In recognition of her services in the field of women empowerment and preservation and promotion of the phulkari, she has been honoured with many awards such as the National Award for Excellence in MSME (Micro, Small, and Medium Enterprise), 2014; Priyadarshni Award, 2001; NABARD Award for Rural Women Entrepreneurship, 1999; and National Mahila Excellence Award, 1996.

Rekha Maan has always believed in looking ahead, as she feels that work and dreams never come to an end. She still has plans for the future. She feels that the traditional art form of phulkari has to be preserved with the help of modern technology and she further wants to develop a software to use it for different purposes. This is all aimed to preserve the art, create new designs, and impart knowledge and training to the younger generation through online programmes, so that they can develop interest in such skills. She also wants to start a phulkari college where she can devise academic programmes with her own course content. These are some of the methods by which she wants to involve urban women in this enterprise. She also has ideas for expansion within a bigger international market as well as reaching out through online portals and social media.

RAJASTHAN

85

Moomal and Mahendra

The love story of Moomal and Mahendra is as old as time. One day Prince Mahendra of Amarkot and his friend Hameer from Gujarat went hunting for game. They spotted a deer and just as they were about to spear it, the deer ran towards the Kaak River, on the outskirts of the kingdom of Lodrava and took refuge in it. The two friends noticed an exquisite garden across the river. On the riverbank stood a double-storeyed palace. They were astonished to see such a magnificent palace in a desolate area. They dismounted from their horses, crossed the river, and entered the garden, all the while wondering why they have never heard of the existence of such a place in this area.

This palace belonged to a princess by the name Moomal. As Mahendra and Hameer approached the palace, Moomal looked out of the window upon hearing voices coming from her garden. Seeing the two well-built men, she called for her maid and said, 'These men seem to be gentlemen. Hurry downstairs and ask the servants to take good care of them.'

As per Moomal's instructions, the servants took care of the two gentlemen. As they sat down to eat the meal that was laid before them, one of Moomal's companions asked the guests who they were and where they have come from. Hameer introduced them both and in return asked, 'Whose companion are you? Who is our gracious host?'

Moomal's companion replied, 'Have you not heard of Moomal? Moomal the famous princess and loved by all in Jaisalmer. She lives here alone with her friends and to her belongs this beautiful palace and garden.'

Saying this, Moomal's companion left the room. Later, a maid, who had come to clear the dishes remarked, 'Miss Moomal lives in her own world, away from the stares of men. Several handsome, courageous, virtuous, and wealthy princes and kings have sent marriage proposals, but she did not even glance at them. She has sworn to marry only for love or else, she will not marry at all.'

Soon Moomal's companion returned and informed the two men that Moomal wishes to speak to one of them. Mahendra volunteered. He picked up his spear and started following the companion. Just as they reached a crossroads, the companion disappeared leaving Mahendra alone. He saw a massive lion sitting at the crossroads. He threw his spear at the lion and it suddenly fell down and burst open. It was a stuffed lion and was filled with fodder. Mahendra was impressed by this ingenious idea to test him. When he reached the palace, he was awestruck by Moomal's beauty and could not look away from her. Her eyes were like cauldrons filled with liquor. Her complexion resembled the colour of molten gold.

Entralled by Moomal's beauty, Mahendra blurted, 'Neither can a temple have such exquisite sculpture, nor a king own such beauty in his harem.'

At the same time, Moomal wondered, 'Such sharp eyes piercing into my soul.' Moomal and Mahendra looked at each other mesmerized. They stayed up the whole night gazing at each other and talking all night long unaware of the passing hours. In the morning, Hameer sent Mahendra a message saying that they must leave immediately. Mahendra reluctantly left Moomal promising her that he would return every night to meet her.

When Mahendra returned to Amarkot, he could not stop thinking about Moomal. His days were spent listlessly, and the nights became unbearable. Finally, Mahendra went to his cameleer and asked for a camel that would take him to Lodrava and bring him back the same night. Ramu the cameleer said that they do have such a camel. His name was Cheetal and he would take the prince to Lodrava at night and bring him back early in the morning. For the next eight months or so, Cheetal took Mahendra on his rendezvous with Moomal in her palace. He would start early in the night and return just before the first crack of dawn. His absence was, however, noticed by Mahendra's seven wives who went and complained to their father-in-law, Rana Visalday. Upon hearing the complaints, the rana called the youngest wife and asked her if there was anything peculiar about Mahendra when he returned. She replied that his hair would be wet. The father-in-law instructed her to collect the water from his hair in a container and bring it to him. The next morning, when the daughter-in-law brought a container to him, the father-in-law tasted the water and said, 'This water is from the Kaak River. It means that Mahendra is visiting Moomal in her palace.'

The seven wives were livid. When they found out that Cheetal carried Mahendra back and forth every day, they gave orders to chop off the camel's legs. That night, Mahendra kept waiting in vain. Finally, he heard from Ramu what had happened to Cheetal. Nevertheless, Mahendra was provided with another she-camel. But as this camel was not used to long journeys, Mahendra was late that night. He reached Lodrava just before the third phase of the night was about to end. In the meantime, Moomal was waiting for Mahendra and playing a game with her sister, Soomal, and her friends. Soomal had disguised herself as a man for the game. Finally, tired from the games, all of them went to sleep. Upon reaching Lodrava, Mahendra saw the disguised Soomal leaving Moomal's quarters. He was so outraged that he lashed the floor with his whip, and left.

Mahendra returned to Amarkot but could not take his mind off Moomal. The thought of Moomal with another man bothered him greatly.

Early next morning, Moomal found Mahendra's whip lying on the ground. She realized that he had come the night before but did not understand why he had left without meeting her. She wanted to find out and waited for his arrival that evening. Alas, Mahendra never came visiting again. Moomal grew pale longing for Mahendra. Finally, she sent a bard to Mahendra. Though the bard faced many hindrances along the way, he finally reached Mahendra and told him that Moomal was languishing waiting for his visit. Mahendra, however, was undeterred and replied, 'Go and tell Moomal that I am not a fan of her beauty. That night I got a glimpse of her character. I do not wish to be associated with her any longer.'

Moomal was shocked on hearing this and decided to meet him. She immediately left for Amarkot. When Mahendra got to know about Moomal's arrival, he realized that there might have been a misunderstanding and sent her a message that he would meet her the next morning. This filled Moomal with hope. However, the next morning, Mahendra devised a plan to test Moomal. He sent a servant with instructions. Accordingly, the servant arrived at Moomal's doorstep and said, 'Last night, a black serpent bit Prince Mahendra and he has passed away.' As soon as Moomal heard these words, she fell on the ground in shock. She took her last breath whispering Mahendra's name. When he heard the tragic news, Mahendra lost his mind. For the rest of his life, he lamented and grieved for his love.

Even today, the Kaak River near Jaisalmer sings of the eternal love story of Mahendra and Moomal.

86

Through the Eyes of Buaji

Once upon a time, there lived a king called Pradyuman Singh. He had a swan. The king loved the swan so much that he fed him pearls. Every evening, the swan would fly around the palace in whichever direction he felt like.

One evening, the swan landed on the terrace of one of the king's ministers. The minister's daughter-in-law, who was pregnant at the time, had heard that if a woman eats swan meat during her pregnancy, her child will grow into a powerful, intelligent, and lucky person. Her mouth watered as she saw the swan sitting on the terrace. She caught hold of the swan, took it to the kitchen, cooked the meat, and ate it. She made sure that no one, including her mother-in-law, father-in-law, or even her husband got a hint of this incident because now she was afraid that if the king got to know what she had done to his beloved swan, misfortune would befall them.

Meanwhile, when the swan did not return to the palace that night, the king and the queen were distraught. Search parties were formed and sent to all four directions, but they could not find the swan. The king sent word to the neighbouring cities and villages that if anyone brought any information about his swan, he or she would be handsomely rewarded.

A fortnight passed. Still there was no news of the swan. Since the king and the queen loved the swan dearly, their despair knew no bounds. One day, a procuress arrived at the palace and said to the king that she could locate the whereabouts of the swan, although she would need some time.

The king replied, 'Neither the priests nor the astrologers of my kingdom have been able to do find the swan. Even the most skilled soldiers have failed, so how will you manage to do so?'

The procuress replied, 'I am confident of my capabilities. If Your Highness commands, I shall fetch the stars. Please give me some time and provide me with the required money. I assure you that even if I cannot bring back the swan, I will at least inform you about its whereabouts.'

The king agreed and the procuress set out on her mission.

First, she collected information about all the wealthy families and if any women were expecting a baby in those families. She was familiar with the fact that some pregnant women craved swan meat during their period of confinement. She was also aware that no ordinary woman would dare to capture the royal swan and that it was the doing of a wealthy person.

After much investigation, she found that the minister's daughter-in-law was pregnant. Therefore, she deduced that perhaps the swan had landed on their terrace and the pregnant woman had killed the swan.

The procuress devised a plan. She knew that in order to form a close bond with any woman, it was imperative to know about her background. Thus, she went to the daughter-in-law's village. On reaching, she enquired the names and all the important events of the daughter-in-law's family. She discovered that one of the aunts had left home with a sage at a young age. Therefore, she planned to visit the minister's daughter-in-law pretending to be her long-lost aunt and that way, she would be able to get all the information. It was a great plan!

The procuress went to the minister's house. Displaying motherly love and affection, she said to the daughter-in-law, 'Child, I am your aunt. Today we meet for the first time. You must be aware that I had left home a long time ago with a sage. I returned recently and when I met bhaiyya, he told me that you are now married and that your father-in-law is the minister of this kingdom. Upon hearing this, I longed to see you, so I decided to come and see you. I am delighted to meet you finally. May God keep you happy and bless you with a strong and powerful son. I will return day after tomorrow, but I will visit again with bhaiyya and bhabi to shower our affection on your kid.'

The naive daughter-in-law believed her and said, 'Buaji, please stay for a couple of weeks. Why do you have to go back in such a hurry?'

What else could the procuress-turned-buaji ask for? She gladly accepted the invitation. Within a couple of days, the niece and the aunt got along pretty well. One day, the aunt casually mentioned, 'Dear daughter, if a pregnant woman eats swan meat during her pregnancy, then the results are wonderful. The newborn child will grow to be strong and powerful. However, swans are only found in Mansarovar, nowhere else. I wonder how we can get one for you.'

Hearing this, the daughter-in-law confided in bauji about her incident with the swan. The buaji replied, 'Child, it is surprising that your king even had a pet swan. Whatever you did was right. However, you should not mention this incident to anyone. Perhaps, you shouldn't even have mentioned it to me. But that's all right, I won't spill the beans, so you should not be worried.'

A few days later, the procuress said, 'Dear child, if you confess to God about eating the swan, then not only will he forgive you, but he will bless you twofold. I will talk to the temple priest and make sure that while you confess your sin, there will be no one except us, not even the priest.'

The daughter-in-law agreed.

The procuress stealthily went to the king and said, 'As per the promise I had made, I have identified the whereabouts of the swan.' She further went on and narrated the entire story to the king.

The king cried, 'Where's the proof?'

She said, 'On such and such day, you should come to the temple and hear the swan eater's confession.'

The king agreed to the plan.

On the agreed day, the procuress went ahead and hid the king in a drum on an elevated platform. Later, the aunt and the niece arrived at the temple for the confession.

The doors of the temple were open. Neither the priest nor any soul was present there. The aunt asked, 'So child, what happened that day?'

The minister's daughter-in-law began to narrate the incident. But before she went any further, a thought struck the procuress. She was worried if the king was listening and signalled the drum and said, 'Dhol re dhol, sunn re bahu ka bol!' Dear drum, listen to the daughter-in-law here.

It was at that moment that the niece had an epiphany. She realized that something was fishy; probably she was conned. She did not utter a single word.

Buaji prodded her on, 'So child, what happened next?'

The niece replied, 'It so happened next that I woke up from my dream.'

And at these words, the aunt's soul woke up too; it weighed heavier than the pregnant niece.

87

Khichan's Demoiselle Cranes and a True Reflection of Atithi Devo Bhava

As dawn breaks over the sleepy village of Khichan during the winter months, the palatial havelis wake up from their deep slumber to the chaotic 'krok-krok' calls of thousands of demoiselle cranes in the skies above. The scene appears spectacular for visitors, but for the villagers it is just another morning of celebrating life with the winged visitors during the winter months every year. These are migratory birds—the demoiselle cranes. Every year towards the end of August, just after the monsoon rains have ceased, they fly in flocks from their breeding grounds on the plains and steppes of Eurasia and Mongolia to the Thar Desert. All of a sudden, the sleepy village of Khichan is transformed into a chaotic, noisy place. The birds descend upon the village to feed and rest throughout the day, only to retire for the night on a nearby mound. The next morning, the cranes are back again. A large space has been demarcated and fenced to feed the cranes every morning. Every day throughout the season, between November to February, 500 kilograms of grains are spread on the ground for the birds. This is all paid by monetary donations from the Jain community in the village. After the cranes have had their breakfast, they gather beside a pond.

The story of Khichan's association with the migratory birds is ancient, but their conservation effort is only five decades old and has a connection with Odisha. It all started with Ratanlal Maloo's uncle, who was originally from Khichan, but had settled down in Odisha. One day, he left Odisha for Khichan, along with Ratanlal Maloo, to take care of his ageing grandmother, who was ailing and had recently celebrated her hundredth birthday. Little did either of them know at that time, that the decision of returning to their roots would change not only Ratanlal's life but also the lives of thousands of innocent birds.

Once in Khichan, Ratanlal found it difficult to sit idle and his uncle entrusted him with a job—that of feeding grains to pigeons, sparrows, and peacocks that frequented a particular place on the outskirts of the village. Being devout Jains, both Ratanlal and his wife liked the idea. They carried sackful of grains to the feeding ground and distributed them amongst the birds. Initially, there were only squirrels, sparrows, pigeons, and occasionally peacocks, but one fine day in September, he saw for the first time, a dozen of large black and grey birds feeding. On enquiring, the villagers told him that they were migratory birds that frequent Khichan every winter. They were called demoiselle cranes or kurja in Rajasthani.

Ratanlal started observing them closely. Their numbers increased to eighty by November, but in February all of them disappeared overnight. He had to wait for another year. This time their number was 150 or so. This number kept on increasing and at present, there is a staggering number of around 25,000 cranes who frequent the area and feed and reside during the migratory season.

In the initial stages, it was not an easy task for Ratanlal. As the number of cranes increased, often the village dogs would attack the cranes, leaving the cranes either dead or badly injured. To protect the birds, Ratanlal first convinced the village panchayat to allocate a suitable space on the outskirts of the village. Later, he coaxed the local people from the Jain community to help him build a six-foot high fence. The enclosed area was called the chugga ghar, feeding home. Ratanlal then got a granary made to store grains with donations that started pouring in from members of the Jain community. He also got a room constructed to treat the injured cranes.

Today, in the winter months, standing on a nearby terrace beside the chugga ghar at the break of the dawn, one can witness a beautiful spectacle. Flocks of demoiselle cranes marching towards the chugga ghar. Apart from being a spectacular display of wildlife, it is associated with a spiritual connection aptly described by the Sanskrit phrase 'Atithi Devo Bhava'. A visitor is like God.

After they have been fed, the cranes head off to the nearby lake, Vijaya Sagar. Here they can be seen gobbling copious quantities of pebbles that are found in abundance on the lake shore. A strange habit it may seem, but this process aids digestion. Since the grains are eaten whole, the pebbles act as a digesting agent. Just before sunset, the cranes call it a day and fly away to Malher Rim, a sand dune about 25 kilometres away from Khichan, where they spend the night, standing on one leg. The next morning, these beautiful birds are back in Khichan.

SIKKIM

88

Lepcha Folk Belief on the Origin of Insects

A long time ago, in a village near the forest was a lee, a traditional Lepcha hut. In that hut lived a nikung, grandmother, and her little granddaughter. Both of them loved each other very much. The parents of this little girl were poor and had other children to look after. Since the grandmother lived alone, she brought the little girl to live with her. This arrangement also helped the girl's parents as they had one less mouth to feed.

The village had very few people, and the houses were located very far from each other. Every morning, after a heavy meal of rice, vegetables, and meat, the little girl set off to a nearby school. In the afternoon, Grandmother would keep lunch ready for her by the time she returned from school. Together they worked in the field and sowed buckwheat, corn, beans, soya, and other grains. They would go to the forest in search of yam and other wild vegetables. Sometimes they would trap small animals in the snares too.

In one corner of the house, there was a hearth. This hearth was used for cooking, cutting meat, and hanging strips of meat over the fire. This was also a place where stories were narrated. Every night after supper, Grandmother would tell stories to her granddaughter. Many a night, while listening to her grandmother's stories, the little girl would fall asleep on the warm floor beside the hearth. This little girl had also learnt by heart almost all the prayers that Grandmother had taught her.

One afternoon, as usual, the little girl returned from school. She found her grandmother in bed. She was ill. So that day, the little girl had to go all alone to the forest to collect firewood. As she was leaving, Grandmother told her about the malevolent spirit of the jungle and said that she must not giggle and stay quiet.

As the little girl was collecting firewood, she suddenly felt that someone was watching her. She looked around but did not see anyone. After a while, she heard a strange noise and she was terrified. Slowly the noise became louder and louder. Within no time, she saw a giant walking towards her. She was so frightened that she dropped the firewood and ran back to the hut. The little girl narrated everything to Grandmother who realized that it was the evil giant who had made her sick and was trying to eat her granddaughter. Grandmother hurriedly closed the doors and windows and told the little girl to remain quiet. Grandmother then started heating the cornerstone in the hearth.

As expected, the giant arrived at the hut and stood outside the door. Grandmother said in a loud voice, 'Oh! Where has my granddaughter gone! She has not reached home yet.' She wanted the giant to hear this and replied in her granddaughter's voice, 'Grandma, please open the door. I am right here outside.'

Grandmother answered, 'Wait, my dear, Grandma is getting out of her bed.'

After some time, the giant again said, 'Grandma, Grandma open the door. I am in trouble.' Grandmother replied, 'Please wait. Grandma is putting on her slippers.'

Meanwhile, Grandmother and her little granddaughter were heating the stone. After some moments, the grandmother replied, 'Please wait, dear, I am taking out the thorns from my feet. They are killing my feet and I cannot stand up and walk.'

Thus, the giant asked her to open the door several times and wanted to come in, but Grandmother kept refusing under various pretexts. After a while, the giant again begged her to open the door. This time, Grandmother told the giant to go to the lower level of the hut where essential household items were stored and to sit just below the window of the upper level. She then told him to open his mouth wide so that she could surprise him with a special delicacy. The giant did as Grandmother instructed.

Grandmother asked once again, 'Have you opened your mouth?'

By this time, Grandmother was standing at the window with the hot stone in her hand. Looking up with his wide-open mouth, the giant answered, 'Yes.'

The moment he said yes, Grandmother dropped the hot stone into his mouth.

Like a fireball the stone went straight to the giant's stomach. Cha ta ta ta ta ta -Pa-tash- Pa-tash....

The giant died instantly. His body started decaying and different kinds of insects such as mosquitoes, leaches, bugs, lice, and so on, crawled out of the giant's body. According to Lepcha folk belief, all these blood-sucking insects were born from this evil giant's body, and they multiplied on earth. Since they originated from an evil body, they cause trouble to human beings and other living creatures.

89

Ageing: A Child's Tough Question

Once upon a time, an old mother and her family lived in a village. This family had a son, a daughter-in-law, and a small grandson. It was a happy family. The mother had become a widow when her boy was only a child. After the death of her husband, she struggled a lot and often felt lonely, but the thought of her little boy kept her going. She devoted her entire life to looking after her son.

When the son grew up, his mother arranged for his marriage. Soon, the son became a father. The old woman was blessed with a grandson. Her son and daughter-in-law used to work in the fields to meet the needs of the family and the old woman took care of her grandson. She found great joy in taking care of the baby. She would play with him, sing to him, tell him stories, and put him to sleep. The bond between the grandmother and the baby grew stronger each passing day.

Apart from looking after the child, the old woman also cooked for the family, fed the cattle and, kept the house neat and tidy. Both her son and daughter-in-law loved her. They knew the house was in good hands so they would go work at their jobs without any stress. However, as days turned into years, the mother became very old and weak. There came a time when she could no longer work as before. One day, while playing outside with her grandson, she got drenched in the rain and fell ill. Her son called the local witch doctor, the shaman, to cure his ailing mother, but it was all in vain. A shaman from the nearby village knew that she was possessed by the jungle spirit and with his powerful amulets tried to cast out the evil spirit but the old woman still did not get well.

With the mother-in-law sick, the responsibilities of her daughter-in-law increased substantially. She had to look after her house, her son, and take care of her ailing mother-in-law. Matters became worse as the old mother was completely bedridden.

Though the daughter-in-law knew that she had to take care of her mother-in-law, she was beginning to feel exasperated with the situation. She forgot all that her mother-in-law had done for the family and her little son all these years. She started complaining to her husband every day. She would say, 'She is going to die anyway, what's the use of taking care of this log? Take her to the jungle and leave her in the cave. We have tried everything to cure her, but nothing seems to work.' Finally, the son and the daughter-in-law decided to take the old mother to the jungle and leave her there alone.

One evening, as planned, the son lifted his mother from her bed and put her in a doko, basket. Suddenly the grandson asked, 'Why do you want to take my beloved grandma to the jungle?' He asked his parents many more questions. Both parents tried to assure the child that his grandmother would soon return home after she regained her health in the forest, but the grandson was not happy at all. He also decided to go along with his father to the jungle. So, he followed his father, who was carrying his ailing grandma in the doko.

When they reached a particular spot in the jungle, they found a cave; the father took his mother into the cave and left her there alone. He also threw the doko nearby. The grandson knew that his father would leave his grandma in the forest but did not understand why his father threw the doko in the jungle. So he asked his father, 'Father, why are you leaving this doko here?' The father replied, 'I'm leaving my mother here in the jungle, so what is the use of this doko now?' His son answered thoughtfully, 'Father, when you and Mother grow old one day, I will have to bring you both to the jungle. So, which doko should I use to carry both of you?' This question troubled his father deeply. He realized that if you harm others, you will be harmed in return.

Ageing is not a curse but a natural phenomenon. Everyone will experience this process of ageing sooner or later. The father was ashamed and put his mother back in the doko. Grandmother, Father, and the grandson trudged back home silently.

....

90

Tikalal Niroula: An Eminent
Personality from Sikkim

A society preserves the memory of a person who makes a positive contribution towards it. There is a Nepalese saying that goes, 'A crow can also manage his life'. So, a question arises, what is the aim of man's life? Is it only to manage one's life or to do something good for others too? To do a kind deed is not only dhamma but it also gives meaning to one's life. Tikalal Niroula is one such person who made his life meaningful and is alive in the memory of the people of Sikkim.

Tikalal Niroula was born in 1919 in Central Pandam in East Sikkim. Sikkim at that time was ruled by a king. For the masses, the thikadars were their lords. Sikkim was like France before the revolution. The life of the poor peasants was hard, and they were not in a position to work freely in their fields. Different systems of bonded labour such as jharlange, kuruwa, bethi, and kalobhari were prevalent. The peasants did not get enough time to work in their fields as they had to spend a good part of their working hours in their landlord's estates. They were also harassed by the kar or tiro, a tax system. Tikalal Niroula was a Brahmin and received his education at home. He was trained to become a priest. As he visited many places and families carrying out his religious duties, he became aware of the then current political environment and the growth and development of the nascent feelings for democracy and also the state of affairs outside the kingdom of Sikkim.

After 1945, the people of Sikkim demanded the representation of the people and also an end to the thikadari system. From this time onwards, Tikalal Niroula identified himself as one of the workers of Sikkim State Congress. The influential Congressmen in Sikkim at that time were Tikalal Niroula, Brihaspati Prasai, Adhiklal Pradhan, Narendra Nar Singha, and Chandralal Adhikari. These leaders are always highlighted in the pages of history, but the role played by the ordinary man remains hidden. To make people aware about the happenings in the country, Tikalal Niroula started the pad yatra (march), going from door to door informing the people of Sikkim about the political situation around the country. He knew everybody in Sikkim and everyone knew him and called him Pandam's Tikalal Niroula.

In order to make people realize about the political situation in India and what was happening outside Sikkim, Tikalal Niraula took his fellowmen to the Indian National Congress's annual meetings at Patna, Guwahati, and Calcutta. The Sikkim State Congress took the initiative to abolish the thikadari system. In the 1974 election, Tikalal Niroula filed his nomination as a Congress candidate, but the party gave the ticket to Kehar Singha Karki. Tikalal Niroula did not oppose the party's decision but wholeheartedly supported the party's candidate, Karki. His association with the Congress party continued over the years.

Apart from this contribution to the politics of Sikkim, local folk remember his contribution to social work. If anyone fell sick in the villages, Niroula would take them to hospitals either in Gangtok or in the neighbouring regions of Kalimpong or Siliguri. He would leave the patients in the hospital only after making sure that they were in good hands. He sometimes acted as a guide to those who wished to go on pilgrimages. His most significant contribution was the establishment of schools. He would visit villages and towns and tell the local people about the need and value of education. Soon he started building schools. After constructing a school, he looked for teachers. Sometimes, teachers were brought in from outside Sikkim as well. In order to pay the salary of the teachers, he would call for meetings with the village folk and encourage them to raise funds for a good cause. He would visit the government offices urging authorities to recognize schools and bear the expenses of running the schools.

In Central Pandam, all the schools, except the school in Duga and Rangpoo, were established by Tikalal Niroula in the 1940s. He even went to Bermoik in West Sikkim and established a school there. He appointed an educated youth from Central Pandam in order to teach in Bermoik. His family members say that there are around forty schools established by Tikalal Niroula. For his contribution towards education, the Government of Sikkim has named the Central Pandam Higher Secondary School Tikalal Niroula Higher Secondary School.

Tikalal Niroula's thoughts were inspiring. K. N. Sharma, who knew Tikalal Niroula, shares a childhood memory about him. Sharma narrated that when he was young, a person died in his neighbourhood, and they had to perform the death rituals. They called on a priest to perform the rites, but the priest declined to do so because the deceased belonged to a poor family and they could not meet his village fees. Sharma's bereaved neighbour's family members were very sad and narrated the episode to Sharma's father. Tikalal Niroula came to know about this from Sharma's family and Niroula asked the priest to perform the rituals for one rupee. He stated that for the performance and continuity of religious and cultural rituals and rites, priests have equal responsibility towards the preservation and promotion of cultural and religious heritage, so a priest should perform his duty irrespective of the economic or social status of the family. Sharma recalls Niroula saying, 'If we, under the pretext of low economic or income bracket, force someone into a very tight situation and compel him to leave his traditional religion and adapt to a new faith, then we have to bear the burden of sin.'

TAMIL NADU

91

The Righteous King

In the Chola kingdom, around 205 BCE, King Manuneethi Cholan was known for his strong adherence to the principles of justice. He was known as the one who was fair towards both friend and foe when it came to dispensation of justice and his commitment to it was unconditional—without fear or favour. His impartiality was evident in a case concerning his own son, when he had to deliver a verdict. Till today, this story is retold as a lesson on fairness, honesty, and integrity.

In front of his place, King Manuneethi Cholan had a large metal bell installed in order to help him dispense justice efficiently. Anyone who sought justice could ring the bell. Once the bell was rung, the king would respond by hearing the case and deliver his fair and just verdict. One day, a cow marched towards the palace and rang the bell, pleading for justice from the king. The king came out and was informed that the cow had lost her calf. The king was informed that the calf lost its life after it had come under the wheels of the chariot of king's son, Prince Veedhividangan.

The prince was riding in his chariot on his way to the temple. People were lined up on the streets and cheering the prince amidst the loud beating of drums. In the midst of this commotion, a calf strayed onto the path of the chariot and accidentally came under the wheels and in the process, it lost its life. The cow was in a terrible shock to see her calf dead and thus went to the king to seek justice. Though it was a terrible accident, Manuneethi Cholan was deeply moved by the plight of the cow. The king deliberated with his council of ministers. They were unwilling to be a part of the king's ultimate decision and at the end, the king made his decision. The ministers advised the prince to perform rituals as a mark of penance as per the sacred texts. However, the king was not convinced. He refused to accept the decision of his ministers and drove his chariot over his son's body. This action of the king perplexed his subjects but Manuneethi Cholan's action had underscored his philosophy—everyone is equal before law, both humans and animals.

92

The Story of Thirunaallaipovar
He Who Will Go Tomorrow

In ancient Tamil Nadu, during the time of the Chola kings, in Adanur village in Thanjavur district, there lived a man called Nandanar. He was a great devotee of Lord Shiva. But since he belonged to the Paraiyar subcaste, one of the most oppressed of the Dalit castes, he was not allowed inside a temple to pray.

Nandanar earned his living making musical instruments such as the drum out of leather. He was skilled in music and dance. He often worshipped Shiva by singing spiritual songs and dancing in divine ecstasy. Yet his devotional offerings were always confined to the grounds outside the temple. Nandanar yearned to see his Lord even if it was from outside the temple precincts. He visited several temples and would stand outside, singing hymns to Lord Shiva. He would often go into ecstatic dance when his emotions took over.

One of the temples he visited was Sivalokanathar Temple in Tripunkur. As usual, he stood outside the temple, hoping to get a darshan of his Lord. As visitors to such temples are aware, Lord Shiva's faithful mount, Nandi the bull is placed opposite Shiva's statue, across the sanctum, as if ready to be mounted at the Lord's will. Nandi, at Sivalokanathar Temple, had become enraged at the Dalit devotee's presumption in approaching his Lord. He had attempted to thwart the darshan by growing in size, attempting to block the view of the Lord from his devotee. As Nandanar stood outside shedding tears, the Lord compassionately intervened on behalf of his devotee and told Nandi to step aside. And so, to this day, in Tripunkur, an oversized Nandi sits a little to the side of the main deity, instead of directly in front of him—placed so on the Lord's orders that his devotee may see him. After fulfilling his cherished dream of getting a darshan of his Lord in Tripunkur, Nandanar returned to his village.

In those days, the biggest Shiva temple in the region was in Thillai, in present-day Chidambaram, where Shiva is worshipped as Nataraja the cosmic dancer. After having visited several temples including Sivalokanathar, in the areas surrounding his village, Nandanar's greatest desire was to have a darshan of his Lord at Thillai. However, the entire area of Thillai was off limits for Dalits and if any Dalit entered the temple premises they could be punished with the death penalty. However, his desire and yearning remained strong, even though he knew it would most likely be a futile effort and even a dangerous one. Every day he would console himself by saying, 'Tomorrow, I will definitely go to Thillai.' That is how he was given the moniker, Thirunallaipovar—he who will go tomorrow.

One day 'tomorrow' finally dawned for him, when his yearning overcame his diffidence. He made the pilgrimage on foot to Thillai but was not allowed entry into the city. Thus, he could not even reach the temple which was at the centre of the city. He circumambulated the city several times, just as he would have circumambulated the temple and then he fell asleep exhausted on the street. Lord Shiva appeared to him in a dream, he was granted permission to enter the city gates by the Lord himself. 'I will inform the Brahmins who guard the temple of your arrival. They will let you in, have no fear. They will prepare a sacrificial fire for you to walk through first. Walk through it triumphantly and come and join me.' So said Shiva lovingly to his devotee and disappeared.

When Nandanar woke up, he realized to his disappointment that it was but a dream. Nevertheless, he decided to try his luck. When he reached the city gates, he was amazed to see a group of Brahmins already waiting for him. They had been apprised as promised by the Lord, to make way for his devotee. They had prepared the fire as per the stipulations of Lord Shiva and Nandanar walked through it, emerging on the other side with a brilliant visage of light. He was thereupon escorted with much honour and pomp inside the temple. Thus, at last, Nandanar had a darshan of his beloved Lord inside the temple.

His travails of gazing at the Lord from afar were over. The Lord took him unto Himself as one of his truest devotees. There, at the Thillai temple, Nandanar merged with Lord Shiva, leaving behind his physical body. And thus it was that a Dalit devotee attained the status of a saint in Tamil Nadu. Among the sixty-three canonical Shaiva saints known as Nayanmar in Tamil, he is the only Dalit. He is also the eighteenth, amongst the sixty-three. The remaining saints who came after him in the canon, often Brahmins, sang praises of the Dalit saint in the canonical literature they had left behind.

93

Insatiable Fire

Darkness and fear engulfed the vast swathe of paddy fields dotted with small huts. It was a cold December night. In fact, it was Christmas night and the next day in some parts of the world would be filled with Boxing Day revelry. But tonight, the air was foul. Things have fallen apart. In the dead of night, Kumaran and his elder sister were walking in the midst of the farmland, singing a popular song from a Tamil film to drive away fear. It was already well past 10 p.m. and they were returning from a neighbour's house. All of a sudden, the eerie silence was broken by the sound of gunshots. From a distance they could see armed henchmen of the landlords, holding torches, rushing towards the huts.

Stories of men and women in Keezhvenmani being kept in illegal detention, canned and forced to drink water mixed with cow dung for any act of indiscretion was nothing new. Occasionally, the henchmen would come and pick up people on one pretext or the other. Their parents, like the other Dalits, accounted for a substantial chunk of the population in Nagapattinam district, remained landless labourers struggling to survive in the face of perpetual distress.

The conditions of the labourers in the fertile Cauvery delta remained the same, even after the change of government in 1967 when the Dravida Munnetra Kazhagam (DMK) took power over from the Congress. Of late, comrades of the red flag party used to frequent their huts at nights and the recent past has witnessed a protest demanding a hike of half a measure of paddy for the harvest of every gunny bag. The usual share of the coolie was only one measure.

As such, the gunshots that broke the silence on the night of 25 December 1968 rattled Kumaran and his sister. In mortal fear, the small boy clasped his sister's hands and both of them stopped, unable to move ahead. 'Hey, thambi, we will hide here rather than getting killed,' she said and held him closely as they took shelter in a field. They remained silent and held their breath as some men came very close by their hiding spot. They were the landlord's henchmen, numbering 100 or so. Closing escape routes, these men started firing indiscriminately, fatally wounding two men. Some wielding sickles and wooden clubs attacked those trying to escape. People ran helter-skelter and many of them took refuge in Ramiah's hut.

Today, at the age of fifty-six, Kumaran, who works in a sawmill in Keezhvenmani, recalls, 'Only Ramiah had patta for his hut. Others didn't have the patta for their huts since the entire land belonged to the landlord. All those who took shelter there entertained an illusion that it would be spared as it was on patta land. But the henchmen bolted the door from outside and set it on fire.'

'Soon after committing the crime, they reached the police station seeking protection and the police obliged,' says Kumaran.

Forty-four lives were lost that night; twenty women, nineteen children, and five old men were burned alive. A pall of gloom descended on the village. The police arrived at the scene a day after the horrific incident. Initially a case of internal rivalry was booked against the miscreants. It created ripples across the country. Within a couple of days, CPI (M) political party stalwarts, Jyoti Basu and B. T. Ranadive arrived at Keezhvenmani and the Left trade unions launched massive protests in Coimbatore and Vellore, forcing the DMK government to book a few landlords, including Gopalakrishna Naidu, the prime accused.

The trial went on for two years in Nagapattinam and

the Sessions Court in 1970 awarded ten years prison term to Gopalakrishna Naidu and others. However, to the disappointment of the victims, the Madras High Court overturned the judgement and acquitted them in 1975. '...there was something astonishing about the fact that all the twenty-three implicated in the case should be mirasdars (landlords). Most of them were rich men, owning vast tracts of lands and Gopalakrishna Naidu possessed a car. The evidence did not enable their lordships to identify and punish the guilty', reads the judgement.

However, this was not the end. A group of young people wedded to the ideology of Marxism and Leninism, propagated by Charu Mazumdar in distant Bengal and living underground with aliases got friendly with Kumaran, though he was unaware of their purpose. As a youth, he too got converted to that ideology. Months later in December 1980, Gopalakrishna Naidu was murdered and pamphlets hailing the CPI (ML) and Vinodh Mishra were strewn around. Well, for some it was poetic justice but, though the fire has been extinguished the embers still linger on.

TELANGANA

94

Fists Against Spears

People in Medaram village were sad; they thought that a curse has befallen them. A drought loomed over the region for years, over the dried-up Godavari River, and the entire forest region. The Koya community looked at the clouds hoping for a drizzle. Sammakka was revered as a goddess among the Koyas. She sat in deep contemplation after a few of her people consulted her and sought her help to tackle the drought. She consoled them but wondered what could be done to solve the problem.

She was flooded with memories of how people had been so fond of her from her childhood. Her father had narrated to her how she was found as an infant, guarded by a pride of lions, and how they regarded her as a gift from God and raised her with great reverence. This story instilled in Sammaka a great sense of responsibility and commitment towards her village. As she grew into a woman, her compassion for villagers had grown over the years. Her hands were magical, and her words were soothing. Many villagers consulted her for advice. Their worries were warded off as soon as they spoke to her. However, the devastating drought tormented her.

Sammakka was married to Pagididda Raju, the chief of the Koya tribe, and they were blessed with a daughter, Saralamma, and a son, Jampanna. Pagididda Raju sensed his wife's anxiety about the drought but could not ask any further questions; he knew that she had other children to worry about, apart from her own.

In these stressful times, one day, a messenger arrived on

horseback from the Kakatiya royal court. The messenger met Pagididda Raju and his son-in-law, Govinda Raju. Sammakka and her children sat listening to the conversation between the men. Suddenly, in a stern voice, Pagididda Raju said to the messenger, 'If your king wants to end the peace by imposing taxes ruthlessly on our people, let it end. My people would never extend their hands to beg although they are at the jaws of death caused by this prolonged drought. Tell your king that hunger can take away our lives but not our honour. We are peace-loving people, but we are also capable of responding to pressure tactics and meaningless violence.'

The messenger smiled crookedly and rode away towards the capital.

Sammakka and her family gathered together as Pagididda Raju tightened his grip on the handle of his sickle, signalling an imminent period of unrest.

Soon, word spread through drummers and horn-blowers about the impending war with the Kakatiya king. People prepared and waited patiently with sickles, axes, spears, and other available weapons to face the Kakatiya army. With the rising sun, Pagididda Raju and his Koya tribe bravely faced the soldiers of Kakatiya army. They slew as many soldiers as possible. However, the increasing number of dead Koya warriors signalled an impending defeat. Pagididda Raju, his first wife, Nagulamma, daughter Sarakka, and son-in-law, Govinda Raju, were killed one after the other. Jampanna was butchered and thrown into the Sampangi Vagu, and the stream turned red with his blood. Sammakka, however, continued her fight against the Kakatiya soldiers. Her aggressiveness threatened the Kakatiyas and they sent her a peace proposal which she declined.

The Kakatiyas finally devised a plan to finish off Sammakka, especially to save themselves from being defeated at the hands of a tribal woman. Sammakka was attacked with a spear from the back, and she was mortally injured. Soon, the word about her injury reached her people, who gathered around her with tears in their eyes. She motivated them to continue their fight, to liberate themselves from the clutches of oppression. She appealed to them to remember her in their struggles. To escape death at the hands of the enemy, Sammakka rushed towards a hillock called Chilakala Gutta and disappeared. Her will power, and determination became a source of motivation. Even the enemy king, Pratapa Rudra, became one of Sammakka's devotees, after her martyrdom.

95

Lalu Sardar: The Short Man

Once upon a time in a village, there was a man named Lalu
Sardar. He was very short. One day after grazing cattle in
the field, he came to his mother and asked her to delouse his
hair. His mother told him, 'Apply some oil on your hair, go
to your elder brother's wife and ask her to remove lice from
your hair.' Lalu Sardar accordingly left for his elder brother's
house. When he asked his sister-in-law to delouse his hair, she
scolded him and sent him back to his mother. Lalu Sardar felt
sad and told his mother that he wished to get married to a
beautiful girl. His mother replied, 'You are a very short person,
who will marry you?' Lalu Sardar told his mother, 'In Bhukya
Thanda, I have seen a beautiful girl and I want to marry her.'
His mother went to the girl's house in Bhukya Thanda and
saw the beautiful girl and returned home. When Lalu Sardar
asked her, she replied, 'The girl was beautiful, but she is taller
than you, how could you marry her?' But Lalu Sardar had
made up his mind. He said, 'No, I will only marry her,' and
left the room in a huff.

Lalu Sardar's father had a horse named Hasaloghodo. One
day Lalu Sardar went to his mother and told her that he wanted
to go for a ride on the horse. His mother said, 'Maat, beta,
maat (no, son, no), you are a short person, how can you ride
a horse?' But Lalu Sardar did not listen to his mother and
went to the horse. The horse did not allow him to sit on it at
first. Finally, after many attempts, Lalu Sardar managed to sit
on the horse. Anticipating an accident, the mother asked him
to get down. He replied, 'If you burn nine bags of agarbattis

and benzoin sticks, then I will get down.' Accordingly, the mother bought and burned in a pit nine bagful of agarbattis and benzoin sticks. Lalu Sardar got down from the horse. Again, he told his mother about the girl he wanted to marry. His mother told him that the girl's parents would not agree to give their daughter to him. He did not listen to his mother and went to the girl's house in Bhukya Thanda with his aunt.

When Lalu Sardar approached the girl's father, he was outraged, 'Savahaat admina maar chwari chavnuka? (With your height, you want to marry my daughter?) They went to the nayak, village head, of Bhukya Thanda, and asked him to solve their problem. After listening to them the nayak said, 'You are such a short person, and our girls are much taller than you. How can you get married?' The nayak and girl's father finally reached a decision and set a task for Lalu Sardar. They told him to look after the maize field for a day and a night and not to allow any bird or animal to eat the corn. Lalu Sardar agreed. Upon reaching the field, he saw a bear eating the maize. He killed the bear and took it with him to Bhukya Thanda and presented it to the nayak. The nayak and the father of the girl were surprised to see this tremendous achievement by a short man and did not believe him. They gave Lalu Sardar another task and asked him to take 560 cows and buffaloes for grazing and bring seven bundles of firewood. Lalu Sardar went to the forest with the animals. In the forest he encountered a ghost, which was ready to eat all the animals. He fought the ghost and killed it. He let the animals graze till evening and collected seven bundles of firewood. He returned to Bhukya Thanda with the firewood, ghost, and animals and showed them to the nayak. But the nayak still did not believe him. Once again, the nayak and the girl's father gave Lalu Sardar another task. 'My daughter will bring seven pots of water, balanced on her head, one on top of the other. You should drop all the pots on the ground.' Lalu Sardar agreed to this task. As Lalu Sardar sat thinking, 'I am shorter than her. How can I topple the pots over?', a man came forward and said, 'Do not worry. I will go and ask her to give me some buttermilk. When she bends to give me buttermilk, you sit on my shoulder, and topple the pots.' Lalu Sardar could easily tilt all the pots and finally the girl's father was impressed and agreed to give his daughter to Lalu Sardar. They got married and Lalu Sardar took his wife and went home happily.

96

Water, Forest, Land

In the first quarter of the twentieth century, Komaram Bheem was born into a tribal family who lived in Adilabad district in Sankepalli, a forest area in North Telangana which was under the rule of the Gond kingdom of Chandrapur and Ballalpur. The area belonged to the Gond community who spoke Gondu, a Dravidian language similar to Telugu. Komaram did not recieve any formal education nor did he know much about the outside world, but he grew up understanding the problems about his community. He experienced the exploitation faced by his community at the hands of the police, zamindars, landlords, and the officials of the Nizam. Komaram also knew that in order to protect themselves from the oppression of the Nizam, his community often had to be on the move. There was hardly any moment's respite. Often, the crops produced by them were forcefully taken away by the officials and they were forced to follow podu (shifting) cultivation.

Often the authorities falsely charged the Gonds on accounts of illegal felling of trees and deforestation. They were punished by having their fingers chopped off. They also faced forceful tax collections, failing which they met with terrible consequences, including brutal physical torture. Komaram Bheem's father was a brave man. He fought against the injustice of the authorities and fought for their rights as aborigines. When he was brutally killed by the officials of the Nizam of Hyderabad, Bheem was only fifteen. The murder of his father greatly influenced him during the course of his future work. Soon after the incident, the family shifted to Saradapur village. In the meantime, the cultivated crops as well as the podu cultivated lands were being taken away forcefully from the Gonds. Komaram Bheem organized a secret group of the Gonds to fight against the authorities.

One day, two officials of the Nizam, Laxman Rao and Siddique came to Bheem's village along with ten people. They started beating the men on charges of tax evasion and it led to a fight between the officials and the tribals, headed by Komaram Bheem. At the end, Siddique was killed and Bheem and his friends fled from the village. He went to Chandrapur and on his way he met Vitoba, a printing press owner. Vitoba invited Bheem to work for him. Vitoba published a magazine and spoke against the British and the Nizam. Bheem started assisting Vitoba in the press. He learned English, Urdu, and Hindi. Unfortunately, one day Vitoba was arrested, and the press was shut down. Komaram Bheem decided to go to Assam. On reaching Assam, he began work in a tea plantation and stayed there for four years. During this stay, he heard about Alluri Sitarama Raju, a freedom fighter and leader of tribal rebellion in Andhra Pradesh. He was deeply influenced by the guerrilla fight under the leadership of Sitaram Raju. Bheem organized the workers in the tea plantation and fought for their rights. He was jailed by the authorities but escaped and managed to reach Ballarshah.

Soon after his return from Assam, he shifted to Kakanghat with his mother and brother. He became an assistant to Lacchu Patel, the head of Devadam village. He married a village girl named Som Bai. Soon, Komaram Bheem became famous as he successfully helped to settle a land dispute between Lacchu Patel and Ameen Saab. Later, he shifted, along with his family, to Bhabejhari. Here, they started cultivating crops but, at the time of harvest, the officials of the Nizam, demanded the entire production and also ordered Bheem's family to leave the land. Bheem decided to speak with the officials to settle matters amicably but was not allowed to do so. Provoked by the injustice done to him, he decided to follow in the footsteps of Alluri Sitarama Raju. He realized that rebellion was the only remedy to solve their problems. He formed an army of twelve young Gond men near Jodeghat and launched agitations against the Nizam. This guerilla army of young Gonds demanded a separate state for themselves. They fought for restoring their rights to the land and attacked the officials who were working for the Nizam. Bheem formulated the slogan 'Jal, Jangal, Jameen' (Water, Forest, Land) while protesting against the callousness of the administrators. Through the slogan, he reminded everybody that the real inheritors of water, forest, and land were the aborigines and not the invaders.

Komaram Bheem's activities were centred mostly around Jodeghat. His speeches inspired many and they joined the guerilla army to fight for their land and freedom. The continuous guerilla attacks on the landlords of Bhabejhari and Jodeghat became a big headache for the Nizam and in an attempt to settle the dispute, the collector of Asifabad was sent to Bheem for a discussion. Bheem demanded the release of the tribals arrested by the officials and also put forward his new proposal for a separate self-ruling state of the Gonds. All these demands were dismissed and an army of 300 was deployed to arrest Bheem and his associates in the Jodeghat hills. As all attempts proved futile, the army sought out an informer, Kurdu Patel, from the Gond community, and following his information, a troop was deployed, under the leadership of the Talukdar of Asifabad. They arrived and surrounded the hiding place of Komaram Bheem and his guerilla fighters. A severe fight ensued and though Bheem and his associates fought bravely with axes, sickles, and bamboo sticks, they could not match the guns of the police. In this struggle, Komaram Bheem was shot dead along with his fifteen brave fighters.

TRIPURA

97

How a Brother and His Sister
Transformed into Elephants

Once upon a time, a father and a mother were accompanied by their son and daughter as they tended to their jhum fields. As the parents were carefully reaping the paddy harvest, the children helped them in collecting the harvest, piling them up, and preparing them to be carried home. From the early morning hours, the parents and their two children worked tirelessly. By afternoon, the sun was hot, and the parents told the children to take the harvest home. 'You're both tired. Go home, have a bath, and eat your lunch. Take the crops and keep them carefully and return after you have rested,' instructed the mother. After a pause, she added with a tone of caution, 'Remember, on your way you will see two waterfalls on either side of the road. Do not have a bath in the waterfall that is to your left, but only have a bath in the waterfall on your right. Remember this.'

Thus, the siblings left, taking the crops with them. On the way, as mentioned by their mother, they saw two waterfalls and immediately remembered their mother's warning. So, they went towards the waterfall on the right but were greatly disappointed to see the sorry state of the waterfall. The water was muddy, and the area was overgrown with weeds and creepers. As soon as they saw the muddy waterfall, they turned towards the waterfall on the left and saw that it was flowing with sparkling water and surrounded by soft grass. Now, witnessing the difference between these two waterfalls, the siblings started to discuss amongst themselves, 'I think Mother mixed up the

two waterfalls. Anybody can see that the waterfall on the right
is unsuitable for a bath. Let us have a bath in the waterfall
on the left,' and so the siblings went to the waterfall on the
left and started bathing.

As they stood under the clear, sparkling water they felt
their tired bodies relax. They were enjoying themselves so
much that they did not realize how quickly time had passed.
Suddenly, they noticed that it was almost evening and they got
scared, lest their parents came searching for them. Thus, they
hurriedly started to get out of the waterfall. But as soon as
they came out of the water, they started to itch all over their
bodies—hands, legs, feet, face, back, and chest. They were each
scratching themselves and also scratching each other. Each one
of them noticed that the other's body had started to swell up.
Soon they realized that their noses swelled up, hands, legs, feet,
head, ears, and belly. Their clothes did not fit them any more
and were ripped apart as they tried to put them on. Suddenly,
each one noticed that the other had turned into an elephant.
At this, both were terrified and they decided that they could
not return home in this state and that they should stay back
in the forest. They sat down and started to cry.

In the meantime, the parents got worried as their children
had not returned. They went looking for them and could not
find them at home, which made them more worried. Then
they realized that they must have had a bath at the waterfall
on the left. Some neighbours got together and lit torches made
of short wooden stumps, and accompanied the parents to the
waterfall. Upon reaching, they discovered the torn clothes of the
children and also the crops and realized that they must have
been cursed by the waterfall. Suddenly, a neighbour noticed
the trees rustling at a distance. On reaching, they discovered
the brother and sister elephants sitting and crying. The mother
could identify her children and went up to them and requested
them to return home. Though the siblings were reluctant to

return home, yet after much persuasion by the parents and neighbours, they started off for home. On reaching, the entire village came to see the elephants. They were all teary-eyed as they knew that they had to bid farewell to the elephants as they will soon leave to live in the forests forever. Thus, everybody got gifts of fruits and flowers and garlands. Finally, the siblings bid farewell to their parents and the villagers and they left for the forest to live there forever.

98

The Owl Delivered the Good News All Night Long But the Woodpecker Got the Reward of the Golden Crown

This is a story from the old days. There was a severe drought on earth and all plants and animals were on the verge of extinction. The weather had turned harsh and unsuitable for survival and mankind was suffering. The news of this severe condition reached heaven and all the gods were worried. Biyatra, the son of Gangi Ma (Ganga), was worried and descended on earth to witness the condition. He was shocked to see that the trees were standing all bare and dry, the grass had all dried up, and many animals were dead. Only the jagya dumur (Indian fig) tree, stood on the banks of the river. Upon seeing this, Biyatra asked the jagya dumur trees if they could provide mankind enough food to keep them alive. The trees replied that they could help sustain mankind. However, this became difficult as all of mankind finished all the fruits of the jagya dumur in two-and-a-half days. This made Biyatra very angry and in a fit of anger, he kicked the jagya dumur trees. The trees bent down and ever since jagya dumur tend to bend as they grow.

Biyatra kept thinking of how to solve the problem and finally decided that he should persuade Goddess Lakshmi the deity of prosperity to come down to earth and bless mankind. He felt that this was the only way to solve the drought problem. He sent Kaliya to heaven to explain to the goddess and ask her to descend on earth. Kaliya went to heaven but got busy drinking alcohol. Soon, he was completely intoxicated and forgot all about his duty until much later when he suddenly remembered his task. He rushed to Goddess Lakshmi, but the goddess, upon seeing the inebriated state of Kaliya, refused to accompany him to earth. Kaliya returned to earth and delivered the news to Biyatra. Biyatra decided to approach Goddess Lakshmi himself and thus, he went to heaven and spoke to the goddess. This time the goddess agreed and soon sent word through the bharati bird about her arrival. The bharati bird was sent down to earth and it informed the owl about Goddess Lakshmi's arrival and also told the owl that all of mankind should be informed of this happy news. The owl, like an obedient messenger, travelled all through the night, hooting and informing everybody about the good news of the goddess's arrival. People heard it all through the night and were very happy. They felt that their anxieties would soon come to an end and they wanted to reward the bird for bringing the happy news. Thus, in the early hours of the morning, all of mankind came out in search of the bird to reward him. However, at that moment, the tired owl had just finished his work and returned to rest within a hollow in the bark of a tree. None of mankind could spot the owl, but saw another bird instead, a woodpecker hunting for insects and they mistook it for the bird who was the harbinger of good news. They picked up the woodpecker, put him on a special pedestal, and put a golden crown on its head. Then all of mankind worshipped the woodpecker. Thus, till date, the woodpecker has a yellow tuft on its head as a sign of the golden crown that was placed on its head long, long ago.

99

Gymnast Dipa Karmakar: Inspiring the Youth

Dipa Karmakar who hails from Tripura has brought Indian women's gymnastics into the limelight all over the world. Over less than a decade, Dipa's name has become synonymous with not only gymnastics and world rankings but has also become an inspiration for many young girls from not only the state of Tripura but the entire nation.

Most success stories of India, related to sports, hardly take into consideration gymnastics—often considered an obscure sport for Indians. Adding a degree of recognition to this niche sport, Dipa Karmakar's story is an inspirational one.

India and the world first noticed Dipa when she won a bronze medal at the 2014 Commonwealth Games in Glasgow. It was a glorious moment as she became the first Indian female gymnast to do so in the history of the Commonwealth Games. This was followed by two consecutive participations and awards—both of which were a first-ever attempt by India—a bronze medal at the Asian Games Gymnastics Championship in 2014, followed by a commendable fifth rank in the World Artistic Gymnastics Championships in 2015. In the following year, while competing at the 2016 Summer Olympics in Rio de Janeiro, she became the first ever Indian female gymnast as well as the first Indian to compete in the Olympics. She won a fourth position in the Women's Vault Gymnastics event with an overall score of 15.066. In 2018, Dipa became the first Indian gymnast to win a gold medal at a global event when she topped the vault event at the FIG Artistic Gymnastics World Challenge Cup held at Mersin in Turkey. Noteworthy are her exceptional skills which shone like a beacon at the 2016 Olympics when she landed on the Produnova vault. Dipa is the fifth woman in the world to do so. The Produnova vault or the handspring double front is currently regarded as the most difficult vault in women's gymnastics.

For her commendable efforts and achievements, Dipa was awarded the Padma Shri in 2017 and the Rajiv Gandhi Khel Ratna Award in 2016. Dipa continues to be an inspiration for many young athletes throughout India and beyond.

UTTAR PRADESH

100

Panduk Chidiya

It was a hot summer morning, and all the deep and cool branches of the thick and verdant trees were occupied with a variety of birds. The parrot was busy pecking at the mangoes. The pigeon was cooing loudly. The little panduk chidiya was relaxing too, amidst the thick shade of the leaves. The crow was cawing continuously and the squirrel, which was used to the rhythm of the birds, was popping in and out of its nest in the bark. The little gauriya, house sparrow, was hopping from branch to branch and she was fondly referred to as chapala for her effervescent spirit. The koel was chirping sweetly. The little panduk said her little prayer, 'Data tu hi, data tu hi....' (Oh Lord! You Are, Oh Lord! You Are....) and set off looking for her day's meal. The rest of the birds continued their busy chirping. They all lived happily on the tree.

One afternoon, as all the birds were either resting or loudly discussing the morning's events with each other, little panduk was sitting forlorn on a branch. The bubbly gauriya noticed this. She came over to panduk and said, 'Sister, why are you sitting so quietly today? What is the matter?' Panduk did not reply but little gauriya did not give up and started to chirp and hop all around panduk. Inspite of all efforts, little panduk did not cheer up. Now, gauriya was worried and she called a meeting of all the residents of the tree, including the crows, koels, and the squirrels and told them to find out why panduk was so sad. They tried their best to cheer up panduk chidiya. The parrot wondered if panduk chidiya had a headache and offered to massage panduk's head. The squirrel said that it was ready to fetch headache medicine. The pigeon said that it was ready to put a cold pack on panduk's forehead to relieve her of the headache. Finally, the crow mentioned that it knew a human doctor, who can prescribe medicine for a headache and all the animals started to request panduk chidiya to visit the doctor. However, panduk chidiya refused to go and started chirping, 'Saputi kurkut de, saputi kurkut de.' None of the animals understood. They asked the koel to explain the meaning who said that she had no idea what panduk chidiya had just said and that the best person to ask was panduk chidiya herself. Finally, panduk chidiya revealed that she had not eaten for two days. She said that her mother-in-law had seven sons and thus, she was asking her to feed her, 'Acchhe saat putron wali ma, khana de, arthat, saputi kurkut de.' (The mother of seven kids, please feed me). Hearing this, the squirrel ran and got some grains from his burrow, the pigeon fetched some millet and wheat, the parrot got scraps of sweet and sour mangoes, the crow fetched a roti with a generous layer of ghee on it that he had snatched from a man's hand that afternoon. The koel put all the edibles together on a large leaf plate and gauriya fed little panduk chidiya with much love and affection. Panduk chidiya was very happy and ate to her heart's content. The koel started to sing a beautiful song and all the birds started to dance merrily.

....

The Hurricane and the Foolish Leopard

Once upon a time, in a village, there lived an old woman and her son. Every day, the son would take their cattle for grazing. One day, while he was in the fields, his mother came and shouted that a hurricane was approaching and that he should return home with the cattle. Now, in the same field, a leopard was hiding and biding his time for the right moment to snatch a calf. When he heard the word 'hurricane', he was curious. He had never heard the word before. He was wondering what it was and grew determined to find it, but he was sure it was a terrific thing as the mother had warned her son about it. Thus, he merged with the herd of cattle and gradually moved along with them to their shed.

In the stillness of the dark night, three thieves crept in to steal a calf. However, they found the leopard and thought it to be a chubby calf and tied it with a rope. Then they tied the leopard to a bamboo stick and carried him away. The leopard who was terrified by the thought of a hurricane thought that the hurricane had come to tie him with a rope. The poor leopard was petrified and instead of resisting, he submitted readily hoping that the hurricane may spare his life. At dawn, when the thieves realized that they had instead carried off a leopard, they immediately left the leopard and ran for their lives and hid inside the hollow trunk of a nearby tree. The leopard freed himself and ran for life, lest hurricane came to gobble him up.

On the way, he met a bear who asked him why he was in such a hurry. When the leopard said that he was running away from the hurricane, the bear assured him that nothing can be so frightful. The leopard took him to the hollow tree where the thieves were hiding. With caution, the bear dipped his tail from the top of the hollow branch. Now, the clever thieves, who were still hiding inside, tugged with all their might at the tail and it got bruised and scratched in the process. The bear was convinced about the ferocity of the hurricane. Both the bear and the leopard ran as fast as their legs could carry them into the forest.

On the way, they met a tiger, who asked them why they were running, looking so frightened? When the bear and the leopard explained about the hurricane, the tiger took it upon himself to assure them that there was no such thing. He mentioned that he had lived many years in the forest and had never seen anything more ferocious than him. So, the tiger was taken to the spot of the hollow tree. All the three animals stood close to the tree trunk and the tiger started to growl loudly. Now, as the thieves saw the approaching animals, they grew frightened and climbed to the top of the tree trunk. Suddenly and out of fear, one of them fell off and landed right on top of the tiger's head. In great fright, the thief quickly clasped the tiger's eyes, so that he could sit still on the tiger's head. Now, the tiger was frightened as he could not see. He started to run hither and thither and he was convinced that the hurricane had got hold of him. The bear and the leopard had already vanished into the forest and the tiger started to run wildly towards the direction of the forest. Meanwhile, the thief somehow managed to get off the tiger and rolled onto the forest floor.

After running for some time, the tiger, bear, and leopard, congratulated each other on being able to run away from the hurricane and promised that they would never meddle with such a creature ever again.

102

Guns That Were Kind

Tension spread in the small, sleepy district town of Sultanpur in Uttar Pradesh, like an oil spill in an ocean, quietly, stealthily. It was new and scary, even though the wrestling competition that was part of the annual carnival was neither. On the contrary, it was a spectacle the townsfolk greatly looked forward to. Bringing great excitement in their otherwise dreary lives, the wrestling competition never fell short of their expectations. Names of the wrestlers were announced a month before the event, people chose their favourites, placed bets according to their whims, and screamed themselves hoarse during the dangal. The atmosphere was always that of joy, excitement, and anticipation with malice towards none. But this it time was different.

The dangal had started as always: the announcements, leaflets, the wait and then the much-hyped event. The two finalists looked like mountains on wheels and while in the arena, they looked into each other's eyes like two angry cobras about to start a duel for their lady love. The trophy was to be handed over by the district magistrate and that was reason enough!

They looked so alike in appearance and objective; it was difficult to discern their different faiths. Nor did it matter. Even during the partition of the country not so long ago, Sultanpur had remained calm, like a well-anchored ship in turbulent waters.

Then why did this year's dangal acquire a communal colour?

It was politics. The two wrestlers supported two different

party candidates and the significant thing was that both were of the same religion. Yet, the spectators were divided into two groups according to their allegiance to the political parties. Cheering changed into slogan-shouting and slogan-shouting into abuses hurled at the wrestlers and each other. Words were replaced by brickbats. The wrestlers jumped out of the arena and lunged at the crowd. Mayhem ensued.

Shopkeepers pulled down the shutters when they saw people running helter-skelter through the main bazaar, and panic spread fast through the lanes and by-lanes. Rumour has its own ways, one that defies comprehension. In no time, the town was abuzz with news of a communal riot.

Chhote Lal Gupta shut his shop and found his way home. He panicked seeing some people running with blood-streaked faces through the bazaar seeking vengeance. A sigh of relief escaped his chest when he found his neighbourhood unruffled, his family still unaware of the events of the day. His mohalla in Majorgunj was primarily a Muslim one. Of the forty odd houses, only ten belonged to Hindus: the majority community was the minority in Majorgunj. It had never been a problem before; life here was peaceful.

Chhote had heard gruesome stories of riots from refugees settled in towns under rehabilitation schemes. Neighbours had turned on neighbours, sparing none. His imagination worked overtime: would he meet a similar fate?

Quietly he figured out a way to safety; for himself and his Hindu neighbours. They could not be left to the bloodthirsty mob, and he had to ensure that, he thought, walking past Hakim Sahib's house.

Hakim Khaliq Ahmad was a practitioner of Unani medicine. A garrulous middle-aged man, affectionately called Bhaiyya by everyone, he was usually seen sitting on the large open veranda of his clinic, surrounded by friends or patients. There weren't many today, lured away to the wrestling arena, but a couple sat there, narrating their troubles.

Hakim Sahib loved shikar, especially bird shooting, and reading. Sometimes he went to the nearby jungles at the cost of his medical practice and returned with bagful of game birds. In addition to medicines, he dispensed wonderfully descriptive accounts of his shikar to friends and patients alike, along with game meat.

For now, he was talking excitedly about disposing off one of the several old guns and buying a rifle instead, so he could kill the wolves which at times plagued the nearby villages.

He spotted Chhote walking past with hurried, furtive steps. Chhote Lal heard the word rifle and panic gripped his heart.

'Hey, Chhote, what's wrong? You look worried.' Hakim Sahib called out.

There was no reply.

Sensing the unrest, Hakim raised his voice. 'Stop, Chhote Lal. What is happening? Come here.'

Chhote could not but obey. He came closer and blurted out what he had heard and seen in the market. Just then, a police jeep followed, announcing a curfew.

'Bhaiyya, let me go. I will inform others and we will go to some safe place before it is too late,' he said and made to leave.

'Go home. No one is leaving the mohalla.' Hakim Sahib understood what Chhote Lal had meant by 'we'.

'It will be a slur on me if some families leave because they think they are unsafe here,' he continued. 'Who are you scared of?'

'Certainly not of you, Bhaiyya, but there is this settlement of meat-sellers close by. They are not like you....' Chhote stammered.

'I do not trust them.'

'And you think they will now trade in human flesh?' Hakim Sahib was angry and everyone around tittered. Chhote felt a little silly.

'Go to the other families. But do not ask them to flee. Give them my message: if anyone dares as much as looks askance at Hindu families living here, my guns will not be trained at birds this time. I will not tolerate any perpetrators of violence, who harm in the name of religion.'

His voice, firm with conviction, quietened the tumult in Chhote's mind. No family left Majorgunj, and nothing untoward happened in the town either. An alert administration had seen to it.

A week passed.

One day, a group of people, along with a local political leader, with Chhote Lal in tow, came to Hakim Sahib's clinic. They had not come to consult him for any affliction.

'What then?' Hakim Sahib raised his eyebrows.

'We have come to request you to contest the election of ward commissioner, on behalf of the political party we represent. You will surely win and the next step will take you to the assembly.'

'Politics is neither my cup of tea nor my goal in life,' Hakim Sahib said, with his characteristic firmness. And then he laughed. 'Invite me for duck shooting; I will come in a flash. And rest assured, you will not be disappointed.'

He called his servant in the same breath, 'Hey, Munna, go and get some hot tea for all of us.'

UTTARAKHAND

103

Pyonli

In the foothills of the high snowy mountain peaks that appear to pierce the sky, in a lush green forest, full of cedar, birch, and ringal, there lived a girl in a deep and unknown cave. Her complexion was a mix of raw turmeric and pink buransh, rhododendron. There was no human habitation, and she was all by herself in this wilderness. Her only kin was nature—the wind and the birds of the forest, the bees and the butterflies, big and small creatures, tiny flowers and plants hugging the earth, and tall trees, kissing the skies. All of them affectionately called her Pyonli[36]. They could understand each other's language well. They would whistle and sing her name in the thick fog of the incessant rainy days of chaumasa—the months from July through October of the monsoon season following the seasons of aashad, sawan, bhadon, and kwar—or during the snowy winters. On the cold days, they would make a cozy corner for Pyonli. Birds would spread their soft feathers to make a comfortable bed for her. All the animals surrounded the cave entrance and kept it warm.

With the arrival of spring, gradually the snow melted, streams began to flow once again and in the warmth of the spring sun, the whole forest bloomed with colourful flowers. Bees sang to call Pyonli out of the cave; butterflies brought

---

[36]A common wild flower, found in the hilly regions of northern India and also in parts of the Western Ghats. Its botanical name is *Reinwardtia indica*. It flowers between November–May. The yellow flower is an endearing symbol of spring.

to her their own world of scented flowers holding her delicate hands graciously like a princess. Pyonli jumped with joy and played with them roaming the jungles.

One day, as she sat dipping her feet in a stream, humming a song with a monal, she heard a voice. She looked around and saw a man standing behind her. He walked towards her and said, 'I am thirsty. Can I get a drink of water?' Pyonli withdrew her feet from the water and stood up. She kept looking at the handsome young man. He must be a prince, she thought. 'You have come here to hunt, haven't you? You only know how to destroy the forest and its inhabitants. You don't do anything to protect them,' she said boldly. The young man was exhausted. Seeing this, Pyonli requested him to rest for a while. He finally said, 'Yes I came here for hunting but lost my way. My companions are far behind.' He was spellbound by the untouched and infinite beauty of nature and remarked, 'You are blessed to stay here in the midst of nature, in the companionship of a chorus of birds,' he continued. 'It is a lovely relationship that holds all of you together.'

Pyonli replied, 'But you live in a palace. We don't have such lavish facilities in our jungle.' And they sat talking till the rays of the evening sun started playing on the treetops. The young man spent that night on the side of the stream on a wide pathal, a stone plate. The next morning, with a heavy heart Pyonli departed with the young man. She left behind her jungle, winds, and birds, to find a different melody with her prince.

New people, novel surroundings, new lifestyle, and her longing for love created a whole new colourful world around Pyonli. Time flew and soon, Pyonli started to miss her natural surroundings. The thoughts cast a gloomy spell on her. The pink colour of the buransh and the fragrance of raw turmeric were soon gone. She fell sick and became weaker by the day. Her beloved prince did everything to revive her. He spent his days and nights sitting beside her, but with every passing moment Pyonli's condition worsened. One day, as she held her beloved's hands, she said, 'Please forgive me. This palace is not for me. I could not value your love. I am a wild flower that can bloom only in the forest. I was a floating sound, drifting from one tree to another. How can I flourish in these suffocating walls of captivity? This land is not for me. When I am dead, please bury my remains in the same peak. Do not hunt animals any more. They all are my companions.'

The prince was perplexed. Pyonli passed away and he buried her in the same peak where he had met her the first time. As the spring season approached, a tiny yellow flower slowly opened its eyes in the wilderness. Trees and plants, winds and birds sang in a chorus with the monal and named that flower Pyonli. Since then, across every hilly field and in every corner of the jungle, flakes of tiny yellow pyonli flowers bloom and witness the arrival of spring in memory of the beloved Pyonli.

Even today the daughters of the land, who are unable to visit their parents, hug these pyonli flowers and remember their good old childhood days spent in the land where they were born and brought up so lovingly.

104

The Moon and His Light

The nights in the month of Kartik from October to November are so brightened by the flimsy streaks of moonlight that even the tiniest granules of the yellowed grains of kharek trees are clearly visible. The village folk—aunts, mothers, grandmothers, and daughters-in-law—relax. They have completed their task of storing the harvest. Now, they have to gather and store away the firewoods for the approaching winters. Then they can relax for a while longer. With a relaxed mind, the mothers tend to their household chores and grandmothers narrate riddles to the children: 'A white calf went to drink water. On her return she turned red. Say what?' Sitting in their mother's lap, the kids would shout out: 'A fluffy poori! What else!' The children laughed, played, and clapped and the mountains echoed with their laughter, alongside the sound of chirping crickets. This was a time when burning twigs was not required at night. These twigs were too precious a thing for simple village folk. It was the pivot of their life and an important resource too. For them it was a valuable gift bestowed by Mother Nature.

In those days of full moonlit nights, men from the villages would go to faraway marketplaces to purchase things they could not produce in their fields such as salt, jaggery, and clothes. A popular proverb prevailed—one should return the borrowed salt once the dhakari[37] comes back. There were no bullock carts or horses and people had to move on foot. On one such

---

[37]A person or a group of people bringing the necessary items for the fellow villagers from faraway marketplaces.

moonlit night, some men packed their ration for a week or
so and set out for the city. The path was clearly visible, and
they moved in a single file. On the way, menfolk from other
villages also joined them. They kept moving on past midnight.

Wherever these dhakaris would move on, the moonlight
showed them their path. After walking for two nights, they
realized that the moon accompanied them till dawn when the
sun rays finally showed up. One of the dhakaris noticed this
and became a little anxious, but could not share his doubts with
anyone else. By noon they arrived at the town of Najibabad.
They cooked a meal and left for shopping.

It was night-time again and there in the city too, the bright
moon was shining in the firmament. Now, the good old man
could no longer resist sharing his doubts with his fellow village
folks, 'I have been noticing this for the past three days,' he
said with concern, 'the moon has accompanied us. I wonder
how our womenfolk are staying back in village without the
moon. Ohh...! See this has stayed back with us here tonight.
Don't know whether it would go back with us or not.'

Oh poor men! A grocer was listening to the conversation of
these innocent people. He was clever and cunning and thought
of fooling these villagers. He said, 'O Sir! This is so strange. I
don't think this moon would return to the mountains now. Last
year also it went away with some dhakaris and now exactly
after a year it has returned with you folks.'

It was a matter of great concern for the villagers. 'To hell
with this moon. It came behind us so quietly that none of us
noticed it,' one of them uttered in quite a perplexed manner.
The clever grocer thought it was time to make his next move.
Acting thoughtfully, he said, 'I have an idea, if it pleases you!'
The poor simple village folk had in the meantime turned pale
with tension. They looked at the grocer for a solution.

The moon was their only light in the deep dark nights
back in the countryside. Though for a few days in a month

it went away to some unknown place, but it finally returned to fill their nights with its bright light.

'Everyone will make fun of us in the village if we leave this moon here. Somehow, we have to take it back with us,' they thought.

Closely observing the villagers, the grocer told them that they would have to spend some money to take the moon back to the mountains. Thus, they started bargaining for the moon. At last, they bought some salt and jaggery with whatever little money that was left with them after bargaining and hurried back to their village as soon as the moon appeared in the sky. What if the moon backed out, they thought. They were satisfied to see the moon accompanying them.

They entered the village and narrated this story to their fellow people and told them how they bought the moon back. People in the village were amazed. There were bright moonlit nights when dhakaris were away. 'You fools! You bought one more moon instead of salt. We were happy with one. Why do we need another one?'

They said, 'Shut up all of you. You don't know how we fooled those people in the city and bought their moon. From now on our nights would be brighter than ever.'

Since then, it is believed that in the hilly areas the moon appears bigger and rounder and its light fills the snowy surroundings with sparkling silver.

105

Tinchari Mai: An Ascetic with a Difference

Eighty years ago, in the village of Majyur, in Tailsain Block of present-day Uttarakhand, Deepa was born. She came to be known as Ichhagiri Mai and later on as Tinchari Mai. Her parents were Ramdate Nautiyal and Rupa Devi. When Deepa was two years old, her mother passed away and by the time she was five, tragedy struck once again as her father too passed away. A distant uncle took pity on her and raised her.

Young Deepa grew up in her foster home but was deprived of education. However, she was a jovial and naughty child. At the age of seven, she was married to a man, who was seventeen years older to her. Child marriage in the region was common in those days. Deepa's husband was a havaldar, stationed at that time in Rawalpindi (in present-day Pakistan). She hardly realized the meaning of marriage and was extremely happy to witness the pomp and splendour of the entire marriage ceremony, sequinned clothes, flowers, and jewellery. The couple left for Rawalpindi the very next day.

Though a child bride, Deepa was blessed with a kind husband. He used to bathe, dress, and feed his young bride every morning before leaving for work. Deepa would often spend the whole day playing with children of her age, but her husband never scolded her for her childish pranks and behaviour. He would even coax her to bathe or eat, whenever she threw tantrums. Unfortunately, this happiness was only to last for a brief while as her husband died fighting in a battle. A widow, Deepa started to think about her future. In the meantime, she was summoned by her husband's superiors to receive some money, which was dutifully her husband's earnings. She was accompanied by another officer to Lansdowne. The officer led Deepa to another senior officer's house and handed over the money to him. This officer deposited the entire amount in Deepa's name in an account in the post office. A few days later, he summoned the pradhan of Ganvani village to help Deepa reach her in-law's place.

At her in-law's, Deepa witnessed what she had anticipated. Nobody welcomed her back and she was seen as a burden and an extra mouth to feed. Finally, one day, she left for Lahore. She took refuge in a temple where she met a sanyasin. This sanyasin took Deepa into her fold and gave her the name of Icchagiri Mai.

Deepa severed ties with her old world and began life anew with a new name. In 1947, she reached Haridwar and stayed at Chandi Ghat for nine months. She was outraged to witness the behaviour of several sham ascetics and monks in Haridwar, who spent their time smoking opium and indulging in drugs and alcohol. She thought of exposing these sham spiritual gurus. However, she faced opposition as these men found it hard to believe that a woman was waging a war against them. Deepa, however, did not give up and continued her work against social evils.

This was the beginning of her work against drug abuse and alcoholism. Soon, from Haridwar, Deepa reached Sigaddi Bhabar in Kotdwar. Residing in a self-made, thatched hut, Deepa soon noted the severe water scarcity which plagued Sigaddi village. Though she made many appeals to the deputy collector, all was in vain. Finally, she reached New Delhi and sat in protest outside Prime Minister Jawaharlal Nehru's office, inspite of several attempts made by the guards to drive her away. Finally, on meeting Nehru, she placed her request for a proper water connection for her village. When she met Nehru, Deepa was burning with fever. Nehru promised her that he would look into the problem of water supply in her village and arranged for some clothes and also sent her to a hospital. By the time she returned, the village had a proper water supply. Deepa had single-handedly achieved what nobody from the village could achieve.

From Sigaddi, Deepa went to Motadhak. Here, she was given shelter in a local schoolteacher's house, who also aspired to build a school for the children of the village. Deepa knew the value of education. Within three to four months, she raised enough money to build a school. Today, this school has become an intermediate college and still stands as a symbol of Deepa's hard work.

From Motadhak, she travelled to other places, including Badrinath, Kedarnath, and finally to Pauri. One day in Pauri, as Deepa was resting on the porch of her house she witnessed an incident, which changed her name to Tinchari Mai. There was a tinchari, a country liquor shop, across the road. An inebriated man came out of the shop and started teasing some women on their way to the forest to collect firewood. This incident enraged Deepa. She immediately went to the deputy commissioner's residence and brought him to the spot to witness the situation. She appealed to him to stop the sale of tinchari. The deputy commissioner did not pay any heed and in a fit of rage, Deepa burned down the tinchari. For this action, the deputy commissioner detained Deepa briefly in his residence and in the evening, drove her to Lansdowne.

Once in Lansdowne, Deepa continued her fight against alcoholism. She urged women to fight against this social evil and raise their voices against all men who drink and beat their wives and children. Deepa came to be known famously as Tinchari Mai. She settled in Chamoli and continued to fight against the social evils of drinking and poverty, at the same time she encouraged the spread of education. She breathed her last on 19 June 1992. Even today, she is fondly remembered in the villages of Uttarakhand for her battle against liquor and continuous work for the general upliftment of the lives of many villagers in the region, especially women.

WEST BENGAL

106

The Story of Madanmohan of Bishnupur

The region of Bishnupur in Bankura district of West Bengal has an interesting story about Lord Madanmohan, the tutelary deity of the Malla dynasty of the Bishnupur royal family. The region was earlier known as Mallabhum and according to this story, one day as King Veer Hambir was returning to his capital from a pilgrimage tour, he came upon an ashram at Brisabhanupur. There was a temple and its presiding deity was Lord Madanmohan. The king was informed by the head priest that the idol of Madanmohan was a gift bestowed by an ascetic traveller. The king was fascinated with the idol and wanted it for his royal temple; however, the head priest was not ready to part with it. Not paying any heed to the priest's resistance, the king left with the idol in the middle of the night. Nobody knew about it, not even the head priest; however, the next morning, when the theft was discovered, the head priest realized that it was definitely King Veer Hambir who had stolen the idol. Upon reaching his palace, the king placed the idol in the chamber of Goddess Lakshmi, in the inner chamber of his palace.

One day soon after, the head priest reached the palace of the king, demanding that he return the idol. The king at first denied all charges, but later on reluctantly agreed as the priest threatened to take his life in front of the king. But the king did not return the idol and the heartbroken priest had to return empty-handed. As the priest was leaving, he cursed the idol of Madanmohan, saying: 'Oh Lord Madanmohan, as You quit me in the lure of Mallabhum, likewise some day, You

will have to leave this holy land as well.' It is believed that
because of this curse, the idol of Madanmohan had to finally
leave the royal palace one day.

The idol became an integral part of the royal family, as
well as the subjects of Mallabhum. One day, during the reign
of King Gopal Singha Dev (1712–48 CE), the fifty-fifth king
of Mallabhum, Madanmohan was said to have saved the
region from the onslaught of enemies. Gopal Singha was also
a great devotee of Madanmohan and had ordered his subjects
to worship Madanmohan thrice a day. One day, one of Gopal
Singha's ministers reported an unfortunate event to him. The
year was 1742 and Maratha invaders, locally called bargees,
light cavalry, under the command of Bhaskar Pandit, were
on their way to besiege Mallabhum. Bhaskar Pandit was the
general of Raghoji Bhonsle from western India (in present-day
Nagpur, Maharashtra). Scared of the Maratha raiders, waiting
at the south gateway of the town, Gopal Singha rushed to
prostrate himself in front of the idol of Madanmohan, instead
of sending an army to the battlefield. Suddenly, Gopal Singha
heard deafening booms of artilleries and canons. Since the
king did not send any army, he was convinced that Lord
Madanmohan was defending Mallabhum against the raiders.
The king was further convinced, when a cannoneer informed
him that in the still of the night, he had witnessed a cavalry
boy in blue, riding an enormous stallion towards the enemy
who was camped at Mundamalar Ghat. The boy had a burning
torch in one hand and held the reins with the other. As the
stallion moved along the dark road, the whole area was lit up
with a supernatural light.

Listening to the cannoneer, the king came out of his hiding
place and reached the Madanmohan temple. On the way, he met
a milkman, who told him that a boy in blue, riding a stallion,
had approached him for the curd which he was carrying for the
idol in the Madanmohan temple. The boy also gave the milkman

a gold bangle. The milkman showed the king the bangle and immediately recognized it to be one of the bangles from the hands of the Madanmohan idol. When the king reached the Madanmohan temple, he saw a gold bangle of the idol missing and also noticed soot-marks on the hands of the idol, as well as an acrid smell of gunpowder on the hands and feet of the idol. The king was convinced that Lord Madanmohan had come out to the rescue of Mallabhum and had attacked the enemy with the Dalmadal cannon, as he had distinctly heard cannons being fired, without any human presence.

Several years later, however, as per the curse of the Brahmin priest, the idol of Madanmohan left Mallabhum, during the time of the fifty-sixth king of Mallabhum, Chaitanya Singh Deo (1748–1801 CE). Chaitanya, along with the idol, spent some years in a rented house in Kolkata. He had to face court cases and ran into debt. Finally, Chaitanya was compelled to mortgage the idol of Madanmohan to a wealthy salt merchant of Konnagar. Thus, the idol of Madanmohan left Mallabhum forever.

Till today, the story of Lord Madanmohan leaving Mallabhum and also coming to the rescue of the region during the time of the bargee onslaught is told in the region of Bishnupur.

107

The Lepcha Legend of the Teesta and Rangeet Rivers

Of the many stories connected with the rivers Rangeet and Teesta, among the Lepchas there is one which is a story of love, acrimony, and reconciliation between the two. According to this legend, Rangeet and Runge-nyu (Teesta) fell in love in their heavenly abode. They decided to meet in the deep forest in Pa-zok (now Peshok, a tea estate by the same name) far below their celestial homes. Both of them took a guide each, Teesta had Pa-ril-bu, the king of the serpents, while Rangeet had a tut-fo, the blue-naped pitta. The serpent king took a straight course and got Runge-nyu, the female partner, to the rendezvous much ahead of time and there she waited for her sweetheart. While the bird, feeling hungry, flew here, there, and everywhere in search of food, making Rangeet's course circuitous and a longer one. Reaching the rendezvous, Rangeet was embarrassed that Runge-nyu had arrived much earlier and was also angry that the passage onwards was blocked because Runge-nyu was lying in wait and was not moving. It was at this juncture that Rangeet blurted out, 'Teestha-nom-tho?' (When did you arrive?) It is said that following this, the Lepcha Runge-nyu came to be called Teesta.

Unable to bear the hurt of his bruised male ego, Rangeet decided to return upstream. Teesta followed, imploring her lover to turn back and to continue their intended journey. It was only when they reached Rangliot and Rangayroon villages that Rangeet realized his mistake and chose to run its original downward course with his beloved Teesta. Very appropriately thus, Rangliot translates as 'the brimful great river' or the brim, top, and edge of height reached by the river. Rangayroon translates from the Lepcha as 'the turning of the great river' and it marks the point where the rivers recede.

....

108

Of Love and Mutual Respect

It was just another one of those wonderful days that little Fathma looked forward to. Trips with her maternal grandmother were always special and exciting as there were surprises galore. Grandma's friends, their houses, the lovely decorations in the houses, a large piano and its wonderful music and most importantly, the aroma of varieties of dishes served by the khansamas. The food was traditional Jewish delicacies which were offered so lovingly that Fathma loved the trips. There were stuffed capsicums with succulent meat, rice, and vegetables, which had its unique taste and finally, there were different types of baked goodies, each one with a distinct flavour.

Fathma used to live in the Bow Barracks area near Central Calcutta. She and her two younger siblings would accompany their grandma often when she went visiting her friends. Fathma's father belonged to the Islamic faith and their house was very close to her maternal grandparents' in the same area. Fathma was born in 1957, a delicate premature baby. Her father feared losing her, but it was the confidence of her grandma, which saved Fathma. She cared for the newborn and fed her with milk soaked in thin cotton swabs and looked after her, till she was confident that the baby was ready to be left alone with the parents. Slowly, little Fathma gained confidence and started to grow up with her siblings but she always shared a special bond with her grandmother. Life was simple, but there was never a dull moment as the house was either full of relatives or guests and their children and celebration of festivals of all religions—something that left its own magic for generations.

Fathma's maternal grandfather, Joseph Assin, was of Chinese origin and a Christian by faith. He owned a workshop called Jessop & Co. in Dumdum near Calcutta. It was mostly a welding workshop of big and small things, but he used to work on other things too. It was these 'other things' which amused little Fathma, as she watched her grandfather's deft fingers at work, preparing ladies cosmetics. Besides his welding work, Fathma's grandfather made face powders and lipsticks. As a child, Fathma was fascinated with the process of lipstick making—the base powder would be gently poured into the metal cast which would then emerge like shining magic in various colours. There was another very interesting fact about her grandfather that Fathma was equally fascinated by. He was famous for his qawwali singing of Sufi songs. Often, there would be gatherings of singers at home with harmoniums rehearsing for various programmes that were held all over Calcutta. Fathma's grandfather was well known for his voice and was famously referred to as Chiney gawaiyya, Chinese singer.

Fathma's maternal grandmother, Matilda Joe Essence, was Jewish. She arrived from Israel in the early 1930s, along with her maternal uncle and her younger sister. They settled in Calcutta in the Bow Barracks region. She worked as a nurse and was the head warden at the prestigious Calcutta Medical College. Very well known for her work, she was also often called over by rich and royal families to personally attend to patients. Matilda was treated with respect by these families and often horse-drawn carriages were sent for her for the trips that she would make to their homes. They all trusted her dedication and loving care. Matilda married Joseph Assin and on 26 December 1935, they were blessed with their elder daughter, Daphne. Five years later, they had their younger daughter, Yvonee. For both daughters, life presented itself in myriad hues, with cultural values that taught them how to exist in unison, through love, mutual understanding and above all respect for all. From a very young age, however, Daphne was drawn to the spiritualism of Islam and was touched by the soulful lyrics of Sufi music. When she was around eleven years old, she was arranged to be married to a Chinese Christian boy. Daphne ran away from home and took shelter in an Islamic neighbour's home. The family already had three daughters and Daphne was almost adopted as the fourth. She continued to live at their residence, following the religion that she felt drawn to. She adopted Islam and became Hamida Bano and was married to Abdul Mughni. Over the years, the couple was blessed with thirteen children. Fathma was the third child. Just like Joseph and Matilda's house, the Mughni household too welcomed all. No religion was excluded, and all religious festivities were observed with equal fervour in both households. Fathma used to particularly love breaking a Jewish fast along with her grandmother, by worshipping the moon. This was done with the help of a special type of Jewish bread accompanied by selected fruits. The harmonious rhythm of the family retained the same beauty which Matilda had experienced at the very beginning of her life, when she had settled down with her husband in their small Bow Barracks flat in Calcutta. The grandchildren grew up, learning the significance of love, mutual respect, and understanding.

When Fathma was around nine years old, her grandfather passed away and Matilda struggled alone in her empty home. Though she found solace amongst her grandchildren, yet she remained restless. She often took little Fathma with her to visit her Jewish friend's home and bakery. This was the famous Nahoum bakery in New Market of Calcutta. Not in service at the hospital any more, Matilda's financial needs were taken care off by a small donation kitty managed by the Jews of Calcutta. She visited the bakery to collect her monthly stipend. The restlessness continued, exacerbated by neighbourhood disturbances from rowdy boys who would often irritate her.

Troubled by the continuous stress of life, Matilda finally decided to leave for Israel. When Fathma was around thirteen, she got married and soon gave birth to her first son in 1975. When the baby was only two days old, Matilda left India for Israel. She was accompanied by her younger daughter, Yvonee D'cruz, son-in-law, Eril D'cruz, and grandson, Kevin. Two years after moving to Israel, Matilda passed away. Matilda's family in Calcutta, her great-grandchildren still remember her fondly and maintain the same pluralistic touches of cultural and religious values taught through generations.

Acknowledgements

It has been an enriching experience to work across fifty-seven languages and dialects over three years and I would like to thank the sixty authors and translators who have contributed their stories and translations to this volume. I would also like to thank my friends Radhika Singh, Dr Radhakrishnan Raman, and Ambassador Rudi Warjri and Ambassador Sarvajit Chakravarti for their guidance and kind help. They remain great sources of inspiration and their contributions at various stages of this work remain vital to the basic conceptualization of the book.

My heartfelt thanks to my editor, Aienla Ozukum, for her guidance and encouragement. My sincere thanks to Bena Sareen for the cover and book design; Apoorva Lalit for the beautiful cover illustration, and Pallavi Goswami for copy-editing the text.

Finally, I would like to thank my parents, Late Dr Tushar Kanti Maitra and Mrs Manju Maitra, for being eager listeners and being great pillars of support and strength, my sister, Dr Gargi Maitra, for always being a keen help and my daughter, Aishani, for being the source of encouragement for this work. When I started my work for this book, my father was excited to see the final result. I would often sit and narrate some of the interesting stories I had collected during my fieldwork, especially stories which had a familiar rhythm to some of the popular folk tales that I grew listening to. The discussions were not only reminiscing, but enriching and helped me to connect a lot of dots to fill gaps while putting together the book. I am sure, wherever he is today, he must be smiling down on me especially glad to see how the storytelling has continued from the simple days of the crocodile and the fox.

Notes to the Stories

ANDAMAN AND NICOBAR ISLANDS

Tatora and Vimaro: This story is originally in Nicobarese/Nicobaric. It has been translated into Hindi by Rajendra Pal Sharma and translated from Hindi to English by Lopamudra Maitra Bajpai. This is a famous story told in every household in Nicobar. It is believed that the deep depression caused by Tatora's wooden sword created two islands. Out of which, one was named Little Andaman, which is quite some distance away from Car Nicobar Island. Today, there is no discord between the inhabitants of Nicobar and Little Andaman, and they live in peace and harmony.

The Fairy Princess of Havelock: This story is originally in Andamanese. It has been translated into Hindi by Rajendra Pal Sharma and translated from Hindi to English by Lopamudra Maitra Bajpai. Havelock Island is located on the south of Port Blair, at a distance of around 20 kilometres. At present, Havelock Island is an important tourist spot and is visited by thousands of people from across the world. In 2018, this island was renamed Swaraj Island after the famous freedom fighter, Netaji Subhas Chandra Bose. This island was once upon a time called Pari Tapu or the land of fairies as it was believed that it was inhabited by fairies long ago. This is a very famous story and is narrated even in present times to the younger generations.

The Legendary Work of A. P. Mohammad: This story is originally in Hindi by Rajendra Pal Sharma. It has been translated by

Lopamudra Maitra Bajpai. The data has been accumulated by Sharma over interaction with Shri A. P. Mohammad. At present, his school has around 1,500 students and its alumni include respectable personalities from various disciplines, including medicine, engineering, and education. The Muslim Education Society School (MES) building in the Azad Nagar area is a testimony to the hard work that went into creating a benchmark in the field of education and knowledge-sharing.

ANDHRA PRADESH

Thinnan: The Story of a Loyal Devotee: The original story is in the Telugu and has been written by Parvathi Chandran. Srikalahasti Temple, the most famous Shiva temple, known as the Kailash of South is located in Chittoor District, Andhra Pradesh. The holy site of the temple is believed to be the spot where Thinnan (Kannappa Nayanar) had worshipped Lord Shiva. The Nayanars, preachers of Lord Shiva, were a group of sixty-three saint–poets who were believed to have lived between the sixth and the eighth centuries in South India. Thinnan is believed to be one amongst them. *Kalahasti Mahatyam* (1954), a Telugu film directed by H. L. N. Simha is closely associated with the legend of Srikalahasti Temple and the devotional life of Kannappa Nayanar. *Bhakta Kannappa* (1976) is a Telugu film directed by Bapu which portrays the life of Thinnan, a hunter turned Shaivite saint.

The Story of Tenali Raman: This popular story, originally in Telugu, has been written by Parvathi Chandran. Tenali Ramakrishna was a scholar, jester-poet, and adviser of Krishnadeva Raya of the Vijayanagara empire. He was well-known for his witty comments and was one of the eminent eight poets (Ashtadiggajas) of Krishnadeva Raya's court. *Panduranga Mahatmyam*, written by Tenali Ramakrishna, is considered as one of the five great literary works in the Telugu language.

Several films have also been made on the stories and life of Tenali Raman in three south Indian languages, namely, *Tenali Ramakrishnan* (Telugu, 1956), *Tenali Raman* (Tamil, 1956), and *Hasyratna Ramakrishna* (Kannada, 1982) by B. S. Ranga. *Tenali Rama* (Hindi, 1990) produced by T. S. Nagabharana was made into a TV serial for Doordarshan.

The Legacy of Mastanamma, the Oldest Food Blogger: This story was narrated to Lopamudra Maitra Bajpai by Shrinath Reddy—a friend of Mastanamma's grandson. The story was translated and transcripted by Lopamudra. Mastanamma's videos are popular on YouTube. She did not follow any trend, as she was least informed about the world of technology, however, she did start the food-blogging trend and cooking in the open with firewood, to encourage food aficionados the world over. Her presentation has inspired many people in the short time that she got to reach out to the world. At the time of her death on 3 December 2018, she had 1.2 million subscribers from various parts of the world. Shrinath Reddy, who helped to provide information for this story, also helped to put Mastanamma's efforts online, along with her grandson K. Laxman.

ARUNACHAL PRADESH

Jaayww Bonv: This story is translated from Galo by Bina Gandhi Deori, after a narration by Mrs Pegi Bam and Mrs Marde Bam. The translator thanks Dr Bomchak Riba for going through the drafts of translations and offering necessary inputs. Mrs Pegi Bam belongs to the Galo tribe of the Lvpaa Radaa district, Arunachal Pradesh. She is a well-known ballad singer of Bam village. A mother of five, she served as the secretary (and teacher) of Anganwadi Worker and Helper Union and Bam Women Welfare Society (BWWS) for five years. She also served as an Anchal Samiti Member. Mrs Marde Bam is a resident of Nyobom village. In the Galo tradition, the story of

Jaayww Bonv is narrated in a ballad form. There are various versions of the story. According to one such popular version, Bwr-Tapuu turned into a fish and made holes in the sand and hid to avoid the poisoned water and that is how he escaped while Jaayww Bonv met her unfortunate end.

Bimbin Tabo: This story is translated from Galo by Bina Gandhi Deori, after a narration by Mrs Pegi Bam. The translator thanks Dr Kenbom Bagra for the corrections required in drafts of the translation.

Gohen Bam: This story is translated from Galo by Bina Gandhi Deori, after a narration of the events from the life of Gohen Bam by his daughters Henpu Lollen (Bam), Henme Loyi (Bam), and son Hengo Bam. Valuable inputs were also received from his grandchild, Shri Pemo Bam. Gohen Bam was an ordinary village boy from Bam village, who dared to dream big and became one of the most well-known entrepreneurs of the Basar region in Arunachal Pradesh. His life is an inspiring example about overcoming shortcomings and rising above difficult circumstances in life. Many young people and interns whom he helped in their younger days are well established in various fields. His friends and village people fondly remember him as thikadar and xikok. His contribution as a pioneer and one of the developers of Basar region is still recognized. His accomplishments as a self-made individual made him not only the most respected in the Bam clan but also one of the most well-known personalities of the region. After a brief illness, he breathed his last in 2005.

ASSAM

The Tale of the Cat's Daughters: This story is originally in Axomiya/Assamese. The Assamese title of the story is 'Mekuri Jiyekor Xadhu'. It has been written by Gulal Salil after a narration in English of the original story by Bitopi Dutta. This is a folk tale which first appeared in the 1911 vernacular printed collection *Burhi Aair Xadhu* (Grandma's Tales) compiled by celebrated Assamese litterateur, Lakshminath Bezbarua. The collection is considered to be a classic in Assamese folk tale culture. Some of the thirty folklores were Lakshminath's own contribution, with a preface dedicated to a narrative about the genesis, movement, and importance of folklores in the world.

The Foolish Son-in-law: The title of this story in Axomiya/ Assamese is 'Jowai' and has been written by Pranab Jyoti Sharma. The narrator first heard this story as a child from his father. This story was also recorded by Lakshminath Bezbarua in his book *Burhi Aair Xadhu*. This story with its tinge of banter and comedy reflects the milieu of pre-modern Assamese society.

Messages Through Wall Art: This story has been translated by Lopamudra Maitra Bajpai and it was narrated to her by Rishi Raj Sharmah. The translator wishes to thank Rishi Raj Sharmah for his narration about Kiran Gogoi. Today, Gogoi is a well-known environmentalist in Assam. He did not receive any formal education in environmental studies but was always driven by a passion to contribute towards nature and his beloved region.

BIHAR

The Ghost in the Hostel Room: This popular story, originally in the Magahi language was narrated by Sukhdev Pal to Dr Ajay, who narrated the story in Hindi to Dr Gargi Maitra who translated the story into English. The translator would like to thank the narrator of this story, Sukhdev Pal.

Harhi Pond: This story is written by Pramod Jha. It is originally in the Maithili language. The author came across this story in

Maithili in the Mithila region. Later on, he also came across this story in several printed publications, including a book by the Sahitya Akademi titled *Mithilak Lokkatha Sanchay*, compiled and edited by Yoganand Jha.

Mother: The original title of the story is 'Amma'. The Urdu version was narrated to Dr Shibal Bhartiya by Syed Shafiuzzaman Mashhadi. Dr Shibal Bhartiya née Fatima, is the daughter of Syed Shafiuzzaman Mashhadi. She helped to edit and translate this story into English. Amma, Wali-ul-Fatima, a woman of steel, is buried next to her husband, Syed Ameeruddin Mashhadi in Gaya. Chhote Abba, Syed Zaheeruddin Mashhadi, died in Chittagong, Bangladesh, away from home and family, and is buried there. The narrator of the story, Syed Shafiuzzaman Mashhadi, is Amma's youngest son who was seven years old at the time of the Partition of India. A retired civil servant, he visits Gaya often to tend to his parents' graves. He broke down many times while narrating this story. Dr Shibal Bhartiya, is an eye surgeon and a single mother to a young teenage boy. She hopes, one day, to be half the woman her grandmother was and find the same faith and resilience in the face of impossible odds.

CHANDIGARH

Mirza and Sahibaan: This story has been written by Jaspreet Mann. It is famous in the region in both languages—Punjabi and Urdu. Punjab is a proverbial land of myth and romance. Poetry permeates the fabric of society at every level, be it the Guru Granth Sahib or poems by Waris Shah. There is a visibly deep influence of art everywhere in the region. The tragic romance of Mirza and Sahibaan is a lesser-known folk tale from the region. A shorter version of the story, immortalized by the seventeenth century Punjabi poet, Piloo, was written by Captain R. C. Temple in 1884 book, *The Legends of the Punjab*. The story of Mirza and Sahibaan has inspired poets, writers, and artists of Punjab over the decades. Even today, Mirza is a metaphor for bravery and courage in Punjabi folklore.

Baba Farid: This story has been written by Jaspreet Mann. It is famous in the region in both languages—Punjabi and Urdu. Sheikh Farid was a great Sufi mystic and teacher (1173–1265). The Guru Granth Sahib contains four shabads and 112 shlokas of Sheikh Farid, popularly known as Baba Farid in the Sikh faith. He is the first recorded poet in the Punjabi language and holds a place of reverence in the hearts of the Sikh community, not only in Chandigarh but across the world.

Amrita Pritam: This story has been written by Jaspreet Mann. The story is famous in the region in both languages—Punjabi and Urdu. Amrita Pritam is not only a well-known name in the Punjab region or across India, but around the world. Chandigarh is a modern city in India designed by the French architect Le Corbusier in 1952. Amrita Pritam had already carved a niche for herself by then and many writers based in Punjab and Chandigarh travelled to Delhi to be in her luminous presence. Even today, as recipient of the Jnanpith Award, Sahitya Akademi Award, Cyril and Methodius Award from Bulgari, and the Ordre des Arts des Lettres from France, Amrita Pritam is one of the brightest literary stars. The Amrita Pritam Hall in Girls Hostel 9 at the Punjab University in Chandigarh, was constructed in her honour.

CHHATTISGARH

The Magical Garuda Pillar: This story is in Hindi and narrates the experiences of the author, Prakash Jha. Danteshwari Temple is located in Dantewada district of the Bastar division in Chhattisgarh. This story is an extract from a tête-à-tête between a traveller (Awara Banjara) and Bharat (Sone ki Chidiya) wherein the former is on a quest to explore the latter's country.

The Mahua Tree: The original story is in Chhattisgarhi and it is titled 'Mahua ka Ped'. It has been translated by Vedanshi Ashok Bhatia and was narrated by her friend, Nirved Verma, who hails from Chhattisgarh. Verma remembers this story being narrated to him during his childhood days by the elders in his family. The language of Chhattisgarhi has attributes of the Bagheli and Awadhi. This is a well-known folk tale amongst the tribals of the region and tells about how the mahua drink was discovered. The mahua drink is considered the heart and soul of the region. It is an alcoholic beverage produced by fermenting the mahua flower. It is a popular summer drink in the region. While preparing the drink, the smell of fermenting mahua flowers and woodsmoke hang heavy in the air. Mahua drink is also an important part of rituals amongst the Adivasi communities of Chhattisgarh, Chota Nagpur Plateau, and some regions of Maharashtra, Madhya Pradesh, Gujarat, and Andhra Pradesh. The Adivasis consider themselves as the guardians of the mahua tree. Birth, death, weddings, and funerals—every important event is sanctified by the mahua drink. Though it remains a minor forest product, it is at the core of a lucrative local business.

Ranjana: The story is originally in Sindhi. It is written by Vedanshi Ashok Bhatia. Ranjana has worked several jobs in her life. Now, at seventy-three, she swears to have 'lived a life filled with colours'. When asked, she says her story is like any other women in Chhattisgarh, whose family had to migrate, but her story is also a lucky and a blessed one. She is well aware about the many hardships people had to face due to Partition and has seen many broken families, but she only focuses on the positive attributes of life. When asked to share any three things that she has learned at her age, she says, 'love everyone, forgive and forget and think positive feelings, and work hard.' Four of Ranjana's siblings are still alive today. Ranjana is a family friend of Vedanshi Ashok Bhatia. She is described as a 'very cool aunt who loves to share her life story'. Vedanshi fondly remembers listening with rapt attention to her many stories as a child along with her several cousins. The original name has been changed.

DADRA AND NAGAR HAVELI AND DAMAN AND DIU

Submergence: This story is famous in the Dhodia, Kukna, and Varlie languages. It has been written in the Gujarati by Kulin Patel and translated by Suhag Dave. The story is famous across a wide geographical region with slight variations across northwest Maharashtra and central Gujarat, including Daman and Diu. The story first appeared in an article by Kulin Patel in *Gujarat Guardian* on 19 August 2012. The story was provided by the author for translation. There is an absence of a written script amongst the tribes of the region and this story is famous across all the tribes with slight variations.

The Divaso Festival and the Evrat Jeevrat Vrat Story: This story is famous in Dhodia, Gujarati, and Hindi. It has been retold and translated from Hindi by Lopamudra Maitra Bajpai. Divaso is a mid-monsoon agricultural festival and falls on the last day of the dark half of Ashad (July–August) of the Indian agricultural month. It is a community festival and is observed by a village or a group. The word Divaso is supposed to have been derived from the Sanskrit term deep puja or worship of the lamp. Often, newly-married women observe this puja till they conceive a baby. On the day of the puja, they fast the whole day, which is only broken at the end of the day, after worshipping the goddesses Evrat Jeevrat. Thus, Divaso day is also called the Evrat day. The festival also observes a mock-marriage between a male and female doll made of cloth. This is a symbolic representation of the association of women for a happily married life. This story has been collected through personal interactions by the author. Details of this story can also be found in *Dublas of*

Gujarat by P. G. Shah, New Delhi: Bharatiya Adimjati Sevak Sangh Kingsway, 1958, pp. 132–33.

The Story of the Preservation of Hoka Trees: This story was narrated in Hindi and Gujarati, over personal interaction with the author and translator, Lopamudra Maitra Bajpai by Ramesh Raval. Ramesh Raval is well known in the region and in media for his conservation work on the lions of Gir National Park and Wildlife Sanctuary. However, his lesser-known philanthropic work is associated with preservation and conservation of the hoka trees. Raval continues his work mostly without any help from others and self-finances his efforts. This is an inspiring effort for a tree which is foreign to the land and refuses to grow at any place, outside of Daman, as Ramesh Raval mentioned during the interaction. The hoka trees are originally considered to be from northern Africa and the Arabian Peninsula and according to popular belief, these trees travelled to the region during the Portuguese colonial times.

DELHI

Delhi Is Still Far Away: The original title of the story is 'Dilli Abhi Dur Hai' and has been narrated in Hindustani by Asif Khan Dehlvi to Sudipta Agarwal, who translated it into English. According to the author, the Hindustani language is an amalgamation of Hindi and Urdu and is associated with Ganga–Jamuna tehzeeb. Dilli Abhi Dur Hai is also a well-known saying about the history of Delhi. It is said that each ruler of Delhi had built 'dedh eent ki Dilli' meaning that every ruler who has sat on the throne of Dilli had tried to build his own city, his own Dilli.

The Loose Nail: The original title of the story is 'Qeeli Dhilli' and has been narrated in Hindustani by Asif Khan Dehlvi to Sudipta Agarwal who translated it into English.

Begum Jamila Khwaja: This story is originally in Urdu. It has been translated and retold by Dr Shibal Bhartiya. Begum Jamila Khwaja, or Phuppho, as the author knew her, had skin like wrinkled parchment: diaphanous, fragile and very, very beautiful. She spoke with emphatic pauses, in impeccable Queen's English, and even more delightful Urdu of the Old Dilliwallas. When the author became acquainted with her, she had already been cheated of her inheritance, and a major part of her story was narrated by the author's baba when she was older. The author's baba also mentioned about how her lawyer had conned her into selling off her glorious home to kaarkhandaars. The author mentions that her baba's memory becomes fuzzy on the question of why she quit medicine; nevertheless, what he did say was that it was decidedly her calling. Perhaps India's Independence and her dropping out of medical school are temporally separated, but according to the author's baba, they aren't. The author remembers visiting her as a kid and ever so often, Phuppho would sneak into the author's tiny hands, sugar candy, out of her bejewelled brocade potlis. Phuppho was old and venerated, and perhaps cruelly, avoided by the kids in the house, because she was, well, old. Eyewitnesses to her bravery and resilience, sadly, are now mostly dead like her, but her life's story of immense courage and self-sacrifice lives on. It would take rare courage and immense strength of character to live the way she did.

GOA

The Potter's Girl and the Divine Cow: The original title of the story in Konkani is 'Kapli Gayo'. It has been compiled and translated by Jayanti Naik. This folk tale was narrated by Late Kushawati Amonkar of Amona, Quepem, Goa, to Jayanti Naik in the Konkani in 2000. The Konkani version of the story was published in *Konkani Lokanio* which was compiled and edited by Jayanti Naik and published by the Sahitya Akademi, New Delhi, in 2000.

The Wicked Mother-in-law: This story is originally in Marathi. It was transcripted by Chandrakant Gawas. It has been translated by Narayan Desai, after the narration in the Marathi by Late Mrs Pirtem Gawas. Pirtem Gawas was a resident of Virdi and had a treasury of folk songs, ritual songs, folk stories, riddles, and so on. Several of these were recorded and included in the book *Humkar* by Chandrakant Gawas. This story is taken from the same book.

1956: A Love Story: This story is originally in Konkani and Hindi and is a personal narration by the author, Ramesh Ghadi about his parents. This is a love story from a difficult time and is still remembered fondly by the people of the place. This story also speaks about respect that should be accorded to a spouse who should be justly treated as a partner and a friend in life and never as an inferior individual. This is the story of Indira and Sau Ghadi who were the parents of the author and who hailed from Saligao, Goa.

GUJARAT

Chamadbhai in the Forest: The original story is in the Rathwi dialect (Gujarati). It was narrated by Ashok Rathwa and Savitaben Rathwa to Diti Vyas, who translated it. This tale is meant to be told by the family/village elders to the children after a tiring day in the fields or forests. This story captures the key elements of the Rathwa lives—ceremonies, songs, dances, dietary habits, religious beliefs, and most importantly, their oneness with the forests and all its inhabitants, as epitomized by the final resolution through becoming a tree. This translation negotiates through the multiple versions of the story that exist among the community and uses the final frame supplied by

Ashok Rathwa and Savitaben Rathwa, who are farmers and forest dwellers from Bapodara village of Panchmahal. This story was archived and translated by Diti Vyas as a part of her current research on the oral narratives of the Rathwa community which is mainly spread in Chota Udaipur, Jabugam, and Nasvadi talukas of Vadodara district and also in Halol, Kalol, and Baria talukas of Panchmahal district.

Dug-a-dug, Dug-a-dug, Digging: The original story is in Gujarati. It was narrated by Gijubhai Badheka to Diti Vyas. This tale was adapted and retold, based on the Gujarati folk tale 'Khadabad Khadbad Khodat Hai' told by a famous educationist from Gujarat, Gijubhai Badheka (1885–1939) in the third part of the *Bal Varta* series. Considered as the founder of Gujarati children's literature, Gijubhai was lovingly referred to as Moochhali Maa for his contribution. After joining Dakshinamurti Balmandir School in Bhavnagar (Gujarat) in the 1920s, he along with his trainees, undertook a massive project of compiling the timeless oral folk tales and used these tales for the purpose of education. These tales were published in the five-volume *Bal Varta*. These stories are noted for their rapid pace, sing-song rhythms, and Gujarati colloquialisms.

Father's Gift: This story is originally in Gujarati. It was narrated by Pundrik Vyas to Diti Vyas, who translated it. This story is based on a series of real-life incidents as reminisced by Pundrik Vyas, a retired bank manager based in Gujarat in the autobiography of his father, Krishna A. Vyas, titled *Kal Yug No Karma Yogi* (The Practitioner of the Theory of Karma in the Age of Kali) published in 1981. Krishna A. Vyas was an additional collector and a Sanskrit scholar. The episodes in Vyas's autobiography capture his experiences as a public servant, spanning the times of colonial India and beyond— from 1921 to 1954 in the backdrop of problems such as wars, poverty, bandits, diseases, and internal strife. The autobiography speaks of statesmanship based on humanitarian principles, honesty, dedication, and social welfare.

HARYANA

Danveer Karna: This story is famous in both Hindi and Haryanvi in the region. It has been written by Jaspreet Mann. Karna is the unsung hero of the Mahabharata who proudly proclaims that 'where there is dharma there is victory'. 'Danveer Karna' may be a mythological character, but he has inspired men to take the path of duty, courage, righteousness, honesty, loyalty, integrity, benevolence, and compassion, no matter what the cost.

An Old War Folk Song: This is an almost forgotten folk song in Haryanvi. It has been translated by Jaspreet Mann. This song has been a part of oral traditions of Haryana and is also well known in the region, especially amongst army men. It is also a part of the book *Haryana Pradesh ka Loksahitya* by Dr Shankar Lal Yadav, published by Hindustani Academy, Allahabad, in 2000.

Kalpana Chawla: This story is famous across Hindi, Hariyanvi, and Punjabi in the region. It has been written by Jaspreet Mann. The late Kalpana Chawla, is a pride of the Indian nation and the world. She is remembered for her contributions to space science. Kalpana Chawla was born in a small town of Haryana called Karnal. This extraordinary girl put her town on the world map. Even today parents hope that their daughters would follow their dreams and display the courage and fortitude that Kalpana showed at every step of her life. The most noteworthy attempt made by Kalpana to contribute to her state in India was the programme started by her which is aimed at sponsoring two school children to visit NASA so that they could not only widen their horizons but also get the same opportunity that she had received.

HIMACHAL PRADESH

The Himalayan Mystery: Shikari Devi: This story is originally in the Mandyali dialect. It has been written by Sujay Kapil. Mandyali dialect is spoken in the Mandi district of Himachal Pradesh. The story is based on local folk tales and popular beliefs. Though the locals believe that the divine energy of the goddess melts the snow, there is no scientific or historical proof. According to another belief, the place got its name from the shikaris who used to worship the goddess on the hilltop to seek blessings for a successful hunt. The Shikari Devi Temple is a popular destination. It is located on a hilltop in the Seraj Valley in the Himalaya Mandi district, Himachal Pradesh, at an altitude of 2,850 metres above mean sea level. The area experiences heavy snowfall during winters and is inaccessible. During summers, Shikari Devi Temple can be reached from Janjheli, Bagsaid, Kandha or Karsog valley via trekking routes. A roadway also connects the temple from Janjheli, which is 18 kilometres away. The reference to the temple is also found in the ancient Indian text, the *Markandeya Purana* and the Mahabharata. According to the *Markandeya Purana*, sage Markandeya meditated and performed tireless worship braving the vagaries of weather and the wild at this place for many years. During meditation he desired to see the worldly forms of Goddess Durga such as Mahishasur Mardani who killed demons like Mahishasur, Rakta Beeja, and Madhu Kaitaba. His unstinted devotion and purity of thought was blessed by Goddess Durga, who appeared in front of him. Goddess Durga blessed the place and said that she would reside there as Navdurga and she would fulfil the wishes of any devotee who visits this place.

Scandal Point: This story is originally in Hindi. It has been written by Sujay Kapil. This folk tale has been narrated across generations in Himachal Pradesh, however, upon close observation, there seems to be no valid evidence to substantiate the story. Lord Curzon was the Viceroy of India from 1899 to 1905. On the other hand, Maharaja Bhupinder Singh was born on 12 October 1891. The narrated incident is supposed to have taken place in the year 1892/1893. At this time, the maharaja was just a toddler and Curzon was yet to be appointed as the viceroy of India. Finally, the author mentions that there is no documented evidence of Maharaja Bhupinder Singh being married to an Englishwoman. Nevertheless, the story lives on through generations. Patiala was a princely state and was known for its power, opulence, and influence in northwest India even during the British Raj. The head of Patiala royal state, Maharaja Bhupinder Singh, was famous for his flamboyance and philandering. He married five times and also had a harem of around 350 women. He was a warrior par excellence and had a penchant for sports, but above all, his reputation as a womanizer overshadowed his other achievements. This could have created a sense of discord amongst the masses for long and thus, the above story was born. The Mall Road is the main street in Shimla. It was built by the British. This road is an almost level road that runs along the Ridge. Today, it is an important commercial, social, and tourist hub of Shimla. The British banned the entry of all vehicular traffic on the Mall Road to preserve it and this continues till date with, of course, with certain exceptions. The Ridge, on the other hand, is equally significant. It is an enormously wide road which runs parallel to the Mall. The Ridge, just like the Mall Road, is a centre of social interaction and cultural exchange. Shimla was declared the summer capital of the British empire in India by the viceroy of India, John Lawrence, in 1864. It quickly became the most favoured destination of the officers of the Raj.

Pahadi Gandhi: Baba Kanshi Ram: This story is famous across Kangri, Punjabi, and Hindi. It has been written by Sujay Kapil. Baba Kanshi Ram's literary work recounts his varied experiences, including his life in imprisonment and as a freedom fighter, his encounters and thoughts on metaphysics, mysticism, romance, and plight of farmers of the hills. His work includes 500 poems, eight short stories, and a novelette. Some of his important poems include 'Smaj ne Roya', 'Nikke-nikke Mahnua jo Dukh Bara Bhari', 'Ujari Kangre des Jana', 'Mera Suneha Bhukhyan Nangiyan yo', 'Na kar Gallan Munuan Kanne Jaane Diyan', and 'Kanshi ra Suneha'. He wrote eight short stories and each one was important and a favourite amongst all readers. Some of his famous short stories include, 'Kunali di Kahani', 'Kanshi di Jawani', 'Nana di Kahani', 'Charu kanne Resho', and 'Pahadiya kanne Chughaliya'.

JAMMU AND KASHMIR

Heemal and Nagrai: The originial story is in Kashmiri. It has been retold and translated by Ashok Dhar. This is a love story of Heemal and Nagrai and is considered as old as the origin of Kashmir. This is an important part of local oral tradition and was often narrated to the narrator by his mother. Kashmir is full of lakes, springs, mountains, rivers and is well known for its natural beauty. These springs are also known as nags, like the famous Verinag (origin of river Jhelum/Vitasta), Sheshnag (near Amarnath Cave), Anantnag, Kokernag, and so on. However, Kashmir is originally believed to have been a large body of water, Satiisar, which was drained by the sage Kashyapa after whom 'Kashmir' got its name. As mythology goes, nagas and serpents are believed to have been the original inhabitants of the valley when it was Satiisar. The nagas were considered to be semi-divine beings who could assume human forms. The story also mentions that the word 'nag' (spring) gets its name from Nagrai. After Heemal snatched a tuft of Nagrai's hair, she wandered around throwing bits of his hair everywhere. These gave birth to the deodar, birch, oak, walnut, bren, pine, and other trees making Kashmir full of dense jungles of green forests known as heewans. This story has been narrated by the famous Kashmiri Sufi poet Shamas Faquir. In his 'Baaz Wala Raaz Hanz', Faquir wrote about how Nagrai, after assuming human form, proved his caste to Heemal and thus, this love is a manifestation of the essence of his very existence. In one such poem, Kashmiris till today, recall the mystic and legendary romance of Heemal and Nagrai.

The Only Son: This story is in Kashmiri. 'Akanandun', The Only Son is a folk tale of Kashmir that has passed through oral tradition which later was written in the form of short story, poem, as well as drama. It has been retold and translated by Ashok Dhar for this volume. This mystic tale leaves readers with many lessons to remember. 'Akanandun' was written by Samad Mir (1894–1959) in fourteen parts. He was a Sufi mystic poet and used Sanskrit and Hindi words. He used this folk tale to tell the syncretic and composite relationship of Kashmiri Shaivism (Trika philosophy) and Sufism (Tassavuf).

The Forgotten Hero: Maqbool Sherwani: This story is famous in the region in English, Urdu, and Kashmiri. It has been retold and translated by Ashok Dhar. The author remembers to have often heard this famous story in his childhood days from his father.

JHARKHAND

The Shepherd and the Tiger: This story is originally in Santali. It has been retold by Pramod Jha. The author came across this story through his various interactions in the region. This story is also found in the book *Santali Lok-Kathayen* (Hindi) published by the National Book Trust, New Delhi.

The Clever Fox: This story is originally in Ho. The version in this volume has been written by Pramod Jha. The author heard this story from his friends who speaks Ho. This story is also found in *Ho Lokkatha-Ek Anushilan* by Dr Aditya Prasad Sinha, published by Vikalp Prakashan, New Delhi.

The Story of the Tana Bhagats: This story is originally in Sadri. The version in this volume has been written by Pramod Jha. The Tana Bhagats are related to the historical Tana Bhagat Movement. They were formed by the Oraon tribe saints Jatra Bhagat and Turia Bhagat. Jatra Bhagat also claimed to be divinely ordained to establish a new sect, the Tana sect, that was remarkedly different from the existing Oraon society and opposed traditional leadership of the pahan (Oraon priest) and mahto (village representative in secular affairs). They also rejected the practices of spirit worship and sacrifice. In the very early phase, the Tana sect was referred to as the Kurukh dharma (Kurukh meaning the original religion of the Oraons).

KARNATAKA

The Story of the Magical Mango: This story is originally in Kannada. It has been translated by Geeta Ramanujam, after a narration by Padmavati, a Hallaki storyteller. This story is part of the oral recital by people from the Hallaki Vokkaligas tribe living in the Uttara Kannada districts of the Western Ghats. The tribe has a vast oral heritage and storytelling is intrinsic to their lives. This story was compiled into a booklet by Bu Da Folklore, a non-profit organization that works to educate, conserve, and document folklore of Uttara Kannada.

Kodai and Poovatha: A Strange Relationship: This story is in Tamil. It has been written by Geeta Ramanujam. Though once a very famous story from the region, it is rarely heard in recent times and is an important part of the oral tradition of the region.

Saalumarada Thimmakka: This story has been provided by

Geeta Ramanujam and retold by Lopamudra for this volume. Geeta Ramanujam referred to this story from *104 Women Will Inspire- Inspiring Stories from Karnataka* by Dr M. C. Mohan Kumari, published by Pramaan Publications, Mysore, 2014, pp. 33–37. Mohan Kumari mentions in the book to have met Thimmakka at her residence in a village called Hulikal about 10 kilometres from Kadur, on the main road from Bengaluru to Kunigal (about 70 kilometres from Bengaluru city limits). Saalumarada Thimmakka is 110 years old and is also called Vriksha Mathe or Mother of Trees. She is well known today as an environmentalist and was listed by the BBC as one of the most influential and inspirational women of the world (according to a *Times of India* report, dated 23 November 2019).

KERALA

The Tale of the Brave Lady: This story is in Malayalam. It has been written by Parvathi Chandran. Ballads of North Malabar are popularly known as Vadakkan Pattukal (songs of the North). They portray the life and valour of renowned warriors of northern Kerala. The legendary heroes in these ballads belong to the Ezhava or Nair caste. One such popular ballad is centred on the fearless beautiful lady called Unniyarcha. Her ancestors are believed to be from Sri Lanka and they were especially brought to guard the local chieftains. Several films in Malayalam are also about these songs and also the story of Unniyarcha, including *Unniarcha* (1961) directed by M. Kunchacko), *Aromalunni* (1972) directed by M. Kunchacko, *Oru Vadakkan Veeragatha* (1989) directed by Hariharan, *Puthooramputhri Unniyarcha* (2002) directed by P. G. Viswambharan, and *Veeram* (2016) directed by Jayaraj.

The Tale of the Lady with the Ruby Anklet: This story is in Tamil. It has been written by Parvathi Chandran. Kannagi's story is the central theme of a Tamil epic poem, *Silappatikaram* (belonging to Sangam literature) written by Ilango Adigal. This is very popular in Kerala and connected with the mythological origin of Attukal Bhagavati Temple and Kodungalloor Bhagavati Temple. Kannagi is regarded as a personification of chastity and worshipped as the goddess of chastity, rain (Mari Amman) and fertility in Tamil Nadu and Sri Lanka. In Kerala, she is revered as an embodiment of Goddess Bhadrakali. The story of the kingdom of Chera (present-day Kerala) speaks of the popular mythology of the origin behind the famous Attukal Devi Temple. The Pongal festival of Attukal Temple (to celebrate the victory of Kannagi over the king of Madurai) is the world's largest gathering of women and has also found its place in the Guinness Book of World Records. The history and origin of Attukal Temple is narrated in *Attukal Amma: The Goddess of Millions* by Lakshami Rajeev (Element, 2016). The popularity of the story of Kannagi has also found its reflection in the popular culture of Kerala. Various films, both in Tamil and Malayalam, have been made on Kannagi, including *Kovalan* (1928), a silent film directed by R. S. Prakash, *Kannagi* (1942), a Tamil film directed by R. S. Mani, *Poomphur* (1964), a Tamil film directed by P. Neelakantan, and *Kodungallooramma* (1968), a Malayalam film on the Kodungallor Bhagavathi Temple directed by M. Kunchacko.

The Revival Story of Navara Rice: The author and translator Lopamudra Maitra Bajpai, gathered information about this story over personal interaction with Narayanan Unny. Currently, Narayanan Unny is working on a book on the Navara rice and collecting artefacts for a museum related to rice and farming, under the Navara Foundation. The aim of the museum is to educate people about rice, its varieties, process for harvesting, technicalities involved, significance in the modern global world, etc. The museum will also be equipped with audiovisual experiences as well as demonstrations of the various stages of rice farming for a real-life experience of the cultivation process.

LADAKH

Tsi-zo Lha-wang and Shing-zo Lha-wang: This story is in Ladakhi/Bhoti and has been retold and written by Lopamudra Maitra Bajpai from a narration by Lhundup Gyalpo. This is a famous story from the collection by Nagarjuna, the Indian Buddhist philosopher who lived during the second century CE. Nagarjuna articulated the doctrine of emptiness (shunyata) and is regarded as the founder of the Madhyamika (Middle Way) school, an important tradition of Mahayana Buddhist philosophy. Nagarjuna's work is an integral part of Buddhist heritage.

The Wish-fulfilling Well: This story is in Ladakhi/Bhoti and has been retold and written by Lopamudra Maitra Bajpai from a narration by Lhundup Gyalpo. This used to be a very famous folklore in the region of Ladakh once however, at present, it is hardly narrated and is limited to folklore within houses, where it is limited to the older generations alone. For the narrator too, this story bears a similar semblance. It was narrated to him as a child by the elders at home.

The Ice Man of India: This story has been collected, retold, and written by Lopamudra Maitra Bajpai after a personal interaction with Chewang Norphel. Norphel's contribution to ecology in the Ladakh region remains significant. The personal interaction with Norphel also revealed how important are his examples for the present generation in the region as Norphel is often consulted by many youngsters even in present times.

LAKSHADWEEP

The Legend of Pampum Palli of Amini Island: The original story is in Jasari. This story has been written by Ubaidulla Thangal for this volume. Pampum Palli or the Snake Mosque has another name—Maula Palli—referring to the qazi who led the act of poisoning of the Portuguese. This story relates to unfortunate events during the Portuguese colonial times in the island. This is a very popular story from the island. *Thuhfath-al Mujahidieen* by Shayk Zainudheen Makhdhum, not only mentions the atrocities of Portuguese in the islands of Lakshadweep in the sixteenth century, but also speaks about the spirit of the local islanders and how they put up a fight against the brutal Portuguese army. In the fight, many became martyrs, including the qazi of the island of Amini. As opined by some of the islanders and reflected in oral traditions, the Portuguese carried out the vehement attack on the island by killing several people in the island of Amini to avenge the Pampum Palli incident.

The Legend of Farangiya Aruta Kunnu of Andorth Island: The original story is in Jasari. This story has been written by Ubaidulla Thangal for this volume. The literal translation of Farangiya Aruta Kunnu is the Hill On Which Portuguese Were Slaughtered. Lakshadweep, the coral islands of India is blessed with natural blue lagoons and pure white sandy beaches and is a tourist heaven, but it was often exposed to tyranny and plunder by the sailors of the high seas. This story as well known as 'The Legend of Pampum Palli of Amini Island'. Both stories are retellings of popular accounts associated with the unfortunate incidents which occurred during the Portuguese colonial times in the island as a result of frictions with the Portuguese army. In the sixteenth century, Vasco da Gama discovered the sea route to India and landed in the Port of Calicut. His arrival in Kerala paved the way for the arrival of the Portuguese sailors in the tiny islands of Lakshadweep. To the Portuguese sailors, the islanders seemed helpless, peace-loving, and simple who did not know the use of firearms. The Portuguese colonial rule was filled with stories of loot, plunder, and harassment of the local population. Left with no authority to turn to, the helpless people suffered incessantly from the atrocities of the Portuguese for a very long time. A historical book of Kerala, *Thuhfath-al Mujahidieen* by Shayk Zainudheen Makhdhum states that the atrocities caused by the Portuguese in the Lakshadweep islands in the sixteenth century was due to their ongoing battle with Arakkal Ali Raja, the king of Arakkal Dynasty of Kannur (Kerala), who was also ruling Lakshadweep at that time. Thus, the common masses suffered as a result of this battle between two political powers. The two stories mentioned in this book have been told and retold in different versions and are part of the famous oral traditions of the island. The author has relied on the most popular versions that have been passed down by generations as legends of bravery and resistance against cruelty and tyranny. The word, 'Farangi' (Portuguese) in the island, has a somewhat negative inference. This also goes to reflect the common hatred passed down through the oral traditions owing to the blood-soaked history of the islands.

Ali Manikfan: A Traditional Scientist and a Genius: This story has been written by Ubaidulla Thangal after his interaction with Ali Manikfan. Ali Manikfan continues to be an inspiration for many in the region, as well as many others across the island including other parts of India. Presently, Ali Manikfan lives with his daughter in Calicut in Kerala. In spite of his old age, he still performs the role of a guide and a teacher for many youngsters across the country. Young visitors come to him seeking advice on various subjects. He is also often invited by many schools and colleges for workshops and academic sessions, especially providing the children with an opportunity to interact through question–answer sessions. Ali Manikfan is truly an unconventional genius. He was awarded the Padma Shri in 2021.

MADHYA PRADESH

The Chudail Who Stayed Back: This story is in Hindi. It was narrated by Madhulika Samanta to Lopamudra Maitra Bajpai who has translated and transcribed it for this volume. This story is often heard in various parts of Madhya Pradesh, with minor variations, for instance, in Kareli, the chudail is perceived as a dancer who marries a peasant. She is thus forced to stay back as her chunri is trapped under a mortar and in due course, marries the peasant and gives birth to two children. She disappears close to the time of the marriage of the eldest son after requesting for the release of her chunri.

The Story of Shaligram and the Butcher: This story is in Bundeli. It has been written by Samvedna Rawat Amitabh. It is customary for Hindu priests to place a black stone along with other idols of deities before beginning the Satyanarayan puja. This black stone is the shaligram. It is a fossilized black stone and is originally found in the riverbed of the Gandaki River in Nepal. Devotees consider the shaligram as a reincarnated form of Lord Vishnu. The story is not only of love, respect, and dedication but also about valuing something even if it is a mere stone. In central India, there are many stories which are a part of the oral tradition amongst women. The author realized early on that these stories formed an important treasury which her mother carried along with her and that they imparted great wisdom for understanding various aspects of life. Some of these stories carry proverbs within them and many also reflect progressive thinking amidst its traditional framework. The author heard this story from her mother, who was a devout Brahmin and followed all rites and rituals. This story expresses the value and intensity of love and dedication.

The Story of a Teacher: This story is in Hindi. It has been written by Samvedna Rawat Amitabh. The author is one of the younger daughters of the teacher mentioned in the story. Years later, after the actual incident took place, the story was narrated by the eldest daughter to her siblings. She was the one who had witnessed all this during her growing up years. She also decided to become a teacher. The teacher was an eminent Hindi poet and writer and also an honest human being, a loving father, caring husband, dedicated teacher, and a great visionary. His name is not disclosed in the story as per the kind request of the author. The name of the young student has also been changed following a request made by the author.

MAHARASHTRA

The Copper-tiled House: This story is in Marathi. It has been written by Rukshana Nanji. This nineteenth century short story has lived in the collective memory of the Christian Mandvi Koli fishing community of Mumbai in lyrical form for centuries. It provides an interesting and rare glimpse into the interface between the Kolis, who were the original inhabitants of Mumbai, and the Parsis, who had settled and thrived there and also the British, who governed the land in the colonial times. The Parsis were the tax collectors and arbiters for the British since they received Bombay (as Mumbai was then called) as part of Catherine of Braganza's dowry. The friendship between the Kolis and Parsis date back to 1692, when Bombay was severely affected by a bout of plague and an attack by the Sidis of Janjira was repelled by a Parsi tax-collector, Rustomji Dorabjee, along with a contingent of Kolis. The British, in appreciation of the brave deed of the Parsi, awarded the title Patel on Rustomji Dorabjee and his descendants. In 1912, an Englishman S. M. Edwardes published a slim volume titled *By-*

ways of Bombay. This volume included a story called 'Governor and Koli' in which Edwardes presented the narrative but said that the original song was lost and only a part of the song was quoted by him, which is as follows:

> *Seaman Koli of simple mould*
> *Hath in his house great store of gold–*
> *Lo! At the order of Topiwala*
> *Koli is peer of Batliwala*

However, in 1923, Edwardes wrote an article called 'A Koli Ballad' in the journal *The Indian Antiquary*, in which he presented the entire Marathi song and story which had been recomposed in 1880 by Antone Dhondu Nakhwa, an old Koli. Surprisingly, the part of the song, earlier mentioned by Edwardes, did not find mention in this version. According to Edwardes, the house in Dongri Street which was occupied by Mahadev Dharma Patel, a headman of the Kolis, in 1906, was the very house with the copper tiles. Once removed from the roof, these tiles were affixed to the wall, since they were so legendary. Unfortunately, no trace of them or the house has survived. The appearance of Juran Patel's name in government land records denote vast holdings and attest to his great wealth.

Friend: 'Maitrn' or 'Friend' is originally in an old form of Marathi, spoken during the time of the Peshwas in the coastal and Konkan region. It has been translated and retold by Lopamudra Maitra Bajpai after a narration by Geetanjali Avinash Joshi. A resident of Gwalior had narrated this story in its original form to the author. It is important to mention that the story belongs to the old form of the Marathi language and particularly belonged to the region of Konkan. This is greatly different from the present Marathi language spoken in the region. Gwalior is at present in the state of Madhya Pradesh but was once ruled by the Marathas.

The Single-handed Legal Battles of Akkatai Teli: This story is in Marathi. It has been written by Sanket Jain. Akkatai has been working as an active member of the Akhil Bharatiya Janwadi Mahila Sanghatana for the past two decades. Through this, she has been actively fighting for women's rights.

MANIPUR

Henjunaha and Lairoulembi: This story is in Meiteilon (Manipuri). It has been translated and retold by Jayanti Thokchom. Moirang is a town in Manipur situated towards the south of Imphal and flanked by the Loktak Lake in the north-east. A historically important region of Manipur as well as of India (the tricolour flag of India was hoisted here by the Indian National Army on 14 April 1944), Moirang has its own rich and distinct cultural heritage. The many myths and legends of the Moirang Kangleirol (lore of Moirang) reflect the age-old culture and tradition of Manipur and are popular throughout the state. The story of Henjunaha and Lairoulembi is one of the nine love stories of the Moirang Kangleirol. Another famous love story is that of Khamba and Thoibi. It is said that these lovers are the langon (incarnations) of God Thangjing and his consort, Paloitabi. It is believed that, all these love stories have been ordained by God Thangjing and are meant to be tragic so that their love would remain immortal. The story of Henjunaha and Lairoulembi is the theme of many Manipuri poems, plays, and ballads.

Galngam: The Thadou Kuki Idol: This story is in Thadou. It was written by Aanandi Kaul. Aanandi Kaul is herself a Thadou Kuki, married to an Indian Army officer who is a Kashmiri Pundit. This is a very popular legend, which has been passed on through generations in the Thadou clan of the Kuki tribe of Manipur. This story is narrated in almost every event, like Kut and during commemoration events of the Thadou. Many of Galngam's exploits are narrated for motivational discourses and for drawing out inspiration for the ambitious youngsters among the Thadou community. Galngam's bravery, presence of mind, friendship, innovative ideas, and love for his clan are always a source of inspiration. There are many critics who debate about the khivui (magical necklace with red pearls) of the Thadou women. It is popularly believed that the necklace came into existence as a result of one of the many exploits of Galngam during his visit to the super-canine world.

Chungkham Rani, the Creator of Rani Phi: This story is in Meiteilon (Manipuri). It has been translated and written by Jayanti Thokchom. The author wishes to thank Anoubam Kalpana Devi (a family member of Chungkham Rani and proprietor of Rani Handloom Industries) and Maibam ningol Anoubam ongbi Pinky (a family member of Chungkham Rani and an employee at Rani Handloom Industries) for providing her with the biodata and information on Chungkham Rani and her work. Manipur has a rich textile heritage. The vibrant colours, intricate designs, myths and legends connected with the various textiles and motifs show its rich history. Handloom weaving is a traditional craft of Manipur and handloom textiles still have great sociocultural and religious relevance. In Manipur, handloom weaving is not merely an economic activity; it has deep-rooted sociocultural connections. Despite the mechanization of textile production, handloom weaving is still thriving, and it is one of the most important cottage industries in the state. In Manipur, handloom weaving is a craft exclusively looked after by women. The skill is passed down from mothers to their daughters. Traditionally, the skill of weaving is considered an essential asset of a Meitei girl, a quality to be taken into account while choosing a bride. Until a few decades ago, parents would give their daughters a loom as one of the awunpot (wedding gifts) on their marriage.

MEGHALAYA

Two Orphans: This story is originally in Khasi. It has been narrated by Dising Marin and translated by Desmond L. Kharmawphlang. Dising Marin is considered one of the best storytellers that the author has worked with. A ritual expert and believed by the village folk to possess the power of becoming a tiger during certain times, he died a perfectly happy man at the age of ninety-three after having seen the flowering of bamboo twice in his lifetime. The story is partly sung and partly narrated.

Grapmangtata: Funeral Song: This story is in Garo. It has been narrated by Winder M. Sangma and translated and written by Venybirth Seng Ch. Marak. This funeral song called 'Chera' is specially sung during Chougin and Saram Chaa ceremony of the Atongs, and Gara-Ganching subtribes of the Garo people residing in the southern part of the Garo Hills in the state of Meghalaya.

The Skull of U Syiem Syad Lukhmi: This story is originally in Khasi. It has been translated by Desmond L. Kharmawphlang. U Wan and U Ksha, after living in the Nonglyngdoh chiefdom for a long time, defending its boundaries, simply disappeared one day leaving behind a body of stories built around them and a megalithic complex attributed to them. Till date, the villagers of Nonglyngdoh believe that the two brothers will return to dwell in their midst. There have also been unofficial reports about the reincarnation of the two in certain families. The author has heard the story being narrated by different people.

MIZORAM

Thangchhawli: This story is originally in Mizo. It has been retold by C. Lalnunchanga and translated by A. Hmangaihzuali Poonte. The Mizos have several folk tales about the keimi (tiger person).

This story has been translated from the book *Ka Pi Thawnthu Min Hrilh Chu* (Stories My Grandmother Told Me), a collection of short stories written and compiled by C. Lalnunchanga, one of the most prolific contemporary writers in Mizo literature.

Chiasung and Manghan: This story is originally in Lai. It has been translated by Lalrinmawii Tochhawng. This is a famous folk tale of the Pawi/Lai people living in southern Mizoram.

Kaptluangi and Rema: This story is in Mizo. The original story is by Malsawmliana. It has been translated by Lalrinmawii Tochhawng. This is based on several incidences occurring during the twenty years (1966–86) of insurgency period in Mizoram when the Mizo National Front (MNF) fought for independence. This work of fiction takes into consideration several such similar occurrences from the period and all characters and places in this story are fictitious.

NAGALAND

Songmo and her Tree-lover: This story is in English and written by Tiatoshi Jamir, after a narration and personal interview with Mr Yentin Ongbou in Hakchang village, on 26 January 2019. The story is also a part of the book *Folklore of Eastern Nagaland*. Changsang Mongku was considered an old Chang ancestral settlement in Tuensang district, Nagaland. This ancient settlement was regarded as an abode of man, beast, and the spirit world that cohabited. The Ao Naga, in ancient Chungliyimti, also shares a parallel folklore similar to the story of a girl and her tree-lover.

A Tale of Two Brothers: The original story is in Lotha Naga. It has been translated and narrated by Chumbeno Ngullie and transcripted by Lopamudra. The story was narrated to the author by her mother. This is one of the popular folk tales of the Lotha Naga tribe of Nagaland told in the Lotha language.

The Spear Cry Out: Narrative of a Naga Archaeologist: This story is written by Tiatoshi Jamir. The author's interest in the work and life of Vikuosa Nienu grew after his visit to the archival exhibition at the Naga Hornbill Festival held in Kohima and locating Nienu's work in a bulletin. Situated within a postcolonial narrative, the text examines the biography of Vikuosa Nienu, a pioneering Naga archaeologist—his formative years at the School of Archaeology, New Delhi, and thereafter his intellectual life nurtured within the Western academia and the major paradigms that shaped his understanding of the historical past of the Northeast, in particular, the Naga Hills.

ODISHA

Stories of the Osakothi Ritual in Ganjam: This story is in Odia. It has been written by Jitu Mishra. Osakothi stories are folk tales in the villages of Ganjam District where Osakothi rituals are performed by so-called lower-caste women during the Navratri festival in the month of Ashwin. Supplemented by murals in a unique style, a fusion of tribal and folk, Osakothi shrines are a link between the tribal deities and beliefs and mainstream Hinduism. The Thakurani goddess is represented as a ghata (pot) and depicted in murals along with other deities. According to yet another folk tale of this tradition, many years after the death of her sons, while going to the river to take a bath on a particular day, Shriya met a woman. She was none other than Goddess Mangala. She told Shriya that if she worships Goddess Mangala, she would get all the things she desired. As instructed by the goddess, Shriya took a pot and worshipped it. With that she revived all her seven sons. She observed osa (ritual fasting) for twelve years. When the queen saw the seven sons of Shriya, she was astonished and enquired about what had happened. Shriya informed the queen who then began the puja of the goddess and was subsequently blessed with seven sons.

There is yet another story which mentions the poet Kalidasa living in Bauri Sahi (street of untouchables). He was banished to Bauri Sahi by the unjust king who was also a womanizer. His kingdom suffered badly because of his behaviour. All his subjects assembled together and thought of an idea to keep the mind of the king from thinking of women ever so often. They proposed to him that he should create a mural of his favourite queen and keep it near him. The king liked the idea and invited the court painter to draw the mural. Everybody appreciated the mural when it was finished, except Kalidasa who intervened and pointed out that the mural was not a complete replica of the queen since there was a kalajai or a black mole on the left thigh of the queen which was missing on the mural. The king was very annoyed, suspecting an illicit affair between Kalidasa and his queen and banished him from his post of the court poet. Kalidasa was left with very few choices and took refuge at the Bauri Sahi. In his new place, Kalidasa started a kothisala. First, he made the mural of Shiva Tandav, followed by the image of Parvati, then Mahisamardhini Durga and then Kali. After that he drew Goddess Mangala followed by Ganesha and Kartikeya, and finally Panchu Pandava or the five Pandava brothers.

Origins of the Dongria Kondhs: This story is originally in Kui. It has been written by Jitu Mishra. Niyamgiri is a high plateau in Odisha's Rayagada and Kalahandi districts and is the abode of the Dongria Kondh, one amongst the three Kondh tribes; the other two being Kutia Kondh and Desia Kondh. Blessed with nature's bounty, the Dongrias of Niyamgiri are truly the children of Mother Earth who possess unique knowledge on environmental sustainability. They speak Kui language of Dravidian origin and treat Niyamgiri as their god who have prescribed rules on sustainable living.

From Khasi Cup to World Cup: A Journey of Odisha's Hockey Culture: This story is in Odia. It has been written by Jitu Mishra. In the twenty-first century, Odisha's capital city, Bhubaneswar, has evolved as a major venue for world hockey. The city hosted Odisha World Cup Hockey 2018 for sixteen participating teams, and it was a grand success. Hockey is today Odisha's new identity symbol. The state has become the official sponsor of the Indian Hockey Team—both men and women for the last five years. The success of Odisha's hockey has its roots in the tribal heartland of Sundargarh district, where missionary activities in early twentieth century was responsible for spreading the hockey culture. In the last few decades, the district has produced some of the finest hockey players of our time. According to Father Isidore Kindo of Jagatmata Church in Sounamara Village (the birthplace of several hockey players including Dilip Tirkey), tribal communities of Sundargarh, which include Oran, Munda, Gond, and Kisan, do not believe in gender discrimination. Most parents do not see their daughters as any less talented than their sons. Today, Dilip Tirkey is a great source of inspiration for budding hockey players of the district. In 2013, Dilip Tirkey organized the Gramin Olympiad Hockey Tournament in Sundargarh in which 800 teams participated.

PONDICHERRY

The Creation: This story is in Tamil. It has been retold and written by P. Raja. This is a folk tale that every Pondicherrian is familiar with. It is a prophetic tale that speaks of the would-be 'cosmopolitan city'. The story speaks of a prophecy, which is believed to have come true as it is well known that Pondicherry has several prominent languages, out of which three are official languages of the union territory of Pondicherry.

Liquor Saves Pondicherry: This story is in Tamil. It has been retold and written by P. Raja. This folk tale is based in history. Ballads and short verses making fun of Raghuji Bhonsle's wife for her love for liquor, are well known across Pondicherry. This story has its source in *A Concise History of Pondicherry* by P. Raja, published by Busy Bee Books, Pondicherry, 2003.

Know God, Know Peace: This story is in Tamil. It has been written by P. Raja. Rev. Fr. A. S. Antonisamy is a living legend in Pondicherry. He is a Diocesan priest and belongs to the Immaculate Conception Cathedral of Pondicherry.

PUNJAB

Baba Farid and Beera Bai: This story is famous in Punjabi. It has been translated and retold by Narinder Jit Kaur. Farid-al-Din Mas'ud Ganj-i-Shakar is reverently called Sheikh Farid or Baba Farid by Muslims, Hindus, and Sikhs of Punjab. He was a twelfth century Sufi preacher and mystic. Some of his hymns have been included in the Guru Granth Sahib, the holy book of the Sikhs. Incidents from the lives of the Bhagats, like Sheikh Farid and others, called the 'saakhis' have been a part of the oral folk narratives of the Sikhs, which were later compiled as *Saakhi Pramaan*. These saakhis are narrated during religious congregations of the Sikhs even today. In Sikh traditions, getting married, leading a family life, and performing familial responsibilities are emphasized.

The Survivors: This story is famous in Hindi. It has been translated by Narinder Jit Kaur and she holds the copyright for the translation. The original story is by Sukhwant Kaur Mann. The translator describes it as a story of grit and indomitable human spirit in the face of adversity.

Women Empowerment and the Colours of Phulkari: This story is in Punjabi. It has been retold and translated by Narinder Jit Kaur, over personal interaction with Rekha Mann.

RAJASTHAN

Moomal and Mahendra: This story is originally in Marwari. It is narrated by Asif Khan Dehlvi and translated by Sudipta Agarwal. This is a very popular love story from Rajasthan. It is often narrated in the areas around Jaisalmer (Sindh). Though there are no different versions of the story, there are different ways of presenting the same story. In some places, it is enacted, whereas in other places, it is narrated with the help of musical instruments.

Through the Eyes of Buaji: The title of the story in the Bagri, Dhundhari, and Malwai languages is 'Buaji ki Aankhein'. It has been narrated by Asif Khan Dehlvi and translated by Sudipta Agarwal for this volume. This story was told to Asif Dehlvi, the narrator, by Katyani bai-sa on one of his trips to Mewar. It is a bedtime folk tale, which is often told to children by their grandmothers.

Khichan's Demoiselle Cranes and a True Reflection of Atithi Devo Bhava: This story is in Marwari. It has been written by Jitu Mishra. Situated on a major trade junction from the times of medieval India, the Thar Desert of Rajasthan has been a stronghold of Jainism for over hundred years. However, by the beginning of the twentieth century, as trade diminished, large numbers of Jain merchants moved out in search of work to places as far off as Chennai, Mysore, Kolkata, Delhi, and Mumbai. The roads of Khichan have several palatial havelis, which have been abandoned and left behind. Sometimes, the residents pay an annual visit, during the chaumas for a couple of months. Today, Ratanlalji is a legendary figure as he alone had taken care of the conservation of thousands of demoiselle cranes that came to the sleepy village of Khichan every winter from time immemorial. It was because of Ratanlal's dedication and vision that the cranes got the food they needed in the chugga ghar and therefore did not ravage the farmlands of Khichan and the surrounding villages. As a result, they have become guests who are received warmly.

SIKKIM

Lepcha Folk Belief on the Origin of Insects: This story is originally in the Lepcha language. It has been written by Anira Phipon Lepcha. It was narrated to her by her grandmother, Late Premkit Lepcha, when she was a child. There is an important moral associated with this story—Evil can be won upon, but it is never dead. Late Premkit Lepcha was from Rinchenpong, West Sikkim and died in 2014 at the age of eighty-six.

Ageing: A Child's Tough Question: This story is in the Nepali language. It was narrated by K. N. Sharma and has been written and retold by Anira Phipon Lepcha. K. N. Sharma is from Pandam, Sikkim, and is a well-known writer and has published many books in the Nepali language. He is associated with a number of social and literary organizations. There is an important moral associated with this story—As you sow, so shall you reap.

Tikalal Niroula: An Eminent Personality from Sikkim: This story is in the Nepali language. It was narrated by K. N. Sharma and has been written and retold by Anira Phipon Lepcha.

TAMIL NADU

The Righteous King: This story is originally in Tamil and has been written by R. Radhakrishnan for this volume. Another popular version of this story from the region goes on to narrate that God, being pleased by the dispassionate conduct of the king, restored the lives of both the prince and the calf, thus alleviating both the king and the cow from their respective agony and sorrows.

The Story of Thirunaallaipovar: He Who Will Go Tomorrow:
This story is originally in Tamil. It has been written by
Thulasi Muttulingam for this volume. Nandanar's story of
deep devotion, overcoming humble beginnings, has inspired
several folk tales, folk plays, dramas, films, literature, and
songs in Tamil Nadu. It still continues to inspire many down
the ages. His story has been extant from the eight centuries
and gained popularity after it was published in *Periya Puranam*
of Sekkizhar in the twelfth century. The *Periya Puranam* is
a biography of the sixty-three canonical Shaiva saints, of
whom Nandanar is the only Dalit saint. Depending on who
is telling the story, it is one of either condoning Brahmanical
supremacy (Nandanar had to purify himself by walking on
fire to be blessed by the Lord with a new body and so on)
or celebrating it. In recent centuries, the focus is on criticism
of caste hierarchies and the story that Nandanar was loved
by the Lord, who paid no heed to his caste and overrode
Brahmanical supremacy to allow him access to Himself, speaks
volumes. No matter who tells the story, it is very much to his
credit that both Tripunkur and Chidambaram temples have
temple lore corroborating the story from the eight century
onwards, despite caste hierarchy reigning supreme there. These
temples remained closed to Dalits for centuries thereafter,
even though such temple lore glorifies Nandanar. To have
made it as a canonical Shaiva saint over a thousand years
ago, is a very important achievement. He remains one of the
most popular Shaiva saints, inspiring generations with his
faith and devotion, as well as his determination to overcome
the social blockades which prevented him from fulfilling his
heart's desire, until he overcame them so successfully that he
merged with the divine.

Insatiable Fire: This story is in Tamil. It has been written by
M. C. Rajan. On the night of 25 December 1968, forty-four
Dalits were burnt alive in a hut, where they had taken shelter

from the henchmen of the landlords. This horrendous tragedy took place in Keezhvenmani in Nagapattinam district, Tamil Nadu. The Dalits, landless coolies, who worked in the farmlands of the landlords organized under the CPI (M) political party. They demanded half a measure more for wages. A tripartite meeting, including representatives of agricultural workers was also held. This enraged the landlords, who detested the coolies demanding more rights for themselves. The prime accused, Gopalakrishna Naidu, was a famous political party functionary and president of the paddy producers' association and is said to have led the henchmen. The police was also alleged to have not investigated the matter and merely filed a case of internal rivalry amongst Dalits as the reason for the murders and had booked 105 Dalits. Later, under public pressure, a case was registered against the landlords, who were supporters of famous political parties.

TELANGANA

Fists Against Spears: This story is originally in Telugu. It has been written by Srinivas Bandameedi. Sammaka-Sarakka Jatara is one of the most prominent tribal festivals celebrated biannually by the Koya tribe. This four-day festival begins on the Wednesday which falls after full moon day in the eleventh month of Telugu calendar, i.e. Magham and ends on Saturday. Jaya Shankar Bhupalapally district, (earlier part of Warangal district) in Telangana hosts this mega event. More than one crore devotees visit this place during Jatara. Although the story of Sammaka and Saralamma has been regarded as the theological narration by many, it has a strong historical relevance where these women could challenge the powerful monarch. In the present socio-political setup, this story serves as an authoritative source to motivate the socially disadvantaged groups in the assertion of their rights.

Lalu Sardar: The Short Man: This story is in the Lambada language. It has been written by G. Veerya Nayak. The author first heard this story when he was a child from his grandfather, Gugulothu Ramoji.

Water, Forest, Land: The original title of this story in Telugu is 'Jal, Jangal, Jameen'. It has been written by Parvathi Chandran. The popular slogan of today's tribal movements 'Jal, Jangal, Jameen' was first coined by Komaram Bheem in his agitation against the nizam. Puchapalli Sundariah, a politician and head of the peasant revolt in Hyderabad has written a biography of Komaram Bheem. The Gond community observes the death anniversary of Bheem every year on Aswayuja Powrnami, an auspicious full-moon day as per Hindu calendar. *Komaram Bheem,* a Telugu movie, directed by Allani Sridhar, portrays the life and struggles of Bheem. Another television serial titled *Veerabheem* (Telugu) produced by Nagabala Suresh Kumar also sketches the life of Komaram Bheem.

TRIPURA

How a Brother and His Sister Transformed into Elephants: The original title of the story is in the Kokborok language and is called 'Bwta Bahanok Maywng ongwi thagkha'. It has been narrated from Kokborok into Bengali by Chandrakanta Murasingh which was then translated from Bengali and transcripted in English by Lopamudra Maitra Bajpai. The narrator, Chandrakanta Murasingh, had heard this story in his childhood from his pishima (paternal aunt). This is a very popular folk tale in Kokborok.

The Owl Delivered the Good News all Night Long but the Woodpecker Got the Reward of the Golden Crown: The title of the story in the Chakma language is 'Pechya kulkulela khuralya madhat sanar tuk'. It has been narrated from Chakma into

Bengali by Gautam Lal Chakma which was then translated from the Bengali and transcripted in English by Lopamudra Maitra Bajpai. The narrator, Gautam Lal Chakma, had heard this story in his childhood from his mother. The story forms part of a bigger narrative. This story continues to be very popular in Chakma.

Gymnast Dipa Karmakar: Inspiring the Youth: This story is in Bengali. It has been translated by Lopamudra Maitra Bajpai. Dipa Karmakar continues to inspire many young women as well as men in Indian gymnastics. She is also instrumental in training the youth in gymnastics in Tripura.

UTTAR PRADESH

Panduk Chidiya: This story is in Hindi. It has been written by Shakuntala Shami (also known as Shakun Shami) in her book *Panduk Chidiya* published by Indradhanush Prakashan in 2005. Shakuntala Shami is noted for her children stories that highlight the folklore of the region. For this volume, the story has been translated and retold by Lopamudra Maitra Bajpai. The translator wishes to thank Deepika Shami, the daughter of Shakuntala Shami for kindly giving permission to translate the story, and providing this story for this book.

The Hurricane and the Foolish Leopard: This story is originally in Awadhi. It has been retold and translated by Lopamudra Maitra Bajpai. This is a very popular story from the region. A very similar version is also popular from the region of erstwhile Bengal (including present-day Bangladesh). The Bengali version is called 'Buddhur Baap' (Buddhu's Father) was also a part of the edited book by Upendrakishore Ray Chowdhury's *Tuntunir Boi*.

Guns That Were Kind: This story is originally in Urdu. It has been translated by Dr Shibal Bhartiya, after the Urdu narration by Zakia Mashhadi. The author and translator is Hakim Sahib's granddaughter who has inherited his love of the jungle and is, like him, a medical practitioner. She also claims to have inherited his sense of humour and love for all that is wonderful about the plural sociocultural fabric of India. Zakia Mashhadi is Hakim Khaliq Ahmad's eldest daughter. Hakim Khaliq Ahmad was born in 1916 and was the alumnus of the famous Takmeel-ut-Tibb College in Lucknow. He moved to Sultanpur to set up his practice as a fresh college graduate. Sultanpur is a small sleepy town in Uttar Pradesh, about 30 kilometres from Ayodhya. He passed away in 2008, surrounded by friends and family, aghast at the events that had unfolded in his homeland, and at the bitterness between Hindus and Muslims. Chhote Lal's grandchildren and Hakim Sahib's youngest son continue to live in Majorgunj with their families.

UTTARAKHAND

Pyonli: This story is originally in the Gharwali and Kumaoni languages. It has been written by Geeta Gairola and translated by Smita Karnatak. This folk tale is famous in Gharwal and also in Kumaon. The author heard it from her paternal grandmother.

The Moon and His Light: This story is originally in the Gharwali language. It has been written by Geeta Gairola and translated by Smita Karnatak. This story was narrated to the author by her grandmother. Referring to dhakaris and sharing food items, she adds, she had heard from her grandfather that in earlier times, salt and fire were the only two things that people would borrow from each other.

Tinchari Mai: An Ascetic with a Difference: This story is in Hindi. It has been retold and translated by Lopamudra Maitra Bajpai and she would like to acknowledge the contribution of the personal communication with C. S. Lakshmi of SPARROW, Mumbai, who helped to compile this story. C. S. Lakshmi had also written an article in *The Hindu* (4 June 2000) on Tinchari Mai. Further, Lopamudra Maitra Bajpai also wishes to acknowledge the reference provided by C. S. Lakshmi for this story 'The Emancipated Womenfolk of Uttarakhand' by Chhaya Kunwar and published in 1997 by the Himalayan Action Research Centre (HARC), Dehradun and The Society for Participatory Research in Asia (PRIA), New Delhi.

WEST BENGAL

The Story of Madanmohan of Bishnupur: This story is in the Bangla language. It has been translated and retold by Lopamudra Maitra Bajpai. The story was collected by the author during her ethnographic fieldwork in the Radh region (consisting of the western part of West Bengal). The erstwhile Mallabhum, ruled by the Malla kings of Bishnupur, flourished during the reign of Hambir Malla Dev, popularly known as Veer Hambir (1565–1620 CE), the forty-ninth ruler of the Malla dynasty. He was a contemporary of Mughal emperor, Akbar (1542–1605 CE). According to popular belief, Hambir converted from Shaktaism to Vaishnavism after listening to the recitation of Bhagavata by Srinivasa Acharya, the Vaishnava saint and thus, later on Madanmohan became the tutelary God of the Malla dynasty. In later years, Gopal Singha's policy of forcing the worship of Madanmohan in his region did not go down well with his subjects. Thus, the subjects infamously referred to this act of forced worship as 'Gopal Singher Begar' (forced and unpaid labour done for Gopal Singha). Finally, with reference to the story related to the Dalmadal cannon, there are no historical evidence of the folklore. It is often critiqued that the cannon could have been fired by either a soldier or the prince, who had dissented with the father. The Dalmadal cannon is preserved, at present, by the Archaeological Survey of India on an oblong altar, surrounded by iron railings in an open space, adjacent to the Chinnamasta Temple in Bishnupur. It is still revered as God's artillery. The word Dalmadal or Dalmardan is a compound of two Bengali words—'dal' meaning horde or group and 'mardan' meaning slayer. Therefore, the name of cannon indicates it was a mass destroying artillery.

The Lepcha Legend of the Teesta and Rangeet Rivers: This story is originally in the Lepcha language. It has been retold and written by Sonam Wangyal. Most river names in Lepcha begin with the prefix 'rang' (rung) which according to K. P. Tamsang means, 'stretched out', 'widespread', 'extensive' or 'extended'. The names generally end with 'ung' (aoong) which simply means water. Addressing a river as 'oong' is not common nowadays. Teesta and Rangeet have always been associated with the people of Darjeeling, especially the Lepcha's ardour, ethos, legends, music, history, and even worship. Mainwaring maintains that the nomen proprium of river Rangeet is rungnyit ung, while that of river Teesta is rung nyu. The rung nyu or the Teesta is the biggest river in the district and almost all the rivers in this region are tributaries of it, including the Great (Bara) and Little (Chhota) Rangeet rivers. This story regarding the confluence of the Rangeet and the Teesta is a very famous legend of the Lepchas in the region. The Lepchas have in deference to the two great rivers, a benediction that goes: 'A-do bryang rung-nyu rung-nyit su-re zong mal-la-o' which translates into 'May your name be celebrated as the rivers Rung-nyo (Teesta) and Rangeet'. The Bhutias and the Tibetans call the river Rang-nyit chu ('chu' means water/river). They hold the Teesta in high regard and call it Sang (Tsang)– chu or 'pure water'.

Of Love and Mutual Respect: This story is in the Hindi, English, and Bengali languages. It has been written and translated by Lopamudra Maitra Bajpai, after personal interaction with Fathma Aslam who lives in Kolkata. She fondly remembers her childhood and interactions with her grandparents. Her son,

Ovais Aslam, runs an initiative called the Indian Pluralism
Foundation to help foster friendship between religions in
Kolkata.

Notes on the Contributors

A. Hmangaihzuali Poonte is Associate Professor, Department of English, Government Aizawl College, Aizawl, Mizoram. She teaches English literature and is a keen amateur photographer.

Aanandi Kaul is an alumnus of Handique College for Girls, Guwahati, and completed her graduation in Arts with Political Science (major). She belongs to the Thadou Kuki tribe of Manipur and has been closely associated with cultural activities of her region. An avid wildlife enthusiast and ornithologist, she accompanies her husband on safari trips. Along with their son, they have been on twenty-five such trips in the past seven and a half years, covering the regions of North Bengal, Sikkim, Lower Assam, Nagaland, the wetlands of Harike and southern Himachal Pradesh, southern Maharashtra, north and central Karnataka. She has to her credit a photobook on the wildlife found in Sukna, West Bengal. She currently lives in Amritsar with her Indian Army officer husband and her son.

Anira Phipon Lepcha has done a PhD in modern history. Her PhD thesis is 'Marginalised Autochthones: Understanding the Historical Process of Subversion–A Case Study of the Lepcha'. Her research interests include regional history, especially history of Sikkim, oral history, study of missionaries, tribal history, history of science and technology, and social and political movements. Before joining Sikkim University in 2014, she had worked at Kalyani University, West Bengal, for seven years. She has participated and presented research papers in many national and international conferences and seminars. She has published her research papers in national and international journals and also contributed chapters in many books.

Ashok Dhar was born and brought up in Kashmir and served in the energy sector for over thirty-five years. He has worked in top leadership roles in three Fortune 500 companies in India and abroad. In 2015, he retired from the post of President, Refining and Marketing Division (Petroleum Business) of Reliance Industries Limited. Widely travelled in India and over thirty countries, he takes special interest in understanding the culture, social life, and politics of the places he has visited. His debut book *Kashmir As I See It: From Within and Afar* (Rupa Publications) published in May 2019, has been widely acclaimed. Currently an independent director on boards, Principal Consultant and Director of Akarosi Private Limited, Kolkata, he is also a distinguished Visiting Fellow of the Observer Research Foundation, a leading think tank.

Asif Khan Dehlvi is a storyteller, walk-leader, culture enthusiast, writer, and a dreamer. Ever since his childhood, he has been an observer and believer of Hindustani traditions that has led him to be the bearer of many tales for over eight years. Born and brought up in Chirag Dilli, surrounded by a plethora of heritage artifacts, he immersed himself in the history of Delhi and founded the Delhi Karavan. He also founded the Calcutta Karavan, Deccan Karavan, Awadh Karavan, and Jaypore Karavan, where multiple events and storytelling take place. He has a soul connection with Rajasthan, which plays a pivotal role in the poetry and stories he writes.

Bina Gandhi Deori is Assistant Professor, Department of Ancient Indian History, Culture and Archaeology, Visva-Bharati University, Santiniketan. Born and brought up in Arunachal Pradesh, she was always intrigued by the folk cultures of different ethnic communities of Northeast India.

C. Lalnunchanga is one of the most prolific contemporary writers in Mizo literature. He has published six novels of which *Pasaltha te Ni hnuhnung* and *Kawlkil Piah lamtluang* received the Book of the Year Award in 2006 and 2015 respectively. The awards were instituted by the Mizo Academy of Letters (MAL), Mizoram. He has also published a number of essays, short stories, short plays, songs, and poetry.

Chandrakanta Murasingh is Director of North East Centre for Oral Literature. He was born in 1957 and is one of the best-known poets from the state of Tripura. He writes in Kokborok and has written several books of poetry. A popular poet in India, he received the Bhasha Samman Award from the Sahitya Akademi, New Delhi, in 1976 for his contribution to the development of Kokborok literature.

Desmond L. Kharmawphlang is a professor in the department of Cultural and Creative Studies, North-Eastern Hill University (NEHU), where he teaches folkloristics and cultural studies. Born, brought up, and educated in Shillong, he has published books on folklore and folkloristics pertaining to Northeast India. Passionate about oral tradition, he extensively travels across lost rural pockets of the Khasi and Jaintia hills, collecting stories and songs. He is involved in several documentation projects, the most recent of which is the Khasi–Welsh Cultural Dialogues in collaboration with the University of South Wales, Cardiff (sponsored by the Leverhulme Trust, United Kingdom), Geo-Spatial Mapping of Legend Sites in collaboration with the Latvian Literature Institute, Riga (supported by the European Union) and Thai–Khasi Cultural Explorations in collaboration with the University of Chulalongkorn, Bangkok. He was the Dyason Visiting Fellow (2018–19) at the University of Melbourne, Australia, and is on the Academic Committee of the Indian Institute of Advanced Study, Shimla.

Dising Marin was a Khasi storyteller par excellence. He passed away in 2012 at the age of ninety-three, after having seen the flowering of bamboo twice in his lifetime. He was also a traditional healer and community priest of the villages of Pahambir and Pahamshken in Ri-Bhoi district, Meghalaya.

Diti Vyas is Associate Professor in Communication at the Adani Institute of Infrastructure Management (AIIM), Ahmedabad. Her PhD in English Literature from the Indian Institute of Technology, Gandhinagar, is titled, 'Gender Politics and Indian Children's Literature: A Comparative Study of Adventure Fiction in English and Gujarati'. She has received national and international accolades for her research work by organizations such as the International Research Society for Children's Literature (IRSCL). Invited to several academic and cultural forums, she has also contributed to international conferences, including the Irish Society for the Study of Children's Literature (ISSCL) and International Research Society Children's Literature (IRSCL) in Ireland, Netherlands, Canada, and England. She has been on the board of the Ahmedabad International Literature Festival and Reviewer Board of Young India Books. Her research interests include gender politics, children's literature in translation, culture, comparative literature, and Indian literature in English, critical theory, collecting and archiving oral narratives and communication.

Gargi Maitra is Consulting Pulmonologist at Fortis Memorial Research Institute, Gurugram. She has years of dedicated service towards pulmonary and critical care medicine. She has been instrumental in helping to organize several workshops and conferences related to pulmonary and critical care medicine at national levels and appreciated for her diligent work for the resourceful handling of her area of work from an early stage in her career. A first class first in the MBBS exams from North

Bengal Medical College, Siliguri, West Bengal, she completed
her MD in Pulmonary Medicine from Government Medical
College, Amritsar, followed by Critical Care Fellowship from
PGI, Rohtak. Her interests include music and reading (across
a wide range of genres). An ace and trained pianist, with
distinction from the Royal School of Music, London, she loves
to travel, explore, meet new people, and explore new cuisines.

Gautam Lal Chakma is editor of *Tripura Sadak,* a Chakma
language newspaper published by the Government of Tripura.

Geeta Gairola is a celebrated author and an advocate of
women's issues in Uttarakhand. She specializes in collecting
and narrating folk tales from Uttarakhand. She currently lives
in Dehradun.

Geeta Ramanujam is an internationally renowned master trainer
storyteller, educator, academician, and administrator. She is the
Executive Director of Kathalaya Trust established in 1998
which is the culmination of her vision and wisdom. Geeta is
a pioneer of the storytelling movement in India. She founded
Kathalaya's International Academy of Storytelling—the only
globally recognized academy for storytelling in the world with
accredited courses affiliated to USA, Scotland, and Sweden. She
has completed 135 batches of the certified beginners' courses
and twenty-seven diploma courses so far. She is an Ashoka
fellow and has widely travelled to over forty-three countries
around the world and twenty-seven states in India to establish
storytelling as a tool of learning and also to set up centres.
She is the Indian Coordinator for both the Indian Storytelling
Network as well as the International Storytelling Network RIC.
She has won several accolades including the Bangalore Hero
Award twice and recently the International Award for the Best
Storyteller at the BoCaDeu storytelling festival at Brazil and the

Governor's Award in Tamil Nadu for the Best Story Narrator. She was recently mentioned and referred to by Prime Minister Narendra Modi in the Maan ki Baat for her contributions to the storytelling field. Over 85,000 people have undergone her training programs. She is also an education consultant on the board of several educational institutions and storytelling canters both in India and abroad.

Geetanjali Avinash Joshi was born in 1949. She is a renowned Marathi writer and daughter of well-known Marathi writers, Padmabhushan Shri N. S. Phadke and Shrimati Kamala Phadke. Her maternal aunt, Indira Sant, was also a well-known poetess. Writing from the age of nine, she is known for her writings about Amrita Pritam, Begum Akhtar, Roy Kinikar, amongst others. She has six books to her credit: *Geetanjali: Collection of Poems, Shattarka* (compilation of hundred poems by women writers over 800 years released on the occasion of her aunt's birth centenary in 2014), *Uttsav Veglepanacha* (translation from English into Marathi of short stories of special children), *Kamala* (her mother's biography), *Keshracha Mala* (*The Saffron Fields,* 2018, edited and co-authored by her with writings of twenty other authors, covering different aspects of her father's literary works) and *Shardiy Morpise* (2019, about the lives of thirty Marathi poets and works).

Gulal Salil writes under the pseudonym, Lal Poster. He is a journalist, researcher, graphic designer, and artist with roots in poetry and anthropology, hailing from Bhopal, Madhya Pradesh. At present, he works as a graphic journalist with the data journalism website IndiaSpend. He is an alumnus of SIMC (UG), Pune and TISS Guwahati. He has worked in various print and broadcast media houses, including, the Golden Sparrow, Pune, BBC Hindi, *Indian Express*, *Pune Newsline*, and Zubaan Books, and in various NGOs. His research project for his Master's in Social Anthropology from TISS Guwahati was titled 'Without Permission: Urban Art in Response to Neoliberalisation of Guwahati City Spaces'. This was a micro-ethnography study which focussed on the unpermitted acts of graffiti and street artists in the city of Guwahati with its affects, legal aspects and spatial politics.

Jaspreet Mann is a writer, poet, avid blogger, and educator. Mann's short stories, poems, and articles have been published in numerous anthologies and journals in India and abroad. She is an international educator who has been teaching English literature for the past sixteen years. Her first collection of poems *Monsoon Showers* was published by Writers Workshop, Kolkata. She has the honour of being recognized as a 'promising' poet from the Commonwealth nations. She also writes for *Thought Catalog*, New York. Six collections of poems, a collection of short stories and two novels have made sure that between her 'finger and her thumb, the squat pen rests; snug as a gun'.

Jayanti Naik is one of the most prolific Konkani writers and folklorists of Goa. Since 1989, when her first collection of short stories *Garjan* was published, she has authored more than forty books. These are scholarly works related to folklore or works of creative literature. Her creative writing includes short stories, drama, poetry, and children's literature. Her own stories have been translated into Hindi, Marathi, Telugu, Kannada, Malayalam, and English. Her work is also referred to in both graduate and post graduate studies. She is the recipient of a number of state and national awards, most notable of which are Kala Academy (Goa) Literary Award, 2002, and Sahitya Akademi Award, 2004. She is associated with Goa Konkani Akademi as a folklore researcher. She is the editor of *Ananya*–a six-monthly literary journal of the Goa Konkani Akademi.

Jayanti Thokchom is a researcher on the history of Manipur. She completed her PhD on 'Vaishnavisation of Manipur: A study primarily based on the Bijoy Panchali' from the Centre for Historical Studies, Jawaharlal Nehru University, New Delhi. She was a Junior Research Fellow at the Indira Gandhi National Centre for the Arts. She was also a recipient of the Junior Research Fellowship from the Indian Council of Historical Research. She has curated a multimedia module on Vaishnava temples of Manipur at Sahapedia. She has published articles on Manipur's religious history and has participated in many national and international conferences. Her areas of interest include textual tradition of the Meiteis and cultural and religious history of Manipur.

Jitu Mishra earned his master's degree in Ancient Indian History, Culture and Archaeology from Deccan College Post-graduate and Research Institute, Pune. He is co-founder of Sarna Educational and Cultural Services LLP, a Bhubaneshwar based enterprise, working in the areas of immersive tourism, sustainable craft, and experiential education. He has a passion for education and has been working in the areas of history, culture, and heritage studies.

Kulin Patel is a resident of a small village, Kos, under the zila Surat of Gujarat and is a poet of the Dhodia bhasha (language). By profession, he is a farmer, photography enthusiast, and also a freelance journalist. He has worked to observe, study, and reflect upon the tribals of southern Gujarat region and has been writing on the same in various dailies. He has also presented his views across the radio station, *Akashvani,* of Ahmedabad and Baroda. He also helped to formulate the book *Aha among Dhodia.* This book looks into the Dhodia tribes who reside in southern Gujarat and northern Maharashtra. He is also a co-editor of the book *Dakshin Gujarat na Adivasi Nrityon.*

Lalrinmawii Tochhawng obtained her MA (English) from JNU, New Delhi, M Phil from Madurai Kamaraj University (MKU) Madurai; PhD from IGNOU, New Delhi in 2015. Her PhD thesis is titled 'Tell Me Your Story: A Study of the Oral Folk Tales in Mizoram'. She teaches English Literature as Associate Professor and Head of the Department in the Department of English, Government T. Romana College, Aizawl, Mizoram. Her fields of special interest include folk literature and the rambuai (Mizo insurgency) period. She has been actively involved in research and production of insurgency literature. She is the author of The *Mizo Uprising: Assam Assembly Debates on the Mizo Movement, 1966-1971* published by Cambridge Scholars Publishing in 2012.

Lhundup Gyalpo is an alumnus of IIT Bombay and a writer from Ladakh. He recently published his debut collection of stories titled *Betty's Butter Tea: Stories from Ladakh*. His work has appeared in *Sheeraza* magazine published by Jammu and Kashmir Academy of Art, Culture, and Languages. He has also contributed to the *Indian Literature* journal of Sahitya Akademi. He was one of the top twenty-five LitMart finalists at the Bangalore Literature Festival, 2018.

Lopamudra Maitra Bajpai is a visual anthropologist, author, and international columnist. She works on history, popular culture, and the intangible cultural heritage (ICH) of India and South Asia. She was recently deputed as the Culture Specialist (Research) at the SAARC Cultural Centre, Colombo, Sri Lanka, and has also been a Research Grant Fellow of the Indian High Commission, Sri Lanka. A former Assistant Professor from Symbiosis International (Deemed University), Pune, she continues to teach at universities in India and abroad.

M. C. Rajan was born in a village nestled between the Kolli Hills and Pachamalai Hills in Salem district, Tamil Nadu.

He received his education from St. Joseph's College Trichy, Jawaharlal Nehru University, and University of Hyderabad. Travel and politics remain an abiding interest for him. He is a journalist by choice and is based in Chennai. He has worked at the *Hindustan Times* as an assistant editor, reporting on Tamil Nadu, with a focus on social issues and politics, which continue to be his passion. He had a stint in Madurai and was earlier with *Indian Express, UNI, Mail Today* (India Today Group) and the television channel, *News18 Tamil Nadu*. He has extensively toured to cover the widespread caste clashes between Dalits and Thevars which rocked the southern districts of Tamil Nadu in the 1990s and the December 2004 tsunami, among other events. He is at present a Bureau Chief at ETV Bharat, Chennai.

Madhulika Samanta is currently Director, Archaeology, at the Archaeological Survey of India, New Delhi. She has a PhD in Geo-archaeology from Deccan College Postgraduate and Research Institute, Pune, and is an alumnus of the Institute of Archaeology, UCL, London. In the course of her career, she worked with the people of West Bengal in the Ajay River basin, independently excavated archaeological remains of the Bharuch and Vadnagar in Gujarat, worked with the tribes of Rewa, Madhya Pradesh and Singrauli and Dang, Gujarat. She worked in Laos as a part of the UNESCO project on the Plain of Jars. She writes in Bengali and English and also has a penchant for writing poetry. She has also been honoured by the Government of West Bengal for her poetry.

Malsawmliana was born in 1976. He obtained his MA (Ancient Indian History) from NEHU, Shillong in 2000 and PhD from NEHU in 2011. Currently, he is Professor in the Department of History, Government T. Romana College, Aizawl. He has published a number of research papers in journals and contributed chapters/articles in edited books. He is currently President, Mizo Archaeological Society and Assistant Secretary, Mizo History Association. His books include *Megalithic Culture of Mizoram* (published by Research India Press, New Delhi, 2016), *Social, Economic and Political History of the Mizo* (published by Eastern Book House, Guwahati, 2011), *Politics of Regionalism in North East India*, (published by Mittal Publications, New Delhi, 2014). He has also published two books in the Mizo language—*South Sabual Chanchin* (2002) and *Thuziak Thlankhawm* (2002).

Narayan B. Desai is a writer and translator in Konkani, Marathi, Hindi, and English. He has been awarded the Sahitya Akademi Translation Prize (2018) in Konkani for *Rajwade Lekh Sangraha* (a collection of research articles by V. K. Rajwade in Marathi). A former school principal in Goa for three decades, he has also worked in various sociocultural organizations in Goa, creating awareness of environmental conservation, mobilization of youth for social and educational development. His PhD was on the Konkani script. He has worked in committees of colleges and the Ministry of Human Resource Development, Government of India. His recognized translation work includes a book each for the National Book Trust and the Sahitya Akademi, Goa Konkani Akademi. He has also contributed to anthology of Konkani poems, a translation of short stories, and to the Goa volume of People's Linguistic Survey of India (PLSI, 2018). As a columnist, he has contributed to local dailies in Marathi and Konkani. A collection of his articles in Konkani has been published in *Jagarayache Kunkare* in November 2019.

Narinder Jit Kaur is a writer and translator in English, Hindi, and Punjabi. Born in 1953, in Patiala, she has done her masters in English and History, and MPhil in English from Punjab University, Chandigarh. She has been a teacher of English

Literature (graduate and post-graduate levels) for thirty-one years in different government colleges of Punjab and retired as associate professor in 2011. Her articles and poems are regularly published in various newspapers and magazines in the Punjab region. She has translated five books, novels, and short stories, from Punjabi into English, namely, *Town and the Countryside* (Sahitya Akademi, New Delhi), *Twilight and Mark of the Nose Ring* (National Book Trust, New Delhi), *Voices in the Back Courtyard: Collection of Stories by Punjabi Women Writers* (New Delhi: Rupa & Co. New Delhi), *Anndatta: The Hand that Feeds* and *On the Trails of Fire* (Publication Bureau, Punjabi University, Patiala).

P. Raja was born in 1952 in Pondicherry. He is a bilingual (English and Tamil) creative writer, critic, historian, folklorist, columnist, and editor. More than 5,000 of his works—poems, short stories, interviews, articles, book reviews, short plays, skits, features, and novellas—have been published across several newspapers and magazines (350 both in India and abroad). He has written thirty books for adults and eight books for children in English and fourteen books in Tamil. He has contributed special articles to *Encyclopaedia of Post-Colonial Literature in English* (London), *Encyclopaedia of Tamil Literature in English*, and also to several other edited volumes. He has also written scripts for television. His short stories and poems have also been broadcast from All India Radio, Puducherry. He was a General Council Member (English Board from 2008–12) of the Sahitya Akademi, New Delhi, representing Pondicherry University. He has edited *Transfire*, an English quarterly devoted to translations.

Parvathi Chandran has been working as an assistant professor at the Department of Journalism, St. Xavier's College Vaikom, Kottayam, Kerala, since 2012. She has published articles on cinema in peer-reviewed research journals and regional magazines and also published a book on Charlie Chaplin for the State Institute of Languages, Kerala. She worked as a content developer at the Centre for Digital Imaging Technology, Trivandrum, and was associated with a number of projects at New Media Division. She was an awardee of Media Fellowship of Media Academy, Kerala, 2017.

Prakash Jha is a former corporate banker who one fine day left everything behind to embark upon a journey covering pan-India (70,000+ kilometres spanning 100+ cities across all the twenty-eight states of India) in search of #TheJoyOfLife! The varied explorations moulded him into sort of a traveller/storyteller/writer—one who infuses his experienced stories with a travel-character #AwaraBanjara, whilst expressing them under the pen name #PrakashVaani. He is also a management graduate (MBA from FMS, Delhi University) and an engineer (B.Tech in Computer Science from NIT Durgapur) with around a decade of professional experience across MNCs—Standard Chartered Bank, HSBC, Yes Bank, and Infosys Technologies Limited. In the past, he has also been a consultant, had entrepreneurial pursuits in short films, e-commerce, and also been a restaurateur. He is also a yoga enthusiast and a reiki master healer.

Pramod Kumar Jha is a postgraduate in English Literature and has worked in Akashvani followed by Doordarshan for more than thirty-two years and retired as Director, Doordarshan Kendra, Ranchi, in 2017. He writes in English, Hindi, and Maithili and has been associated with the Sahitya Akademi, New Delhi, and Central Institute of Indian Languages and Basava Samiti, Bangalore in various capacities, including vetter, translator, and language expert. He translated a monograph on Rahul Sankrityayan from English into Maithili (Sahitya Akademi, New Delhi). During the last thirty years, he has produced scores of documentaries and interviewed luminaries like Dr Birendra Kumar Bhattacharya, Dr Bishwanath Prasad Tiwary, and Professor Jagannath, among others. He was a Senior Producer, Prasar Bharti-BBC Anti Leprosy Campaign. Currently, he is the coordinator of the ensuing translation of Vachana, in Angika and a guest faculty at Central University, Jharkhand and is also invited for lectures at ATI, NABARD, CUJ, and IICM.

Pranab Jyoti Sharma is from Hajo in Kamrup district near Guwahati in Assam. He grew up in a small township in Kokrajhar district. He works as an editorial manager at SAGE Publications India, based out of SAGE's Dehradun office and leads the Language Services Division of SAGE. He is actively involved in professional writing and editing of higher academic research papers and books for nearly one-and-a-half decade now. He has a PhD in Archaeology for which he extensively studied and did fieldwork in the Dhansiri–Doyang Valley of Assam to study the development of early historical settlements in the valley. He has several academic, peer-reviewed papers published in journals to his credit, and has also attended several national seminars and conferences across India to present his research work. He has a keen interest in music and performing arts and in the discourses around indigenous communities and society and their current socio-politico-economic situations.

R. Chumbeno Ngullie is an assistant professor in the Department of History and Archaeology, Nagaland University. Her interest lies in ethnoarchaeology, pottery, and oral sources. She has co-edited two books, *Tapestry* and *Taboos, Myths and Legends*. She has also contributed several articles pertaining to Northeast India, especially Nagaland.

R. Radhakrishnan is presently working as a faculty (Political Science) at Symbiosis Law School, Hyderabad. His earlier experience involved work in a political office and research in a think tank in New Delhi, before moving to teaching. He had pursued his masters and MPhil from the Centre for Political Studies, Jawaharlal Nehru University, New Delhi. Presently, he is pursuing his doctoral research on the topic 'Political Communication as Soft Power: Role of Media in India's Foreign Policy', from Savitribai Phule University, Pune. He has co-authored a book, co-edited books, contributed chapters in edited books, articles in journals and has written many web-based articles, apart from the occasional brief comments in newspapers. He has also presented papers in national and international conferences, apart from being invited as a resource person and speaker at international conferences and workshops.

Rajendra Pal Sharma was born in 1955 in Phoenix Bay, Port Blair. He originally hails from Punjab. He is at present, the editor of the regional daily *Info India* and editor–publisher of *Andaman Wave* (English). An experienced journalist, his career spans over forty years and includes various dailies, including *Dainik Vishwamitra, Janasatta,* and others (all from Kolkata), *Sanmarg, Navbharat Times, Khel-Khiladi,* and others (Hindi) and *Navjivan* (from Mumbai). He is a former bureau in-charge of *Hindustan Samachar* and a Press Trust of India (PTI) correspondent. His literary work includes, amongst others, *Andaman Nicobar ki Lok Kathayein* (The Folktales of Andaman and Nicobar), *Andaman ka Ross Island* (The Ross Island of Andaman), *Andaman Paryatan* (Andaman Tourism), *Hello Andaman* (English), *Main hoon Cellular Jail* (I am Cellular Jail). He has been variously involved in local social causes and has also been awarded for his work.

Ramesh Sahadev Ghadi was born in 1964 in Goa and writes under the pseudonym Ramesh Saju Ghadi. A farmer and a fitness trainer by profession, he writes both prose and poetry. He mentions that he became a writer by chance. He travelled for work to the Gulf region in the 1990s and began missing his village. The nostalgia and thoughts of his village encouraged him to write poetry and short stories about his village life. He has been writing poems and prose for the last fifteen years and his poetry, short stories, and essays have been published in leading publications of Goa. He is involved with many environmental groups that are trying to save nature and heritage of the coastal villages of Goa. He is presently working on his poetry collection *Tale Zale Suke* (The Pond Has Dried Up) in Konkani and a short story collection *Gavakadchea Goshti* (Village Tales in Marathi).

Rishi Raj Sharmah runs Maati, a community-based organization working in the field of preservation of art and culture. Maati understands the importance of art as a significant entity and has attempted to carry on various endeavours to help art flourish and find a platform. Developing a community of artists and audiences who are involved for their artistic streak and love for art and culture, Maati also focuses on education and sustainable livelihood.

Rukshana Nanji has a double postgraduate degree in English Literature and Ancient Indian History, Culture and Archaeology. She is also the first recipient of the prestigious H. D. Sankalia Gold Medal. Her PhD thesis (from Deccan College) was published under the title 'Merchants and Mariners: A Study of Early Medieval Ceramics in India', with special reference to Sanjan (Vol. I Sanjan Excavation Reports), by BAR, Oxford. She co-authored a book on Buddhist sites in Gujarat with Professor K. Krishnan and Dr Atusha Irani. Her work includes extensive field archaeologist and ceramic specialist work on several sites in Gujarat, Maharashtra, Rajasthan, Madhya Pradesh, and Karnataka. She has several international and national papers, seminars and conferences to her credit, including research publications. As an independent researcher, she continues her work on early medieval port sites on the western seaboard of India and interactions across the Indian Ocean as reflected in archaeological records.

Samvedna Amitabh Rawat was born in Mysore, Karnataka. She is a Hindi poet/writer and professional storyteller. Founder of Kahaanipur (storytelling initiative), she also has journalistic experiences of nearly ten years in Bhopal in *Dainik Bhaskar, Hindustan Times,* and *ETV Bhopal.* She is also a guest faculty in Sophia Women's College, Mumbai. She has rendered stories and trained students in children's festivals, schools, colleges, and universities of Mumbai, Jaipur, Bali, China, and Portugal. She has a master's degree in English Literature, post-graduate diploma in advertising and public relations, and a diploma in storytelling. She has published a book of poems and received a prestigious award of Hindi literature in 2007. She has also presented papers on storytelling in China and Bali in 2016–17, and conducted a workshop in International Seminar on Fairy Tales organized by Moonluza in Sintra, Portugal (2018–19).

Sanket Jain is an independent journalist based in Maharashtra's Kolhapur district, and a 2019–20 People's Archive of Rural India (PARI) fellow where he documented vanishing livelihoods and dying art forms from the villages of Maharashtra and Karnataka. Sanket whose work has been published in over eighteen national and international publications has reported on an array of subjects including farmers' protests, casteism, gender inequality, human–wildlife conflict, climate change, floods, poverty, etc. He has written for *The Progressive, Baffler,*

Indian Express, *The National*, *Vice*, *Scroll*, *Toward Freedom*, *Byline Times*, etc. He is also the co-founder of Insight Walk, a non-profit that offers teaching fellowships to rural women and make education accessible to children from the marginalized communities. In 2020, one of his stories won the 14th PII-ICRC Annual Awards under the special mention category for best article and photograph on a humanitarian subject. In this story, Sanket had reported from over ten flood affected remote villages and written about how everyday heroes saved thousands of lives.

Shakuntala Shami was born in 1945 in Balapatti, Hathras, and completed her schooling from Hathras, Uttar Pradesh in 1962. Following this, she finished her undergraduate studies and master's degree in sociology from Meerut University. In addition to *Panduk Chidiya*, she has authored a children's book, *Mama ka Gaon* which contains four short stories from her childhood days in her uncle's village. She has also written essays on caste and untouchability which have been published in the weekly Hindi magazine *Manorma*. Further, she has also been part of a Doordarshan interview on the same subject. She has three children and six grandchildren. Presently, she resides in Bhopal, where she has committed herself to mastering visual arts such as painting, sculpting, doll making, and pottery.

Shibal Bhartiya is currently working as a senior consultant in Ophthalmology at Fortis Memorial Research Institute in Gurugram. She trained to be an eye surgeon from Maulana Azad Medical College and the All India Institute of Medical Sciences (AIIMS), New Delhi, and the University of Geneva, Switzerland. Dr Bhartiya is the executive editor of the *Journal of Current Glaucoma Practice*, the official journal of the International Society of Glaucoma Surgery. She is also the editor-in-chief of *Clinical and Experimental Vision and Eye Research*. She has edited and written eleven textbooks on glaucoma, in addition to over a hundred peer-reviewed research papers.

Smita Karnatak has a master's degree in English. Her interests include reading, writing, and translating folk tales, in particular. Some of her writings have been published in several web magazines. She currently lives in Haldwani.

Sonam B. Wangyal is a physician, author, and a renowned researcher on Darjeeling and the adjoining Himalayan region. As a physician, he has worked as Registrar of Medicine (under UNDP) in the Kingdom of Lesatho, Southern Africa, and as Chief of Level One Clinic, UNDP, South Sudan. He was also a columnist for *Nvplus, The Statesman, Himal, Tibetan World Magazine, Flatfile, Himalayan Times*, and *Sikkim Observer*. He is also currently on the editorial board of *Ladakh Journal*. Some of his important books include *Sikkim and Darjeeling: Division and Destruction, Footprints in the Himalayas, Dooars vis-a-vis Gorkhaland*. At present, he is working on his forthcoming book *Darjeeling Stories: Tribes, Natives and Oddballs*, and another book on the visit of Mark Twain to Darjeeling.

Srinivas Bandameedi is an academic, currently working as an assistant professor at Symbiosis International (Deemed University). His areas of interest are English Language Education (ELT) and literature. He has authored several research papers published in national and international journals.

Sudipta Agarwal is an independent researcher. She completed her postgraduation studies in English Literature in 2017. She is currently working on the translation of various texts from Urdu and Hindi to English. Her areas of interests include cultural studies, Gothic literature, translation studies, and Victorian literature.

Suhag Dave has been doing freelancing translation and copy-editing work since his college days. He translated the Gujarati articles for the *Encyclopaedia of Indian Poetics*, an undertaking of the Sahitya Akademi, New Delhi. Proficient in Gujarati, his mother tongue, Hindi, English, and Sanskrit, and with a master's in Linguistics, from the Maharaja Sayajirao University, Baroda (Vadodara), he can work with languages with ease and efficiency. Other than editing and occasionally translating, he also writes short stories and reviews, as well as research articles in Gujarati and English. These are published in various journals and in anthologies. Currently, he is a senior language editor for the premium language editing services offered by SAGE Publications under its MILES vertical and is based in Dehradun.

Sujay Kapil is an avid researcher in the field of communication with several publications in reputed national and international journals to his credit. He has experiences of both industry as well as academics in the field of media and communication. He is an alumnus of School of Communication Studies, Punjab University, Chandigarh. He has keen interest in the field of public relations and likes to explore the social facets of technology.

Syed Shafiuzzaman Mashhadi is a civil servant and has spent most of his formative and adult life in Bihar. He finished his master's in Psychology from Delhi University to join the provincial Civil Services and worked in rural and urban Bihar, until his superannuation. He served as a member of the Bihar Public Service Commission, thereafter. He has since served as the vice chairman of the Bihar Urdu Academy and until recently was the chairman of the Bihar Urdu Advisory Board. He has thirteen books to his credit, including a collection of dramas and four short story collections. He writes in Urdu. He has been awarded several times by the governments of Bihar, Odisha, and West Bengal. He also received the Ghalib Award for his contribution to Urdu literature in 2017.

Thulasi Muttulingam is a freelance journalist based in Jaffna, Sri Lanka. She is fascinated by the concept of stories and storytelling, as well as how stories take on different dimensions depending upon who is telling them. She is currently living in post-war (but still conflict-riddled) Sri Lanka where she experiences first-hand, how victors take ownership of narratives that go down as 'his story'. Her focus, therefore, is all about challenging such 'his stories' as well as including quite a few of 'her stories'. So long as it's only the hunter who can write, the lion will always be vilified. She considers her job as a scribe as an opportunity to give voice to the voiceless—lion, deer, and downtrodden, everywhere. She firmly believes in challenging one-dimensional narratives as narrated by victors.

Tiatoshi Jamir is Professor and Head of the Department of History and Archaeology, Nagaland University. His main interests are prehistory, ethnoarchaeology, community archaeology, and ethnomusicology. He currently directs a research program on the Archaeology of Naga Ancestral Sites and Cave Archaeology in the Naga Hills Ophiolite Formation in joint collaboration with the Department of Art and Culture, Government of Nagaland. He is author and editor of *Archaeology of Naga Ancestral sites* (Vols. 1 and 2) and co-editor of *50 Years After Daojali-Hading: Essays in Honour of Tarun Chandra Sharma*.

Ubaidulla Thangal is a native of Androth Island of the Union Territory of Lakshadweep. He is presently working as Public Relations Officer, Officer (Marketing) and Officer (Marketing) in Lakshadweep Development Corporation Limited. He has completed his bachelor's degree in science (B. Sc. Petrochemicals, First Class) from Al-Ameen College, M. G. University, Kerala, post-graduation in Business Administration from Vishwakarma Institute of Management, Pune University, and LLB from the School of Legal Studies with a First Class from Cochin University of Science and Technology, Kerala. Earlier, he had worked at JK Tyre & Industries.

Vedanshi Ashok Bhatia has a bachelor's degree in Psychology. She is a social worker and is also an anti-bully activist. She is passionate about teaching and is also a theatre artist. Her interests revolve around writing or any form of self-expression to promote better mental health, reading philosophy with particular focus on the concept of moksha. She believes in promoting a healthy mental health environment and is interested in developing techniques within the field of Art Therapy.

Veerya G. Nayak hails from Jayashankar district of Telangana. He holds a PhD in English from the English and Foreign Languages University, Hyderabad. He is presently the Principal of Goutham Degree and P.G. College, Hanamkonda. His areas of research interest include Reading Comprehension and Teacher Education in English. He has published several research articles in national and international journals.

Venybirth Seng Ch. Marak is from Tura, West Garo Hills, in the state of Meghalaya. He obtained his master's degree in Garo from North-Eastern Hill University (NEHU) in 2006. He was awarded MPhil by Gauhati University in 2011 for his thesis 'A Study on Cultural Tourism with Reference to West Garo Hills'. He worked as a research assistant in the Department of Anthropology, NEHU, Shillong (2013–14) and is presently pursuing his PhD in the Department of Cultural and Creative Studies in the same university. He is also the author of *Achikrangni Ringa Minga Aro Golporang* (Oral Songs and Tales of the Garos), a collection of songs, tales, riddles, and proverbs of Abeng, Matabeng, Matchi, and Gara Ganching Garo subtribes of the Garo Hills region. He has a number of literary articles published in the Garo language.

Winder M. Sangma is sixty-five years old. He was born in a remote village of Eman Aruakgre in the district of South Garo Hills which falls under newly created Chokpot Civil Sub-division. He is a gifted folk singer and performer of the chera ringa or sola. Chera song is normally sung during post-funeral ceremonies of the Atong and Gara–Ganching subtribes of the Garo people residing in southern part of Garo Hills in the state of Meghalaya.

Zakia Sultana Mashhadi is a proud recipient of the Sahitya Akademi Award, 2019, for her exceptional translation from English into Urdu. She is one of the most well-known Urdu fiction authors of our time. She is a prolific writer of short stories and has to her credit, more than 150 published stories. She studied and also later taught psychology at the University of Lucknow, before settling for a life dedicated to Urdu fiction. She writes with equal fervour in Urdu, Hindi, and English and has several important translations to her credit. She has published six collections of short stories and a novelette in Urdu. She has been awarded by the Government of Bihar for her contribution towards literature and also by the Government of India for her work in adult literacy. She received the Ghalib Award in 2016 and the Shamim Nikhat Award in 2018.

References and Further Reading

Amubi, Irom (ed.), *Moirang Kangleirol*, Imphal, 1994.

Badheka, Gijubhai, *Bal Varta 3*, Bhavnagar: Sumit Publications, 1998.

Bahadur, K. P., *Folktales of Uttar Pradesh*, New Delhi: Sterling Publishers, 1960.

Bahadur, Mutua, *Traditional Textiles of Manipur*, Imphal: Mutua Museum, 1997.

Bajpai, Lopamudra Maitra (ed.) 'Loksahitya (Folklore), Storytelling and its Myriad Reflections Across the SAARC Region', *SAARC Art*, Issue no. 4, Sept. 2017, available at <http://saarcculture.org/wp-content/uploads/2017/10/issue4.pdf>

____, '100 Years of Thakurmar Jhuli (Grandmother's Bag of Tales): From Oral Literature to Digital Media-Shaping Thoughts for the Young and Old', *Indian Folklore Research Journal*, Issue 7, 2007.

____, 'Childrens' Oral Literature and Modern Mass Media in India With Special Reference to Gradual Transformation in West Bengal', *Indian Folklore Research Journal*, Vol. 5, No. 8, 2009, available at <https://www.academia.edu/442965/From_Oral_tradition_to_digital_media_Folklore_in_West_Bengal>.

____, 'Intangible Heritage and the Dynamic Art of Storytelling: Sustainable Development of Cultural Heritage through Different Expressions', *Book of Abstracts, SAARC Research Programme on Cultural Heritage Tourism and Sustainable Development in South Asia*, Sri Lanka: SAARC Cultural Centre, April 2014, available at <http://saarcculture.org/wp-content/uploads/2016/02/book-of-abstract_chtsd.pdf>.

____, 'Oral-Written Nexus in Bengali Chharas Over the Last Hundred Years: Creating New Paradigm for Children's Literature', *SAARC Culture*, Vol. 3, 2012, pp. 137-171, available at <http://saarcculture.org/wp-content/uploads/2016/02/journal_vol3_2012_3rd.pdf>.

____, 'Stories of Tuntuni from Bengal- Connecting Oral Traditions with The Global Age Across a Century', *Heritage and Us*, Year

2, Issue 1, 2013, available at <http://go.epublish4me.com/ebook/ebook?id=10023475>.

Balfour, H., 'Concerning Thunderbolts', *Folklore*, Vol. 40, No. 1, 1929, pp. 37–49, doi: https://doi.org/10.1080/0015587X.1929.9716805.

Barron, Lt., 'Note on the Stone Implements from the Naga Hills', *Journal of Anthropological Institute*, Vol. I, 1872, pp. 61–62, doi: https://doi.org/10.2307/2841288.

Bascom, Williams, 'The Forms of Folklore: Prose Narratives', *Journal of American Folklore*, Vol. 78, No. 307, 1965, pp. 3–20.

Behari Singh, Huirem, 'A Study of Meitei Folklore' (unpublished PhD thesis), Gauhati University, 1985.

Beck, Brenda E. F., Peter J. Caus, Praphulladata Goswami, and Jawaharlal Handoo, *Folktales of India*, Chicago: University of Chicago Press, 1987.

Bezbarua, Lakhminath, *Burhi Aair Xadhu*, Assam: Banlata Prakashan, 1911.

Brara, N. Vijayalakshmi, *Politics, Cosmology and Society in India's North-East*, New Delhi: Oxford University Press, 1998.

Bronner, Simon J. (ed.), *Meaning of Folklore: The Analytical Essays of Alan Dundes*, Utah: University Press of Colorado, 2007.

Department of Art and Culture, *Fables from the Misty Mountains: Folklore of the Nagas*, Guwahati: LBS Publications, 2009.

Department of Under-developed Areas, Government of Nagaland, *Folklore of Eastern Nagaland*, Dimapur: Heritage Publishing House, 2017.

Devi, Sobita (ed.), *Moirang Kangleirol*, Imphal, 1982.

Documentary of Mizoram War of Independence (1966-1986), MNF Gen. Headquarters, Mizoram, 2017.

Edwardes, S. M., 'A Koli Ballad', *The Indian Antiquary*, Vol. 52, Part 657, June 1923, pp. 127–30.

____, *By-ways of Bombay*, Bombay: D. B. Taraporewala Sons and Co., 1912.

____, *Gazetteer of Bombay City and Island* (Vol. III), New Delhi: Reprint by Cosmos Publications, 2001.

Fischer, J. L., 'The Sociopsychological Analysis of Folktales', *Current Anthropology*, Vol. 4, No. 3, 1963, pp. 235–95, available at http://www.jstor.org/stable/2739608.

Goswami, Nityanandbinod, *Chhele Bhulano Chhara*, Santiniketan: Vishwa-Bharati Publications, 1948.

Gurdon, Capt. P. R and Srijut Hemchandra Gosain (eds.), 'Hema Kosha', *An Etymological Dictionary of Assamese Language* by Hemchandra Barua published under the authority of the Assam Administration, 1900.

Henry, N., 'Medaram Jatara to be National Festival', *The Hindu*, 6 January 2018.

Higgins, J. C. (John Parratt ed.), *Notes on the Beliefs and Customs of Manipur*, Imphal: Manipur State Archives, 1998.

Hutton, J. H., 'A Naga Hills Celt', *Journal of Asiatic Society of Bengal*, Vol. 22, 1926, p. 133.

____, 'Prehistory of Assam', *Man in India*, Vol. 8, No. 4, 1928, pp. 228–32.

____, 'Two Celts from the Naga Hills', *Man*, Vol. 24, 1924, pp. 20–22.

Jha, Yoganand (ed.), *Mithilak Lokkatha Sanchay*, New Delhi: Sahitya Akademi, 2017.

Karaka, Dosabhai Framji, *History of the Parsis: Including their Manners, Customs, Religion and Present Position, Vol. I and II*, London: Macmillan and Co., 1884.

Kipgen, Tingneichong G., *Women's Role in the 20th Century Manipur: A Historical Study*, New Delhi: Kalpaz Publications, 2010.

Kshetrimayum, Otojit, 'Women and Entrepreneurship in North East India: Handloom as an Enterprise', *NLI Research Studies Series*, No.11, June 2016.

Kunwar, Chhaya, *The Emancipated Womenfolk of Uttarakhand*, New Delhi: The Society for Participatory Research in Asia (PRIA), 1997.

Laishram, Rena, *Early Meitei History: Religion, Society and the Manipur Puyas*, New Delhi: Akanksha Publishing House, 2009.

Lakshmi, C. S., 'Reform, Her Middle Name', *The Hindu*, 4 June 2000.

Loktongbam, Mangaleibi, 'Folklore genres of Meitei community', E-Pao.net, 28 July 2018, available at < http://www.e-pao.net/epSubPageExtractor.asp?src=manipur.Folks.Folklore_genres_of_Meetei_community_By_Manganleibi_Loktongbam>.

Mainwaring, G.B., *Dictionary of the Lepcha Language*, revised and completed by Albert Grunwedel, Kathmandu: Ratna Pustak Bhandar, 1979, p. 444a, 335b.

Majumdar, Dakkhinaranjan Mitra, *Thakurmar Jhuli,* Calcutta: Mitra and Ghosh, 1907.

Mojumder, O., 'Celebrtaing Tribal Lives', *Deccan Chronicle,* 5 July 2018.

Naik, Jayanti (ed.), *Konkani Lokanio,* New Delhi: Sahitya Akademi, 2000.

Pandya, Amita and Joymati Thoudam, 'Handloom Weaving, The Traditional Craft of Manipur, *Indian Journal of Traditional Knowledge,* Vol. 9, No. 4, October 2010, pp. 651–55.

Pandya, Mamta, 'Gijubhai and his Tales', *Muse India,* Issue No. 38, 2011.

Paratt, Saroj Nalini, *The Religion of Manipur: Beliefs, Rituals and Historical Development.,* Kolkata: Firma KLM, 1980.

Paratt, Saroj Nalini Abraham, and John Paratt, *The Pleasing of Gods: Meitei Lai Haraoba*, New Delhi: Vikas Publishing House, 1997.

Patel, Simin Jehangir, 'Cultural Intermediaries in a Colonial City: The Parsis of Bombay c. 1860 – 1921' (DPhil Dissertation), 2015, available at <bombaywalla.org/docs/simin-patel-dphil-dissertation-2015.pdf>.

Phenan, Lakhi Kanta, *Juju Budini Sastar* (Original text in Rabha by Lakhi Kanta Phenan, Assamese translations by Dr Upen Rabha Hakacham), Assam: Directorate of Assam Institute of Research for Tribals and Scheduled Castes, 2009.

Purushotham, K., 'Evolution of Telugu Dalit Literature', *Economic and Political Weekly,* Vol. 45, No. 22, 2010, pp. 55–63.

Ragan, Kathleen, 'What Happened to the Heroines in Folktales? An Analysis by Gender of a Multicultural Sample of Published Folktales Collected from Storytellers', *Marvels & Tales,* Vol. 23, No. 2, 2009, pp. 227-247.

Raja, P, *A Concise History of Pondicherry,* Pondicherry: Busy Bee Books (2nd edition), 2003.

Ramanujan, A. K., *Folktales from India,* New Delhi: Penguin Books, 1994.

Rashtriya Pustak Nyas (National Book Trust), Charwaha aur Bagh (The shepherd and the tiger), *Santali Lok-Kathayen,* New Delhi: National Book Trust, 2014.

Reeves, Peter, Andrew Pope, John McGuire, and Bob Pokrant, 'The

Koli and the British at Bombay: The Structure of their Relations to the Mid-Nineteenth Century', *Journal of South Asian Studies*, Vol. 19, Series 1, 1996, pp. 97–119.

Riba, Bomchak, *Unpublished Thesis*, Arunachal Pradesh: Rajiv Gandhi University, 2010.

Rogers, H. T., *First Lessons in Telugu: Comprising Twenty-Five Short Stories, with Copious Notes and Translation*, Madras: C. Foster and Company, No.8, 1889, pp. vi–vii.

Samom, Thingnam Anjulika, 'Chungkham Rani: Weaver, Designer, Entrepreneur', *The Sangai Express*, 22 January 2007.

Shah, P. G., *The Dublas of Gujarat*, New Delhi: Bharatiya Adimjati Sevak Sangh Kingsway, 1958.

Shakespear, J., 'A Manipuri Festival', *Folklore*, Vol. 21, No. 1, 1910, pp. 79–82.

____, 'Customs at Death Among the Manipuris and Cognate Clans', *Folklore*, Vol. 23, 1912, pp. 463–61.

____, 'The Religion of Manipur', *Folklore*, Vol. 21, 1913, pp. 409–55.

____, 'The Pleasing of the God Thangjing', *Man*, Vol. 13, 1913, pp. 81–86.

Shami, Shakuntala, 'Panduk Chidiya', *Panduk Chidiya (Bal Kahaniya)*, Uttar Pradesh: Indradhanush Prakashan, 2005.

Sheppard, Samuel T., *Bombay Place-Names and Street-Names, An Excursion into the By-ways of the History of Bombay City*, Bombay: The Times Press, 1917.

Shobha, H.C., *Moirang and Eputhou Thangching*, Moirang: Mellei Press, 2011.

Sinha, Aditya Prasad, *Ho Lokkatha- Ek Anusheelan*, New Delhi: Vikalp Prakashan, 2014.

Singh, L. Bhagyachandra, *A Critical Study of the Religious Philosophy of the Meities Before the Advent of Vaishnavism in Manipur*, Imphal: L. Jayantakumar Singh, 1991.

Sobita Devi, K., *Traditional Dress of the Meiteis*, Imphal: Bhubon Publishing House, 1988.

Surajkumar, Nongmaithem, 'Manipuri Folktales', *Indian Literature*, Vol. 59, No. 5 (289) Sep–Oct 2015, pp. 161–69, available at <http://www.e-pao.net/epSubPageExtractor.asp?src=manipur.Folks.Folk_Tales>.

Tamang, K. P., *The Lepcha-English Encyclopaedic Dictionary*, Kalimpong: Mani Press, 1980, p. 747b.

Vidyarthi, L. P., 'Folklore Research in India', *Varia Folklorica* edited by Alan Dundes, Paris: Mouton Publishers, 1978.

Vyas, Krishna A., *Kal Yug No Karma Yogi*, Ahmedabad: Gurjar Grantha Ratna Karyalaya Publication, 1981.

'Weaving in Manipur: A Rich Cultural Heritage', *Northeast Window*, 1 September 2017, available at <http://www.thenortheastwindow. com/2017/09/weaving-manipur-rich-cultural-heritage/>.

Waddell, Lawrence Austine, 'Place and River Names in the Darjiling District and Sikhim', *Journal of the Asiatic Society of Bengal*, Vol. 60, 1892, pp. 53–79.

____, *Among the Himalyas*, Kathmandu: Ratna Pustak Bhandar, 1978.

Yadav, Shankar Lal, *Haryana Pradesh ka Loksahitya*, Allahabad: Hindustani Academy, 2000.

Zamawia, R., *Zofate Zinkawngah (Zalenna Mei A Mit Tur Ani Lo)*, Aizawl, 2017.

Zide, Norman and Vishvajit Pandya, 'A Bibliographical Introduction to Andamanese Linguistics', *Journal of the American Oriental Society*, Vol. 109, No. 4, 1989, pp. 639–51.